CLOUD SURFING

BILL AUSTEN

Copyright © Bill Austen 2021

First Published in Australia by Australian Self Publishing Group 2019

All rights reserved. No part of this book may be reproduced or transmitted in any form or by any means, electronic or mechanical, including photocopying, recording, or by any information storage and retrieval system, without permission in writing from the copyright owner.

Publisher:
ASPG (Australian Self Publishing Group)
P.O. Box 159, Calwell, ACT Australia 2905
Email: publishaspg@gmail.com
http://www.inspiringpublishers.com

National Library of Australia Cataloguing-in-Publication entry

Author: Austen, Bill

Title: **CLOUD SURFING**/*Bill Austen*

ISBN: 978-1-922327-87-1 (Print)
      978-1-922327-88-8 (eBook)

Flying and navigating an aircraft is maybe something of a mystery to most people, CLOUD SURFING is a collection of stories and explanations in plain language designed to clear that mystery. There are stories of what it's like, and what the challenges are, to fly a Jumbo Jet along with tales of what pilots get up to on the ground. Funny times, scary times.

The author spent forty-two years and travelled the equivalent of five-hundred times around the world collecting the stories. Please climb on board, fasten your seatbelt and hang on for the ride.

If you don't speak fluent Australian check out the Glossary at the end of the book before you start reading. It will help in understanding confusing Australian English.

Contents

1	Cloud Surfing	7
2	Why Become A Pilot?	11
3	Security Issues	18
4	Cadet Training	26
5	Ailerons	34
6	Unusual Flights	44
7	Flying Near Fires	55
8	Vertigo	64
9	Earth Shadow	69
10	Early Days	74
11	Guns, Diamonds and Cash	82
12	On the Changing Times	90
13	On Space and Stuff	99
14	Problem Passengers	109
15	Vietnam Flying	116
16	Refugees	125
17	Los Angeles Riots	130

18	Melbourne Balloon	137
19	I Only Fight Women Passengers – Almost	142
20	Mars	156
21	Type Wars and Air Shows	163
22	Sex (X-Rated)	179
23	Differences	188
24	Flights with Stretchers	198
25	Lightning	212
26	Not All The Fun Was in the Air	223
27	Flying Skills	239
28	Long-Distance Flying	248
29	The Three-Card Trick	258
30	Antarctic Flyovers	267
31	San Francisco	275
32	Travelling the World	284
33	Great Times on the Ground	294
34	Historical Hilarity	304

Glossary of Terms 311
Acknowledgments 314
Notes 315
Extras 373
Pilot Stories 378
Benediction for A Queen 383

CLOUD SURFING

The weather was getting worse as we approached Auckland and the crosswind on the runway was increasing. The real concern, however, were the reports of severe windshear. To lessen the risk, the rules state that the Captain must take over control from the First Officer — so that is what I did.

Left hand onto the control wheel, right hand onto the four thrust levers, a lot of pushing and pulling of these controls as well as a lot of pushing on the rudder pedals with my size twelves. As the wind sheared and swirled, it increased the risk of the 747 losing lift. The strengthening crosswind had upped the risk of landing with the aircraft not pointing straight down the runway. It also meant the wind might push us onto the downwind edge of the runway.

Usually, on this last part of the landing approach, the controls would be caressed to achieve a nice stable approach. The aircraft's speed and its approach angle would be maintained by very little movement of the control wheel or the thrust levers. If the speed started to reduce on a normal day then a squeeze of power was all it took to stop the unwanted speed drop. On this day it was different. As the speed fell, it fell quickly and steeply, windshear can do that, and it had to be corrected quickly and firmly – no mucking around. As *the arse fell out of it* – this has always been the technical term for this situation – the power had to be shoved up, not caressed. Because the wind component had reduced over the wing, the lift had also dropped and the rate of descent had increased accordingly. No gentle fingertip easing up of the nose to keep the approach angle. I had to pull back hard to get the nose up.

I couldn't have cared less about the nose really, what I was doing was increasing the angle of attack of the wing to the airflow to give me more lift. Higher angle of attack means more drag and therefore even more power is needed. So when the aircraft started to fall, and I could actually feel it at the same time that I saw it, I was pushing forward on the thrust levers – technical term: *a handful of thrust* – as well as pulling back quite hard on the elevators. As I said, no fingertip gentleness this day. Nose up, power up and then suddenly the gusts would change and give me more wind over my wings than I needed – and they're bloody big wings on a Jumbo – so all of a sudden there was too much airspeed and too much lift. I pulled off the power and pushed on the control wheel. Less angle of attack meant less drag, just as I was trying to slow the aircraft. Flying, like life, was never meant to be easy.

While all this pushing and pulling was going on, I was also trying to keep the Jumbo tracking down the extended centreline of the runway and, better still, to actually land on it. But this was getting tricky. The gusts and the change of strength of the crosswind were making me work. The aircraft had to be rolled to turn it and the wings were tending to drop by themselves with the turbulence, making the whole tracking thing difficult. I couldn't really complain; I was the one who had chosen to make my living in these three dimensions.

Having taken over at 1200 feet above the ground, I would normally expect to move the thrust levers a smidgen just a few times before touching down, but on this day I went from no thrust to nearly full thrust and vice versa at least four times. The passengers in the cabin would have heard near silence from the engines increasing to a deep roar as the 240,000 horsepower kicked in. This would be followed by silence again and the sequence would repeat.

Over the fence and the speed and height were where they should be, all I had to do then was flare the aircraft for the touchdown, keep the wings, with their dangling engines, level and then bring the nose around so we were pointed straight down the runway. Sounds easy enough but don't try this at home. In the end I got it pretty right and the aircraft went onto the appropriate spot on the runway with the nose heading straight down the strip. I didn't try for the smoothest of landings, it had been raining and a slightly firm touchdown meant water was squished out from under the tyres, that was a good thing.

To minimise the risk – there's that word again – of the aircraft aquaplaning down and off the runway there are little grooves cut into the concrete to drain the water away. It was still slippery but there was enough grip to slow the couple of hundred tonnes of aircraft, with a touchdown speed of a couple of hundred klicks, almost to a standstill.

After touchdown, the engines, which had been pulled back to idle for the landing, were once again spooled up but this time in reverse mode. This was important because if there was a marked *reduced braking* due to the dampness, then the reverse thrust from the engines would have been very welcome. The auto brakes had been set at a higher than normal setting

– another precaution against the risk of sliding off the end of the runway.

They kicked in at the same time as the reverse thrust. This day, an attachment to the massive braking system also kicked into action. The anti-skid electronics detected some skidding tyres and the system reduced the braking on those wheels. All I heard and felt was the chattering of the wheels as they desperately tried to get a grip.

The brakes worked, the reverse thrust worked and we managed to turn off the runway at the usual place and duly delivered our passengers to the terminal. I was pleased to note as we shut down that there was no adrenalin shaking of my hands. By this time, I was a pretty experienced risk manager – I was 58 years old. After getting to the hotel in this wet and windy weather I enjoyed my usual curry laksa and didn't make it to the bar. The F/O (First Officer) told me the next day that he and the check Captain, who had been sitting behind me watching the approach and landing, had made my wind shear flying the talk of the bar. That was nice but by the age of 58 I had learnt that valuable lesson which all pilots eventually learn: *You're only as good as your next landing, not your last.*

Over my 42 years of flying there were lots of landings and a lot of risk management. I flew a long way – about twenty million kilometres or about 500 times around the world – and nearly two million passengers were delivered safely to their terminals. In the process of doing all this I naturally collected a few stories along the way. I'm not the only pilot with stories to tell. My lifelong pilot mates certainly all have their stories. The following accounts of experiences – both in the air and on the ground are mine though and I would love to share them with you.

WHY BECOME A PILOT?

A young skinny boy growing up in the fifties and sixties really had the world to choose from in a relatively wealthy country, an education was on offer and, in those boom times, it was expected that a job should be available when education finished. I didn't overthink where I was headed as there seemed to be plenty of time to choose a future. Why start thinking before I had to?

I realise in retrospect that, as a young teenager, I was interested in relatively few things. The world was a smaller place then – I wasn't exposed to the complexities of today's world as kids are now. Good thing? Bad thing? I don't know. I did however dream of winning the grand final for my footy team with the last kick of the game, but then 98% of all young blokes have that ambition. The other 2% want to be the umpires. (It's a power thing.) No internet and limited television meant that when I did start to get interested in things, I actually read a lot of the *Encyclopedia Britannica*, the only source of information around at the time.

In these years, I realised I liked finding out how things worked. I made a Meccano contraption with wheels around a little steam engine and had it chuffing up the footpath. With gears and rubber bands, I built a gearing system with a 13.5 to

1 ratio. By coincidence this is about the same ratio that turbo jet drive shafts have to be reduced by to drive the propellers on turbo props, *deedoo deedoo*. I'm glad they don't actually use my system though, the rubber bands would just melt. Yes, I envied the boys who learnt to play guitar so they could sing to the girls at school year parties, but I was too busy exploring this new universe of mechanical things and, besides, I was a bit slow and shy with the girls.

Lots of kids, mostly boys back then, of course, built model aircraft and got right into all aspects of aviation. Not me. I got straight into the mechanics of flight by buying cheap little balsa wood toy aircraft, which needed a rubber band wound up to spin the little plastic propellers. I got a great kick out of flying a little plastic footballer on short flights around the backyard and side street with the limited amount of stored energy in the wound-up rubber band. For some reason, that little plastic footballer had been cast as if he was sitting on the ground, which made him an ideal pilot for the small toy aircraft.

If I stuck this pilot on the single balsa wood rail with a small rubber band, the centre of gravity of the aircraft would be altered and I would have to move the wing along a bit to alter the centre of lift. I didn't know I was doing these things of course, I was just learning about flight from the ground up. (Sorry, I make these atrocious puns all through the book, so watch out!) When some form of sport wasn't happening for me, these engineering hobbies were the go. A bit of information was forced into my brain by reading encyclopedias, but science fiction and James Bond books opened my eyes as well.

The high school I went to was a big 'baby boomer' in the outer suburbs of Melbourne, overstocked with kids, understocked with teachers and other resources. This was a perfect place to learn how to pick locks, open cars, blow things up, and electrify things. All this was taught by fellow pupils as there also weren't enough guards. I heard that Egypt spent more money per head of population on education than then-backwater Australia did. This may or may not be true, but it certainly felt like it in the State system of the time.

Macleod High School was a 1,500-odd pupil – I don't use 'odd' in an obvious way here – co-educational institution, which meant it had girls as well as boys as inmates. Teachers were a mixture of old school (sorry) and young progressives. I did what is now known as STEM subjects with no pretence of being given an all-round education. Science, Technology, Engineering and Maths was where I was put and that's where I stayed. Mind you, I was following my older sister and preceding my younger brother through the school and it would appear that those subjects were the only ones any of us were any good at.

Having only half the teachers needed meant, of course, that it was quite often pointless turning up to school and self-education at home was the way to go. Not recommended, as the only person you can ask if you have a question is the only person on the planet who, you know for sure, doesn't know the answer.

I tell you all about these school-related experiences because they all come together and actually help in later years. For instance, I had been given a healthy education in the capabilities of girls/women when it came to anything. Academics, strength of character, intelligence, of all types, these school girls had it in spades. As a result, I've always been able to talk easily with women. All I had to do was assume their superiority in most things and I got along fine.

Sport, the tougher the better, was all the go and luckily the gene pool that selected me was imbued with enough coordination, speed and size to help in this regard. Because I could run faster than average, I was given responsibility as an Athletics Captain and a House Captain. This apparently impresses future employers as they see you as someone who can take responsibility someday.

Towards the end of the final school year, Qantas Empire Airways were offering pilot cadetships. I knew enough about flying, because my father was an airline pilot, to think that a job flying aircraft may well be a thing to do. I knew that it was a job that entailed skill, challenges and a bit of application of those practical sciences that I was interested in. I was a realist enough to know that getting a cadetship wouldn't be easy. Academic and health standards and the huge numbers of young blokes attracted to this honey pot of a career, as they would have seen it anyway, would be big hurdles to clear. I'd certainly give it a go but what did I or any other candidate really know what a flying career meant? As fate would have it, I got a glimpse as the school year ended.

The senior formal was one of the last social functions at the school. This dance, in as formal clothes as we could muster, was a big deal. The Americans are always making movies about 'the Prom' – this was our version. I was just finding out that I could ask girls out and some would say, 'Yes'. (Co-ed schools are great!) However, this particular dance could have been a disaster for me. In my caution in making sure I had a date, I'd actually invited two girls – both accepted. Not good.

By pure luck, a young pilot mate of my father had arranged to deliver a single-engine aircraft from Sydney to Darwin during the week of the dance. I jumped at the chance to go with him and got my first taste of real flying – hard work, exciting, tiring and exhilarating all at once – and I was saved from a formal that could have been the end of me. Mind you, the midyear formal could also have been the end of me, but that's another story.

The flight to Darwin was an epic. The aircraft was an old forties British aircraft, an Auster. A two-squeezy-seated, high-wing tail dragger with an old Gypsy motor. We flew for hours each day over deserts or tiger country – rough bush or really rough terrain without bits to land in where you know you don't want the engine to stop. An aircraft can glide down, but it's really nice to have a flat clearing and, if you do have to land, hopefully you are in a country without actual tigers.

Walking into bush towns from the airport at sunset, wobbling with the severest case of 'sea legs' I've ever had – you know how the world keeps moving after you get off a ship for a while – was a new experience for me on this trip. Walking back out to the airport before dawn with the only light being weak starlight was also something new and unforgettable. No iPhone flashlights in 1966.

Flying over featureless deserts for hours, keeping a steady heading and hoping the wind wasn't too strong to mess up our navigation, flying under heavy clouds and being hit so hard with the rain that the newly applied paint on the leading edge of the wings was just eroded off, was an adventure. This flying thing was indeed a thing to do. I was lucky – I'd found out that flying an aircraft was a challenge and fun at the same time. Roll on the Qantas testing and interviews.

I mentioned earlier that school experiences have helped in later life. No doubt, 'Maximum Security' High helped in being that little bit more mature. This school encouraged self-reliance and a bit of toughness; it didn't do it deliberately, it just happened. I also mentioned that the midyear dance was a bit dangerous. I'll let you be the judge.

The dance was not out of character for this time and place. First off, on the day of the dance, the senior girls were called to a special assembly by the headmistress. This was expected as they were always being briefed on how not to be de-briefed later that night. Apparently, if they wore red, blokes were uncontrollable. This was conveyed to us boys when Maureen, one of the science girls, a clever wild spirit, ran back into one of the science rooms, leapt onto the big front desk, opened her dark blue parka and flashed the red lining at all of us now quite bewildered blokes. She then ran screaming from the room. She often did this sort of stuff, so it didn't worry us until she then popped her head back in the door and implied in no uncertain terms that obviously we weren't real men because we didn't chase her. Maureen ended up a very respectable, on the surface anyway, doctor.

What wasn't expected that day was that the boys were also called to an assembly. This was odd – we weren't subject to any 'no touch' rules. Even if we didn't actually know how to do this 'touching', we were going to pretend we did. It turned out that the young male teachers charged with running the dance had done the right thing. After threats of violence from some local gangs, rather than cancel the dance, they had come up with a plan – arming a whole mob of over six feet tall footballers, basket ballers and 'sportsmen' with hockey sticks, cricket bats and baseball bats. What with teacher's duty of care and such, this would not happen now anywhere in the world – OK maybe in Russia.

Sure enough, halfway through the dance, while I was dancing with Maureen, who had defied her father's ban and climbed out of her bedroom window, there were two interruptions. First, one irate father stormed in and made a bit of a scene retrieving a daughter. Next, the call went out for 'those boys we organised earlier' as the gangs had turned up. This meant about twenty tall, but way too skinny, kids filed past a teacher as he handed us our bits of wood that may or may not have been of any use. We then formed up in a line – battle formation – behind the footy coach who had opened one glass door in the big wide entrance area. We had a good view of the attacking Visigoths and, while trying to look as tough as we could, there were the occasional murmurs of disquiet. 'Look at that huge fat bastard, he's eating a fucking chain,' was a fairly typical comment.

Nobody got hurt that night. The young footy coach scared the Huns off with threats that he'd let us killers loose on them, and statements like, 'Look at them, all of them footballers, all huge'. We were just hoping he wouldn't aggravate them too much.

This was typical of the area and the times. My dad had been a bouncer at the local youth club and had probably already thumped a few of the gang members on show that night; there had been one occasion when he and three other men took on a chain-wielding gang.

These experiences in self-teaching and learning how to keep yourself safe always helped me in life. The neighbourhood and times taught me one essential skill, how to win a fight by a hundred yards. Flying overseas had its moments, especially in the early days. I was always glad to have a bit of survival training before I started.

3
SECURITY ISSUES

As a fairly new Second Officer (S/O), I was enjoying my time flying the line on the mighty 707 and would jump at any chance to get back up in the air. I wasn't due for a flight for the next few days and had flown down to Canberra to visit my lady friend. We had planned for her to drive me back to Sydney after she finished work for the week. This meant I only had to buy a cheap staff ticket for the flight down. Well, things changed – best laid plans and all that. A flatmate rang to say that Qantas had called desperately looking for a S/O for the following day to do a London trip. Youth, enthusiasm and a misguided sense of loyalty saw me volunteering to be that S/O. I had to visit the Qantas office in Canberra to get a ticket to fly home as soon as I could – this ticket took a very long time to appear. The manager didn't like this unusual request even though it would obviously help the company function better. That was not his job, it would appear. At last I was able to get back to Sydney and set off on the trip to London and back.

The flight to London went via Hong Kong and Tehran, and it was in Tehran that things started to get tricky. The time of departure was scheduled for before dawn which meant the crew arriving at the airport around two or three am to get things ready. Our little bus, that just fitted the four technical and seven cabin crew, duly arrived at the departures area. The scene that greeted us was totally unexpected.

We were in the Middle East and the early 70s was a turbulent time – when isn't it in the Middle East? But this was still unexpected. Two years after this night, the Munich Olympic massacre occurred and another year later the nasty little Yom Kippur war was fought. The Palestinians were in the news throughout this time with various activist groups living up to their description. Hijackings were the go and even pilot emergency checklists had Arabic phrases to help communicate with the bloke holding the gun. On this particular night, one group decided to go for it big time and the faecal matter hit the revolving air mover like it had never done before. The Western world's airlines were attacked in a brand- new way – several aircraft were hijacked at the same time. People were killed or injured and four big jets never flew again. We knew nothing of all this when we arrived at the airport but things were about to go pear-shaped.

When we arrived at the airport, as visitors from a quieter part of the world, we watched in awe. The Iranian Army was fortifying the whole area and it was a sight to behold. Fully armed combat troops were everywhere and if they weren't everywhere there was a squad of them running to fill the empty spot. They were not mucking about. They had bulldozers making ditches so that main battle tanks could back into them and become low- profile armoured gun emplacements. These tanks had serious artillery – big guns designed to stop other tanks or to bring down buildings. At the airport entrance there were lots of guns and we really hoped they wouldn't be pointed at us.

As we got out of the bus, trying to give out the vibe that we were no threat to anybody, two British agents came and met us. These were spooks and we were really glad that someone was able to tell us WTF was going on. Well, we were glad until they actually told us what was going on. They showed us a telegram – for young readers this was something like a text message or tweet printed out – and it was a very official, very secret one by the look of it. It was a warning from British Intelligence to anyone who might be concerned. That was us. I can tell you we were concerned and getting more so all the time. The telegram warned of expected action by Palestinian activists – they were on the warpath and we were in their sights – imminent hijacking attempts on multiple aircraft in the Middle East. They didn't know exactly where, but they expected attempts on American, French and British targets. The most chilling titbit was the phrase 'for British, also read Australian'.

Well, what did we expect? I worked for an airline named Qantas Empire Airways and I had pledged allegiance to the British queen all through primary school. I could understand that some Popular Front strategist might not quite get the subtlety of us Australians making ourselves self-governing while still calling ourselves British. This same strategist was probably just trying to achieve exactly that – self-government – but there was no subtlety about it.

The Qantas 707 had arrived from Hong Kong early. The inbound crew had been whisked off to the hotel and we were told to load up and depart before the airport was shut down. Normally the three pilots did the paperwork in the little Qantas office and the Flight Engineer and cabin crew went out to the aircraft to prepare it. This was 1970, so that meant you really did go out to the aircraft. There were no aerobridges joining the aircraft to the terminal. Passengers and crew either bussed it out to the aircraft or they walked. We were Westerners in Iran. They didn't like Westerners very much even back then — I think it probably goes back to the Crusades. Australia didn't have much to do with the sad events that occurred way back then but trying to explain that to an Iranian when you had the British monarch on your currency was again a subtlety too far. This dislike I'd witnessed firsthand, on my very first stopover in Tehran.

That time, the second most junior pilot took me out to a hole-in-the-wall restaurant close to our hotel. He'd had multiple vodkas and limes but I was off the grog – and just as well. Two local young thugs decided to give us a hard time and tried to pick a fight. They came up to our table and started messing with our main courses with their hands. My mate was happy to find some new friends – vodka and not growing up in an area that had a lot of young thugs will make you do that. I had neither of these advantages and knew exactly what was happening.

The two thugs were suddenly confronted by a bloke who had jumped up, thrown his chair out of the way to give himself kicking room and was brandishing the mean-looking steak knife I had been eating my lamb with. The vision of a big six-footer who obviously was not as drunk as they thought stopped them in their tracks and they quickly re-evaluated taking me on. They made a speedy exit as the owner of the establishment started yelling at them. I'm not sure my mate noticed any of this; he was probably wondering why I had jumped up and thrown my chair away.

On another occasion, I was hurrying through the Tehran airport corridors early one morning to get the little bus out to the aircraft when I came around a corner and nearly collided with an Iranian airport policeman. His look of hatred was one thing but he wasn't going to let it finish there. He drew his pistol, even though by then I was apologising as much as I could and moving pretty fast towards that little bus. Just love the smell of adrenalin in the morning – at least I hoped it was adrenalin I was smelling.

So, what happened next on the night of the long rifles, didn't come as a surprise to me. When we found out that our aircraft was waiting for us well outside the military cordon there was absolutely no security help offered to us. Not a friendly move. The Captain ordered the cabin crew to stay put, the F/O to do the paperwork and the Engineer and myself to accompany him out to the 707. The three of us headed out to the aircraft.

Strangely, the thousands of armed soldiers we'd seen when we arrived were nowhere to be seen. Now, if you were a Palestinian commando squad where would you go? Where the tanks were or where three unarmed Westerners who fitted the description of one of your targets were?

It was really dark out on the apron. The airport didn't have that much lighting in the terminal, let alone the outer reaches. Very warily, as you might expect, we got about our task. We all started to search our assigned areas, the Captain checked out the flight deck, the Engineer the outside of the aircraft and I did the cabin. We were looking not only for freedom fighters with their trusty Kalashnikovs but also for anything suspicious. Were they leaving a cache of weapons in a nice little hidey hole that their people could access after take-off or were there bombs being planted to create confusion? We didn't know, so we searched as much as we could. Opening the toilet doors was my job. Nobody else was around to see how brave I was doing this so I wasn't very brave. I did it and prepared to instantly surrender if gun barrels appeared. What else could I do?

It took us a long time but we couldn't find anything, so the flight went ahead.

Passenger and baggage screening weren't anything like it is today, we just had to accept that we had done our part. The route that we followed after take-off was the normal one, south of the Caspian Sea then just south of the USSR, as it was then – Azerbaijan and Georgia now. It was a strange abnormal flight.

We kept a listening watch on the radio, listening to our normal air traffic controllers but also the emergency frequency that all aircraft should have up on their second radio.

These were VHF radios. Very High Frequency means good clear transmissions but a limit to the line of sight between transmitter and receiver. The higher you were meant the further you could see and the further away you could pick up the signal. If the transmitter and the receiver were both high up, like in two cruising jets, then you could hear each other a long way away.

Well, we heard the *Mayday* call and it was on. An aircraft was telling everyone around them they were now on an unauthorised steep descent, so watch out. He didn't have to tell anybody he was being hijacked; everyone knew. I can't remember whether he actually said who they were or where exactly they were but I do know we put all our landing lights on and searched outside especially above us in case he was coming down on top of us. Around us, jets were being hijacked by people who knew what they were doing; they were aware of secret codes and had enough aviation knowledge to get their captives to a secretly renovated old RAF air base in the Jordanian desert –Dawson's Field

I'll never know how close to all this we had been; we were picking up aircraft hundreds of miles away and I was quite happy if all this stuff in fact stayed hundreds of miles away. I was happy to have a normal flight to London from then on, get off and go to a nice hotel.

There had, in fact, been multiple hijackings and one failed attempt. A Swiss Air and a TWA were diverted to the desert and a Pan Am Jumbo ended up in Beirut. There were a lot of crew and passengers not going to any soft beds like I was. Their ordeal was just beginning. Another jet, this time British, ended up in the desert a couple of days later. Most hostages were released fairly quickly, although some British and Americans were very lucky to live through some serious fighting that erupted between Jordanian troops and Palestinians.

Some Jewish and American citizens were eventually traded for some PFLP (Popular Front for the Liberation of Palestine) prisoners. In the end, only one pilot hostage was actually wounded and one hijacker killed on a failed attempt on an EL AL jet. The four jets, three at Dawson's Field and the Jumbo at Beirut, were all blown up. The Pan Am Jumbo was actually flown to Cairo and blown up. The outcome could have been a lot worse.

On our flight up to London, the Captain got me to write up the facts of what happened, on which he could base his report. I put as much down as I could, it got his approval and he signed my notes. It became the official report that was sent back to Sydney for all sorts of hierarchy to see, review, have meetings over and file. I wish I'd known.

Did we get a hero's welcome when we got back to Sydney? Well, not if my experience is anything to go by. We'd arrived as usual about six in the morning after having no sleep. I was home and asleep by about eight but then a mate from the HR department wakes me to tell me the head of HR is about to call and wants me in his office. Well, yes, big drama on that flight, no wonder he wants to see me. 'No,' he says, 'while you were away, Qantas Security ran a full security check on you. What have you been up to, delivering cars or something?'

'WTF!' (Sorry about the language but I can assure you that expression was around then and I'm pretty sure I used it – not in the shortened form.) He explained that some Qantas staff were making money by delivering vehicles for car dealers around the country. They could then travel home on staff travel cheaply and have a competitive advantage over any rivals. I had obviously set off some alarm bells by getting a staff ticket in Canberra. Using staff travel for business was forbidden. I never was a businessman and had never heard of this minor scam – I'd seen some real malfeasance recently and it didn't involve motor cars.

Forearmed with this information, I was ready for the call from the head of HR. Fred was a big fat bloke sitting in an office and he invited me to come in to his office without saying why. I told him I needed no accolades or rewards for what happened up in Tehran and that I was just pleased to be of help. When he seemed confused what I was on about, I asked if he had seen the newspapers and the film of aircraft being blown up in the desert and if he knew a Qantas plane and crew had been up there and what had gone on. Did he know that there had been absolutely no help from Qantas security, who were all back in Sydney doing fuck all? I then made a deal with him. He would never ring me again while he worked for the company and I would never come into his office – that deal would also apply to his useless, fat-assed security mates as well.

You may gather I was a little miffed and I probably should have waited until I'd had some sleep before going nuclear. Fred obviously got hold of the report I'd written and I never heard another word from him or from security. The pilot managers did note, however, that there was a new S/O who you had to be wary of and who would probably never be asked to join any pilot management team. I was happy with all of these developments.

4
CADET TRAINING

After the end of my final school year I got a call from my sister. A few years older than me, she had moved straight from school into computer programming at Monash university, a big Melbourne uni. She was ringing to tell me the computer she had programmed to tabulate all the state's final-year school results had stopped as my personal number had come up. She had told the computer to stop when that happened. I was getting my results weeks earlier than everyone else and, luckily, they were good enough to get me into any course I wanted at university. It was easier in those days and I'd won some scholarship money to help pay for the fees. My sister also pointed out just how simple it would have been to change my scores. Apparently, then, as now, the people who control the computers control the world.

Until Qantas came up with an offer university was the live option. Nuclear physics and all that quantum stuff was where I was headed. I was at one stage the first student on the roll at the brand-new Latrobe Uni. Somebody named Anderson soon took that honour away from me but I saw the positive of having a name that starts with 'A'. My sister eventually changed universities and ended up in charge of Latrobe's IT section. By then Latrobe was on its way to becoming Australia's biggest tertiary institution.

My final interview for Qantas was held the day after I had competed in a night athletic competition. I had pulled some chest muscles, because of an insufficient warm-up in the cold night air, and turned up for the most important job interview of my life in considerable pain. Captain Bird – I kid you not – was the lead man of three Captain interviewers. He was down from Sydney and bored at the end of the day after too many spotty kids. I was next. Although I didn't know it at the time, Captain Bird was actually in charge of the whole cadet course, but it was obvious to me that he was the power in the room. He was the man I had to impress.

Well, my school results didn't seem to do the trick and my father hadn't briefed me on how aircraft flew. When he learned to fly at the height of WW2 they probably didn't bother teaching trainee pilots too much theory. Anyway, these Captains were more interested in whether I supported the Vietnam War to stop the Viet Cong from taking over Australia. Not being stupid, I went along with them. Of course, I agreed completely. 'Dominoes, dominoes falling all the way across the water,' I was heard to shout.

Then things took a turn for the worse. I hadn't realised it but with the pulled muscles I was actually catching my breath from the pain. Captain Bird just looked at me and asked, 'Do you have a speech impediment there, Bill?' Again, not being stupid, I thought a speech impediment might be a thing that would not enhance my chances of getting a job flying. I quickly pointed out the reason and waited for the next disaster.

Well, it turned out Captain Bird liked athletics. He saved the day for me. He sat up and asked what distance I ran and then asked, tellingly, if I was an even time runner. This meant he knew more than most about athletics. Even time was 10 seconds for 100 yards and, when I confessed to being better than even, I was suddenly his golden-haired boy. The other two Captains were just staring at him, not me.

On the way home, I told my Dad about how being an athlete had turned the interview around.

He then told me how he got the nod from the Air Force back in 1942 to go into pilot training. On his selection into the Air Force, he had done well enough in the maths exam to get into navigator school. This meant air crew and he was happy. The officers making the decision recognised him as being a prominent Australian rules footballer and a top-grade cricketer. They crossed the 'navigator' assignment off and wrote 'pilot'. The thinking was, if you can catch a ball, you can fly a plane – after all hand eye coordination does help. He was a pilot from then on until he retired at sixty.

A future Prime Minister of Australia went into the navigation school about the time my father nearly did. Dad never met him. Another future Prime Minister sat on the flight deck and watched my father's last landing on his retirement day and asked, 'If you could land so well on the last flight how good did you have to be to get the job in the first place?'

Maybe those RAAF officers had the right idea.

Now, before you can fly on the line for an airline, you have to actually learn to fly. My cadet course started just over 50 years ago. I know this because the survivors have just had a huge piss-up reunion in the wine country north of Sydney. Much can be assumed by my telling you that. This was a course that gave its cadets a lifelong camaraderie and esprit de corps. It was challenging, fulfilling – all those qualities you would expect of a quasi- military course where young blokes went from knowing nothing to knowing just how much they didn't know. Believe me, that's a big step.

Twenty super busy months of aviation academics, flying training and flight navigator qualifications up to the highest rating. As well, there was stuff like report writing and English. It would appear that the education of blokes who were good at STEM subjects always missed out on English no matter where you came from.

I won't go into the cadet course too much. I will say that I found it just as hard and as big a challenge as I had expected. I did a lot of growing up in that pressure-cooker environment. There weren't many second chances given and there was a reasonable attrition rate. My cadet mates learnt all the secrets about each other and all our strengths and weaknesses. I once called the course a 'character revealing' one not a 'character forming' one. These heavy experiences where you rely on each other, have each other's back and have a healthy competition will always form bonds that shouldn't be messed with, they are way too precious. Fifty years? It could have been yesterday up in that Hunter Valley resort.

I will say a few general things. One, my fitness level dropped alarmingly even though we were doing the Canadian Air Force fitness regime. It would appear beer and bad food, late nights and more beer will slowly erode things. Who would have thought? I remember I and another senior cadet turned up for a workout with the newest batch of cadets who started a year and a half after us. My mate and I were struggling to keep up with these young bastards when the instructor, a new one, tried to console us. 'Don't worry,' he said, 'you two will soon catch up. It takes time. How long have you been at it – a few weeks?' My mate lying on the floor managed to wheeze out, 'Eighteen fucking months!'

Learning how to navigate using techniques best suited for Captain Cook was weird. We trained for astronavigation using a sextant. The only basic change from the 18th century version being a periscope attachment so it could be stuck up through a hole in the flight deck roof. My son, who has modern-day airline pilot navigation qualifications, refuses to believe we ever did this. We even used the term *cocked hat* for the three lines on the map that the sextant gave. Ideally they would intersect at a point. In reality, they formed a triangle named after what an old 18th century sailor would recognise from above as the shape of his three cornered *cocked hat*.

Pilots also still talk about speed in knots, as in throwing out a little bucket on the end of a string into the ocean and counting the knots tied into the string at regular intervals. As the sand runs out in the egg timer you call, 'Six and a half knots, sir, and avast ye lubbers.'

The real secret to this is that a knot is the equivalent to one nautical mile per hour. One nautical mile is one minute of latitude, a very easy thing to measure on a map that has latitude markings. What is really happening here is a way of using the angular measurements from your sextant and speed readouts from your string to produce a position on a map. I have always known that there are people way smarter than me. It would appear that they were there in the past as well.

Going back to getting a small cocked hat. I had the ability to get them as large as the greater Sydney metropolitan area, and this was from a stationary Perspex dome on the roof of a Qantas building at the airport. This meant I had narrowed the position of the building to somewhere in Sydney. These night-time exercises in the bubble were long and boring and the occasional instructor felt so too. One Nav instructor was just out of the British Air Force, where they had new nuclear bomb armed aircraft of various shapes and sizes. They were all called 'V bombers' however. He'd been on one of them and held a bit of street cred with us because of that. One particular night, he and a few of us cadets trudged across the roof of the big building to the little hut with the Perspex bubble.

It was an absolutely clear night and ahead of us lay a few hours of drudgery turning ourselves into sailing ship navigators. This instructor, once inside, eyed all of us off very carefully before, for some reason, settling on me. He ordered me to get up into the dome. 'See if you can see if the weather is suitable for shots.' Now, he had taken his time before selecting me so I knew I'd better not blow it – my credibility was on the line. 'Sir, I think I can see some wispy clouds out over the Blue Mountains.' I couldn't see any clouds but apparently it was the right answer because we all ran off the roof and adjourned to the pub.

The lesson in the pub was great because the ex-RAF navigator opened our eyes as to why a British jet carrying *a little bucket of sunshine*, as these guys called their thermo nukes, at just below the speed of sound was bloody hard for a Russian missile to hit. The missile would have to fly at just over the speed of sound to chase the bomber and at that speed they had real control problems from the shock waves forming all over the control surfaces and nose. Logical, especially if you think of the turning circles of a faster missile trying to catch something that can out-turn it.

I had an assignment during the cadet course where I had to give a lecture on the mathematics of speed and turning circles and angle of banks and all that, and no Google to help either. I astounded the class – well, I kept them awake – with how big a radius a Concorde would need to go around a corner when it was flat out. Really big. Russia eventually made missiles that flew so fast no amount of British sneakiness would stop them.

Recently, on a cruise, I met an older American who had flown forever and had some great stories. He had started out in the USAF as a navigator on the American equivalent to the V-bombers so he was the American version of my old British navigation instructor. He joined me and another retired Qantas bloke for the obligatory pre-dinner drinks. Pilots have always done this because that way they have an instant audience that understands what they're talking about – electrical busses, false indications, subtle engine failures, cabin fires, grid navigation, pressure pattern navigation – that sort of thing. All conversations like this are referred to as *opening the hangar door*. This term is the only part of these conversations I have never really understood.

The American had flown on a B47, (Not B747) a very early strategic bomber the Yanks had. His job was to navigate from inside a completely enclosed nose cone using, wait for it, a periscope sextant. Once over the target, he looked through another eyepiece attached to a bombsight and became the bomb aimer on the mission. His job was to obliterate a Russian city with a bomb thousands of times more powerful than those dropped on Japan. In my early twenties, I was not doing this. My path was way more peaceful.

The navigation studies on the cadet course had lots of interesting stuff in them. Form of the Earth and Aeronautical Charts (FEAC) was one subject that taught all about how a flat piece of paper could never actually represent the globe we live on, or indeed the oblate spheroid that the earth really is – it's a bit squashed at the poles. There was a great need for tables, graphs, almanacs, logarithms and then more tables. Most of this information fitted into a big book called *Norie's Nautical*

Tables (first published 1803). Remember slide rules ruled in the 1960s. Basic electronic calculators were years away and, in 1803, they probably used quill and parchment. We were indeed old school and probably some of the last old school navs ever trained.

The huge advantage to this book of tables was that it was needed in the exams. The margins in this book soon filled up with very light pencil marks, hardly visible unless you were right up close – like if you had it open in front of you. The arduous task of memorising all the formulas – spherical trigonometry throws up some beauties – was therefore negated as was the need to learn countless facts and figures that were required to pass these exams. More time was freed up for essential drinking sessions and those lovely Sydney girls.

I witnessed a variation on this exam-passing technique some thirty years later. On the last day of a gruelling Jumbo Jet ground school, one of the other trainees turned up for the written exam with his kid's pencil case. It was all covered in graffiti – looked like a stranded train carriage in the morning. I commented on this and he made me take a closer look. Every fact, figure, and formula needed to get a Jumbo into the air and back was cleverly inscribed and camouflaged – brilliant work. This bloke had got some good training in the Air Force.

All in all, I learned a lot on the cadet course. Very important, for instance, to insist that somebody shuffle the cards in front of you before you play a mob of so-called mates at blackjack. It's amazing how some blokes can stack cards and then fall off chairs laughing at a certain naive person who may or may not have been completely taken in by the ruse.

Mates! Lifelong mates.

5
AILERONS

Thirty-nine thousand feet and approaching the main airways that traverse the southern islands of Japan up to the northern reaches. These airways are busy at the best of times but are clogged in the late afternoon peak. The aircraft, a Boeing 767, was on a routine tourist flight taking Japanese passengers home. As the Captain, I was sitting in the left-hand seat on the flight deck. Sitting next to me was the Second Officer while the First Officer was taking a break in the crew's rest area in the middle of the aircraft.

The problem that arose that day had the real possibility of sending about two hundred and forty people to the bottom of the East China Sea. The kicker, if that had happened, is that, even if all the wreckage and the various recorders were recovered, no provable reason for the crash would have been found.

The auto pilot was handling the cruise as is the case in 99% of flights. A little explanation is needed here to tease out exactly what that means because, to fully appreciate the cluster fuck that follows, it is important to understand the role of the autopilot – what it does and does not do.

The autopilot can be operating in various *modes*. That just means the variety of things it can do. At this moment it was holding Flight Level 390 (39000 feet) and, in the other two dimensions, it was holding a track (path over the surface) generated by the navigation system. This track can be seen on the Navigation Display screen as a magenta line. If the aircraft is on track, and proceeding along it, the line can be seen as vertical and in the centre of the screen with the little aircraft symbol sitting at the bottom. The line, and anything on it, like an airport, comes down the screen. The aircraft symbol does not go up – it's all relative. This flight everything was as it should be – until it wasn't.

This particular autopilot system was subject to a minor glitch that was annoying – but only mildly. Every now and then, for some reason, a horizontal yellow warning line would appear through the green NAV indication on the screen in front of me. The yellow bar was supposed to mean the autopilot was having serious trust issues with its interface with the navigation system but my experience with this glitch over the years meant I had a serious trust issue with the yellow bar instead. In the past, every six months or so, this little yellow bar would appear and give the indication that all was not well. In the past, it had always proved to be a false alarm as there wasn't actually anything wrong.

I'd got wise to the yellow bar – all you had to do was disconnect the autopilot. A button on the control wheel was the easiest and the best way to do this because it meant you actually had 'control' at your fingertips when the autopilot disconnected. The yellow bar would vanish and you could reconnect the autopilot by pressing the *on* button on a panel in front of you. Then you could just sit back for the next few months and wait until it happened again. The glitch was in the 767's system and would just show up on any aircraft at any time.

So, yellow bar, aural warning and an escalation in this case – the autopilot shat itself. That is to say, it disconnected with its own visual and aural wake-ups. I put my hands onto the control wheel; the automatic disconnect meant I had to. By doing so, I had achieved one thing in these evolving events – I had gained some control but, most significantly, not complete control.

The Swiss cheese theory of accidents says that all barriers that humans put up against mishaps will have holes in them. People can put more barriers up but they too will have holes and if the holes happen to line up then there is a lovely straight line for the bad stuff to go through. This Swiss cheese theory is taught to pilots so that when things go wrong maybe a well-considered action can form a barrier to any impending mishap; a barrier without a hole.

There was a leaking tap in the centre of the cabin of this 767 – the first hole in the cheese had been found and a pathway started. There is a drain hole at the lowest point in this section of the fuselage to safely get rid of any leaking water. This hole leads directly into the wheel well below it, that is, the space the undercarriage comes up into and where it is stored during the flight. To get the water to the bottom of this space there is a plastic tube fitted from the drain hole to the outside. The tube is stuck onto the hole with some plastic/silicone type of goo. Another cheese hole appeared here – literally a hole in this goo that allowed water to spray into the wheel well and, upper atmosphere conditions being what they are, this water turned to ice pretty bloody quickly. You can see that 'cluster' is beginning to be a very appropriate word for all this.

A safety slice, that would have stopped this nasty pathway dead, is fly-by-wire technology. Fly-by-wire is where the flight controls are moved by computer signals. This system is not available on this aircraft because the 767 was designed when computers were small, weak things just waiting for their spot in the museum. They just couldn't do it. As a result, instead of making the control surfaces work with electrical wires, metal cables are used. That is, a moving wire rather than a stationary one. I'm not saying here that fully computerised controls don't have their problems, they do, they just don't suffer from mechanical lockups.

On this aircraft, one of these moving control cables runs through a big metal pulley attached to the front wall of the wheel well. The cable runs from the control wheel, the one I was hanging onto upstairs, to the little flappy things you see at the rear of the wings and towards the wing tips. These *ailerons* (from the French 'little wing') are not flaps but they do flap. Flaps are flaps but don't actually flap – I didn't name these things.

Ailerons make the aircraft roll and tip over, as when the aircraft goes around a corner. Everybody has seen a motor bike or a bicycle go around a corner. Anything that can lean into a corner, does. I won't go into the explanation for this with graphs, diagrams and all sorts of cool maths, I don't want to make your eyes glaze over. Readers who are ahead of me will have connected the dots to see there may be a problem with the ailerons on this aircraft. The ice had been forming in the wheel well for who knows how long. We were about eight hours into the flight at this stage.

That other well-known theory that has actually progressed to a Law came into play at this stage. 'Murphy's Law' works in aviation better than anywhere else because there is more to go wrong, and if it can go wrong it will. Thanks Murphy. Three dimensions, speed, fuel-burn-induced time constraints and really complicated machinery all help Murphy enjoy his work in aviation. He made sure the spray of water was aimed at the front wall of the wheel well and not the rear and therefore it was all over the pulley. He made sure the conditions were just right to form ice.

Once ice formed on the pulley, it stopped moving. Once it stopped moving, the cable out to the ailerons stopped moving. The pink line wasn't perfectly straight up anymore, the autopilot hadn't been able to fix it and had correctly disconnected itself. The little yellow bar was telling the truth for once. Cluster had happened.

Upstairs, I didn't know this. I was 'hand flying' the aircraft. It was now in a condition the Wright brothers would easily recognise. I had my hands on the control wheel which was attached to a control column and I had my feet on the rudders. I could now move the aircraft in the three axes; pitch, roll and yaw. Every other time I had hand flown an aircraft this was the case but not this time. I could still make the nose yaw left and right with the rudders, I could still make the nose go up and down by pushing or pulling the control column: push to put the nose down, pull to get it to go up. But the roll thing wasn't going to happen if the cables to the ailerons weren't going to move.

At this point I was wondering why the little yellow bar was escalating things and had shut the autopilot off – this was unusual behaviour. Good flight management in these situations means the crew pool their knowledge and hopefully resolve any issues. The S/O and I were racking our brains but it was obvious we must accept what we had, namely an autopilot shutdown possibly associated with its interface with the navigation system. I saw that the pink line was a smidgen off vertical, so I thought I would at least fix that and then apply the fix that had worked in the past. To do this, I would roll the aircraft with the ailerons and turn it so the pink line was vertical and then re-engage the autopilot.

In trying to roll and therefore turn the aircraft I found out I had lost control over the ailerons, the control wheel wouldn't move. It was as if the autopilot was still engaged. I was now very alert but not yet alarmed. This autopilot is just one of three and if it wasn't going to behave, by not disengaging in the roll axis, then I'd make sure it was shut off completely and I'd let one of the others have a go. Triple redundancy is the name of the game and I was all for it.

My alertness level leapt as the usual methods of autopilot shut off made no difference; reconnecting and disconnecting the autopilot and doing the same with the other two, didn't help. Even hitting the 'AUTOPILOT DISCONNECT' bar that shuts off all the autopilots didn't budge it. Now I was a bit alarmed. The S/O beside me had no instant fix, we were both running out of ideas. As I said, good practice is to always check with other crew members in case they are onto something you're not. You might lose a little face if you don't know the fix, better than losing everything.

At this time, I ordered the seat belt sign on and tilted my head towards the flight deck door. The male flight attendant sitting behind us got the hint and skedaddled. I had both feet firmly on the rudders now for a real reason, I had somehow lost roll control and I had reverted automatically to the 'further effects of controls' to regain it. If a wing dropped now I had two methods to pick it up. The first was to apply rudder to make the aircraft yaw in the opposite direction of the dropping wing, this makes the dropping wing move slightly faster than the one going up – it's all relative, remember. Faster, more lift and up comes the wing. The further effect of yaw is therefore seen as roll.

The other method would be to use more power on the engine on the dropping wing, more power, more speed, more lift. This method is much harder because with the time lag in the power coming up or going down, you can easily 'over control'. This means the power/speed may be just coming up when you need it to be reducing and vice versa. Some incredible pilots have actually landed big jets using this method when their controls have lost hydraulic power. Some have even walked away from these landings. Things would have to get pretty scary before I started moving the thrust levers.

Using the rudders to their 'further effect' or 'secondary effect' is easy in a light aircraft. As a flying instructor, I demonstrated it to my students in one of the first lessons. When there wasn't a student on board but another instructor it was sometimes used as a primary way of turning the aircraft – just for the fun of it.

In a big swept-wing jet it's a completely non-fun thing to do. On my first *endorsement* onto a jet, the mighty Boeing 707, I got to do some great flying – the sort that is dangerous enough to only be done in simulators these days. The particular *air work* exercise, done with only a few tech crew on board, involved yawing the 707 to induce the roll. The thing is, on a swept-wing aircraft, things go bananas. It yaws and rolls both ways, the nose goes up and down viciously and the poor trainee flight engineer sitting behind me vomits like a volcano. The aerodynamics of this are very complicated. The lesson being given though was 'watch out for this *Dutch Roll* as it will kill you' and also make sure any jet you fly has a working *yaw damper* – a nifty little device that stops jets getting too far into this scenario. I knew any yawing would have to be gentle.

Thirty-nine thousand feet, boots on the rudders and a frozen control wheel.

Somewhere in the system there is supposed to be a breakaway that will separate my stuck control wheel from the co-pilot's. Maybe if I could break the cable breakaway, this would fix whatever was wrong and his would suddenly start working, or mine would. I would have settled for either.

So, I put two hands on the wheel and turned, and turned. I had been told that the control wheel could take whatever you did to it and I was testing that. After four or five seconds of gritted-teeth effort, it suddenly freed up with quite a rolling jolt to the aircraft. I was relieved but only to a certain degree. I still had no idea what had caused all this and the obvious thought of ice wasn't top of the pops. We hadn't been anywhere near a source of water for many hours; the last clouds we had been through were in the southern hemisphere.

I wasn't going to trust the autopilots. They might be the cause of all this, so I just continued to hand fly. The rest of the flight into Nagoya was conducted with me regularly rolling the wings to give me confidence that I could, in fact, still roll the wings. I was bloody happy not to have to fly, at about right angles, into one of the busiest airways on the planet with a crippled aircraft steered by rudder only.

On this particular flight there were two important Australian tourists heading to Japan for what was, for them, one of several trips they did to that country in their retirement. My parents were the reason I had bid for this trip in the first place. My father, a pilot from 1942 until his retirement from Australian Airlines in 1979, came up to the flight deck for the landing. He'd felt the jolt, 26,000 hours in the air and you get a feel for it. After I explained the symptoms he just said, 'You had ice somewhere in your aileron cable run.'

On the ground, after telling the Ground Engineer all about it, I had to sprint to catch the outgoing Captain before he got out to the aircraft to tell him not to take that aircraft anywhere, at least not until he found out what was wrong. The Ground Engineer meanwhile opened up the wheel well doors as they had shut back up after the undercarriage had gone down, and found the huge lump of ice still in place. I had freed up the pulley so that there was just enough movement for flying.

He alerted his bosses in Sydney. They in turn alerted Boeing and the engineer told me how the next morning his Japanese counterparts from All Nippon ran over to tell him about a big problem with all the world's 767s. Boeing had indeed ordered all 767s around the world inspected after each landing for wheel well ice: this went on for six weeks until the possibility of the same sort of leak was negated with a 'mod' (engineering modification.)

The other fix was an addition to the Emergency Checklists that all Boeing aircraft have. The title 'Jammed or Restricted Flight Controls' says it all; the checklist directs pilots to do exactly what I and the S/O did that day. We had made our mark on aviation history, but we'd rather not have.

Back in Sydney and there were, of course, all sorts of reports – verbal as well as written. I got told two things: 'You done good,' from the Captain in charge of safety; and the Chief pilot, passing me in the corridor, mentioned that Boeing had asked, after seeing the iceberg photos, 'Just how big is this pilot?' Size helps but adrenalin is best.

In telling my story to a group of pilots during an Emergency Procedures day (appropriate) I told them how the Qantas ground engineers were now calling me 'Ice Man' after the *Top Gun* movie that had come out a few years earlier. I said I thought I might use this – after all, the ex-Air Force blokes all had cool nicknames.

Unfortunately, an old mate I'd been a cadet pilot and a flying instructor with was at this meeting. He offered me a deal: if I refrained from referring to myself as 'Ice Man Austen', he wouldn't start calling me 'Brown Pants Austen'. I took the deal.

This mate has always had a way of making you keep your feet on the ground; sometimes this is important for a pilot.

After many years of reflection on this incident, I am glad that, while I know I'll never forget the details, I'm not haunted by the shock of suddenly finding myself with a compromised aircraft. Other pilots who have had similar events haven't always been so lucky. A fellow Qantas pilot who had a nasty control problem with a fly by wire aircraft many years later, has just written a book about his incident. The book not only describes the incident but also his long struggle with PTSD. My incident wasn't anywhere near as scary or as violent but I know I'm lucky not to have been affected by the experience of having an aircraft out of full control. It is a pilot's worst nightmare.

6
UNUSUAL FLIGHTS

Some people find flying aircraft easy. They are what we mere mortals call *naturals* or describe as having *good hands*. Me? I am just one of the majority. I can, or could, fly alright. I was average. Mind you, if I was in practice, I could go up a couple of grades but then I'd go and spoil it all by going on holidays. So, in a way, I pity the naturals. They would never get the satisfaction of slowly getting good at handling a big fast jet and at last conquering it, and themselves, like I did. This challenge, and the satisfaction of at last being good, is a big factor in my love of flying.

A pilot who doesn't have a passion for flying turns his or her career into work. My son, who would ring me from Darwin where he was a young pilot getting his hours up in order to apply for an airline, would always impress me with his latest adventures. His ecstatic description of flying alone inches above some flat wispy clouds (cloud surfing) in the magical light just before a tropical sunrise was what I wanted to hear. It meant he was into flying for the right reasons. I know he gets professional satisfaction from being good at what he does now. Pilots aren't the only people who get this feeling and some professions and occupations must produce the same or better highs – just different. Actually, getting into an aircraft and flying it somewhere is where a pilot gets his or her kicks.

During a pilot's career most flights are routine – that's the nature of the job. The Sydney to San Francisco flight was the same from the first time I did it as the most junior S/O on the 707 to my last flight as a senior Captain on the 747: regular passenger flights one and all, perhaps presenting slightly different weather challenges, approach conditions and those other little things that happen in the air, but basically all the same.

Every now and then I would experience a more interesting flight, one that would stick in my memory, and make flying for a living just that little bit more worthwhile. These flights were scattered throughout my forty-year stint. I'll start at the beginning. Going solo just over fifty years ago is easy to remember. Every pilot either remembers their first solo flight or is so traumatised by the experience it is permanently erased from the memory.

In my case, I recall it quite clearly – lovely day, good flying conditions. My *crash mate* had just made a good fist of his, demonstrating a degree of confidence and professionalism that would follow him throughout his career. I only wish I could have matched him on the day and throughout the rest of *my* career. At gatherings I still call him what he is – 'the bastard'. A crash mate is someone a pilot is paired with to do some major training or upgrade – maybe changing aircraft types or going from S/O to F/O or from F/O to Captain. All I know is that whoever I was paired with was always bloody good and I spent a lot of my time in these situations playing catch up. They made me a better pilot. My solo buddy was just the first in a long string of bastards.

First solo, the only entry in a pilot's logbook that is done in red ink, marks the transition from passenger to pilot like no other point can. If you have gone solo then, my friend, you have flown and nobody can take that away. My big occasion was carried out on a satellite airstrip just south of Sydney. It had a sealed surface but that was all. No control tower or, for that matter, much else, on the airport. It was quiet, air traffic wise, and therefore less confronting to any student – ideal for going solo.

I still remember the instructor's name, a nice careful bloke who made sure we were ready and had completed all the things we had to master. He ensured we were skilled enough to control the little trainer, that we could keep its speed where it should be, that we could actually get into the three dimensions and move the energy around and manage it.

Flying is all about managing energy. Speed and altitude is where we see this energy. The faster you go the more kinetic energy you have and the higher you are the more potential energy you have. This stuff will appear throughout the book so prepare to be energised. (Hey, the *Star Trek* TV show came out just as I went solo, okay?)

The instructor rehearsed our circuit with us until he was satisfied we were ready. He didn't talk about energy. He called it speed and altitude. My mate went solo first and did well. As he relaxed on the grass alongside the strip the instructor checked me out. When he deemed me ready, he got me to stop at the end of the runway and just got out. Suddenly, I was responsible for whatever happened and I couldn't just pull over to the side of the road and think about things if it all went pear-shaped.

Power on. Keep straight using the rudders. Check the instruments. Once the speed was sufficient to supply the relative airflow over the wing to give enough lift, I would fly. Just on this point, this is why you take off into the wind if you can – you get free airflow.

I'm at flying speed, 'Vr' in technical speak, but I just knew it as flying speed. I ease back on the control column and by doing this I alter the angle of attack of the wing relative to the airflow and, whacko, I'm airborne. By altering the angle of attack, I've made the wing give me more lift but at the expense of more drag. Two things happen: I lift off and the speed stops increasing. The engine is still supplying energy but instead of converting it to kinetic energy (speed) I'm now converting it to potential energy (altitude). Am I thinking of this as I do my first solo take off, am I composing fantastic poetry about silvered wings and touching the face of God? Well, no, I'm just trying to stay alive here. Okay?

Up I go, keeping the speed where it should be, turning onto the rectangular *circuit*. This is, by the way, just one of many weirdly named aspects of aviation. For instance, if you *ditch* an aircraft you don't actually land in a ditch. In the circuit there is a lot of levelling off, raising the flaps, turning and adjusting the power. You reduce the power when you get to the circuit height. In a car you take your foot off the accelerator at the top of a hill – same thing, except in an aircraft the ground is a thousand feet below.

A couple of turns later I took energy out of the system by reducing the power further and started going down – let the downward slope provide enough energy to overcome the drag. What I was really doing was letting the drag wipe off some of my energy. Was I thinking of this or imagining myself soaring with the eagles? Well, no, I was still just trying to make it down in one piece, the thinking could come later when I was pissed.

I put some flap out to help in the lift drag arrangements the aircraft was making with the airflow and turned onto final approach. Was I thinking that *final approach* is not necessarily the most reassuring choice of words to describe a pilot's first-ever unaccompanied plummet towards Earth? Well no, see all of the above, about just trying not to fuck up. That is what the instructor had told me: if you fuck it up just go around and have another attempt.

Two things here. If I messed it up the first time, what's to say I wouldn't go on messing it up until I ran out of fuel. The second thing is 'the bastard' hadn't messed it up, so how could I face my mates ever again if I did? I hadn't even finished my first flight but already I'd developed a pilot's ego.

I managed to keep it together enough to arrive at the correct end of the runway with the correct altitude and speed. Things were looking good at this point and I was watching the end of the runway to better judge height and rate of closure. I shut the power off so I wouldn't fly off into the distance forever. Having done all these things right, I should have executed a beautiful landing just like my mate.

Everything was fine. I'd applied the right amount of back pressure to bring the nose up a bit, which does nice things to the airflow, remember, namely increasing lift as the speed decreases as well as increasing drag. So, the aircraft should settle gently onto the ground as the speed gradually reduces to non-flying speed. Well, no. There was one slight problem. This training aircraft was pretty light – light with two blokes in it, even lighter with only one.

If you put the same inputs into your controls when you're alone as you did when there were two on board, you can't really expect the same outcomes. You have, in fact, added a variable without compensating. Was I running all this through my head? Of course not. I was just wondering why I hadn't gently kissed the runway with the wheels yet.

The answer was obvious. I had *flared* normally for a particular weight but that wasn't the weight anymore – it was exactly one instructor's worth less. I was now flying relatively high above the runway and rapidly running out of flying speed. I was high enough so that when the aircraft finally gave up flying, it, and I, just fell a couple of feet.

Have you ever built a ramp up to a two-foot drop and driven your car off it? Well, neither have I but I did something very similar that day. Crunch or bang, I'm not sure what it actually sounded like because that noise was drowned out by the very loud expletive I let fly at the world. A memorable flight indeed and the story of why, even though he rang me on the fiftieth anniversary of our solos, my mate will always be 'the bastard'.

A couple of years later, as a flying instructor, I was very careful to warn my students that, on going solo, there was suddenly a weight difference. Even though I was young and skinny in those days, I had learnt a valuable lesson during my first solo. One of the main things with students at this stage is that you don't scare them and destroy their confidence. I was making it easier for myself. It wasn't because I was a nice guy or anything.

After the first solo, there are further check flights with an instructor to see if the student is maintaining his or her standard and to decide if a second solo is warranted. One Sunday afternoon, at the light aircraft airport in Melbourne, I was carrying out one of these checks on a really good student. Not ideal because, at this time of the week, this airport was crazy busy.

The duty runway was actually three runways running parallel to each other, one for take-offs, one for full stop landings and, in between them, one for touch-and-go landings. The air traffic controllers were so busy on the radio that they couldn't actually answer every call from the departing or approaching aircraft. The student and I were out in this semi- controlled mayhem doing what we could. We were going around doing touch-and-gos on the central strip. Every approach we would radio call at a given point that we were *base, touch-and-go*. Too busy to reply because of all the other aircraft coming and going on the other runways, the controllers would just leave us to it. Aircraft approaching for full stop landings would report and similarly, if there was no problem, would not receive a reply.

Pity the poor student flying the aircraft while desperately watching out and listening out for other aircraft. These were skills you developed, but it took time. A good instructor would have the *situational awareness* thing going. I'm not sure whether we called it that back then but all it meant was you kept a view in your head of what was going on around you – and I don't mean whether one of your co-workers was going through a personal crisis or not. I'm just talking about being alert to where the other aircraft are and how fast and high they are so as to not actually bump into them at some point. Looking out of your aircraft is the best way to see them but that meant not looking at your instruments all the time – students tend to spend too much time *inside*. Experience helped with finding other aircraft – where to look, higher or lower, where should they be, how their speed is relative to yours, lots of variables, lots of caution needed.

One trick came from the old seafarers. If you saw a galleon, or an aircraft, off in the distance in a particular direction and, a little while later, it was still in the same direction but closer, then you had established, wait for it, a line of constant bearing, a nice way of saying a collision course. Continue with this, because if the aircraft is at the same altitude then, obviously, the closer bit eventually gets to be too close.

I was using everything I could to make sure my student was away from other aircraft that day but I wasn't so sure he was picking up on all the clues. It would be negligent of me to think that he should be on top of it all. He was flat out flying, it was all new to him and he was just trying to stay alive. I vaguely remember being a little bit like that when I first started going solo. The student had demonstrated that he was coping and, even with the number of aircraft around, he was demonstrating good procedures. I could let him go off by himself.

We turned onto the base leg for the *full stop* runway and made the appropriate radio call – the base leg is the leg at right angles to the final one. Now things started to get serious. For a start the *situational awareness* now has to include faster aircraft approaching for full stop landings. When the little trainers are all doing their thing on the central runway, they are all zipping along at the same speed. Once you are in front of an aircraft, it doesn't catch you and, in turn, you don't catch the two-seater in front of you – easy-peasy. On the main landing runway, you can have bigger aircraft going way faster and, if its pilot was a *cowboy*, it could be even faster again.

We turned final, this is where the student noticed that he was a bit high on his approach, no, don't go there, it just means he hadn't gone down early enough across the base leg of the approach and he needed to be about fifty feet or so lower at this stage. I had been watching him get into this situation and was waiting to see when he would recognise it and then how he fixed it.

I had been listening very closely to the radio and had heard an aircraft with a call sign I didn't recognise call base after us. That meant he wasn't a training two-seater but probably a bigger, faster aircraft. If he was tracking wider out than us it should be okay. He would have been travelling further and wouldn't have caught us. So, as we were tracking along this base leg, my head was darting everywhere. I was looking for shadows. I was looking out the back, above us, to the sides.

I didn't know it at the time but young blokes have incredibly flexible necks. I couldn't see him but I knew he was there somewhere; he had told me so.

We were now on final and the student announced to me, 'I'm high, Bill. Going to get it down.' His hands were on his control wheel and he was about to push on it, it would've made the houses get bigger. If the unknown aircraft wasn't behind, on the side of or above us and I couldn't see it in front then, wait for it, it must be below us. I put my hand behind my control wheel to stop any pushing and told the student to wait a tick. There it was coming out from under our nose, flying faster of course, that's how it caught us in the first place. You can just imagine the cowboy pilot shouting, 'Yippi ki yay!' at this point, can't you? He had just broken the golden rule of not doing stupid dickhead things with aircraft, and he was enjoying it.

The student freaked as you would expect, and I took over. I had an agenda. The quickest go around and *split arse* circuit I'd ever done was over in seconds – or so it seemed. Don't ask me why a really tight, fast circuit was so named, I just knew if you did one it was so labelled, and I just went along with it. Just as I went along with the description of idiot pilots as *cowboys*. They both just seemed to fit. This circuit of mine was so small and fast that I landed not long after Roy Rogers on his trusty steed, Silver – I may have got my westerns mixed there but no matter. I'd landed and taxied up, probably a little too quickly, behind the now parking aircraft. I was standing outside his hatch as this bloke got out.

He was a private pilot who had an inflated opinion of himself. I pointed out that what he had done by flying underneath me was not only fucking dangerous but was also illegal. His smart-arse reply said it all. He just looked at me and said, 'Well, what you did was illegal too.' I managed to ask, 'What?' through my shock. He was one self-entitled moron and proved it in his answer, he just said, 'You flew over the top of me, that's illegal.' You'll be pleased to know I didn't deck him, although, I must admit, I nearly did. I think I was too much in awe of his stupidity and, besides, I wanted him in one piece when I marched him into the Tower office and got his license pulled. A broken nose and two black eyes would have been very satisfying but may have weakened my case a tad. I was young then and made the wrong decision, I know.

Now to the most serious and sad part of my whole career. Fast forward a generation of pilots, literally in this case, where a terrible accident took the life of a young woman pilot in very similar circumstances on the very same runway as this incident occurred. The young woman was a Qantas cadet pilot flying circuits to get up some hours before being fed into more advanced training. Her parents were, and still are, very good friends with my wife and me. We had known the young woman from birth. She was the daughter of one of my fellow cadet pilots.

The accident happened at night when it was dark and the Tower wasn't operating. This meant that nobody could see that two aircraft were approaching together with one on top of the other. With high-wing trainers this can happen because neither pilot can see the other aircraft. The pilot below can't see through the wing and the pilot above can't see through the floor. If, by a freak coincidence of timing, they turn onto *final* together, and it is night, with what that means for visibility, then they can fly down together all the way to the ground unaware of the proximity of the other aircraft. They will meet, of course, when both aircraft try to land on the same spot on the runway. The young cadet, Holly, was in the trainer underneath. She was the one killed.

This book is dedicated to Holly Smith, an impressive new pilot and a fantastic young woman taken from us far too early. But at least she was living her dream when it happened.

Not to take away from this tragedy in any way, I will point out that aviation, in all its forms, is inherently dangerous – speed, altitude and machines that don't have five-star safety ratings all contribute. Add weather problems and a few other factors – not the least being human frailty in all its forms – and you have something to be wary of. Most pilots know many other pilots who have been killed in accidents. During my time in General Aviation, as distinct from airline flying where almost nobody gets killed, I personally knew at least six pilots who died. I was in GA for only a few years.

Holly's tragedy wasn't the only one to affect my cadet pilot course. One other close mate lost his wife and mother-in-law in a crash and an ex-cadet from the course was killed flying in New Guinea. As I got older I understood my father's initial reluctance when I first announced I was getting into flying. He had learned to fly during the war and he knew that there had been a large number of deaths in training accidents. He had lost mates too, including one who was flying an aircraft he was in when it crashed. Dad was cut up badly and carried the scars and some glass in his chin for seventy-five years until his recent death. Luckily, apart from the cuts, he was basically okay after that crash. Not so the pilot instructor doing the flying.

FLYING NEAR FIRES

I spent the time between the cadet course and being trained on big jets gaining valuable flying experience as an instructor. Being an instrument rated instructor meant I could do to any sort of charter or instruction flights. One summer I was assigned to a series of flights over several days – they were unforgettable. It was bush fire season and everyone knows what that means – things can go pear shaped really fast. It was January of '69 and the weather was dry and hot – is there an Eagles song in there somewhere? It kept getting hotter and on the eighth, two hundred and thirty fires broke out in the Melbourne area. It was one dirty day with temperatures well into the forties (hundreds) and the wind crazy strong and gusty. Humidity was at zilch and huge amounts of dry 'fuel' covered the paddocks and the floor of the eucalyptus bushland all around Melbourne. One spark was all it needed but it appears there were, in fact, hundreds.

There was no flying at the airport I worked at – far too windy and hot for that. Also, the wind direction was across the main runway and the velocity was way over any crosswind limitations on aircraft. This was true for the runways that were at an angle to the main one as well – just too much wind. Nobody was going anywhere.

Early on in the day, word was coming through of fires down on the road out of Melbourne to the coastal city of Geelong. Near Geelong was a north-south airstrip called Avalon where Qantas had a couple of 707s based doing pilot training. If fires approached, they would just take off and go somewhere safe. Not on this day. The wind was from the west at sixty or seventy knots – way too much crosswind – so they were stuck. A good mate was working there as a roster officer while waiting for a placement in general aviation as a pilot. He told me later how they would jump in the aircraft and taxi up and down the strip dodging the grass fires raging in the area. Airports always have lots of aviation fuel all over the place but this one had something extra, at one end was a military weapons storage.

Nobody knew what was in the little dirt and grass covered huts – probably not even the military. My ex-cadet mate was having a day of it, but fate had decreed that the 707s and their crews were OK this day. Twenty-three people were killed on the road a couple of kilometres away instead. These were serious fires.

I can remember preparing a twin-engine aircraft for a senior instrument pilot to take people down to this area to see what was going on. A short time later, I was assigned an aircraft and told to get ready to take a fire observer up to some big fires in the semirural bush just north of the city. Since the airport was closed, the aircraft doing this emergency work had to be crewed by instrument pilots, the smoke was so thick. The CFA (Country Fire Authority) observer teams arrived. They had proper military radios to do their reports. That was fine with me as I was going to be too busy to help with their communications. A lot of CFA fire fighters had been mobilised. I'd heard that thirty thousand were on duty around Melbourne. I got to see a lot of them that day and the teams that turned up with a couple of ambulances at the airport were just the start.

The aircraft I had was a six-seater high-wing Cessna with a strong motor. I was going into some pretty nasty turbulence and knew that having high power-to-weight and being way below the aircraft's weight limits were good things. Two skinny young blokes on board – the fire observer was young like me – and no baggage. The fuel load was only about half capacity so we were nice and light for when the G-forces hit and promptly tripled, or more, our weight in the turbulence. We strapped ourselves in as tight as we could. We were both wearing white overalls so they could find us in the bush if we went in. I only had underpants on underneath – it was bloody hot. When I say strapped in, this aircraft had full shoulder harnesses for us to pull down tight. I knew this would be important. When the bumps start you don't want your head bouncing off the roof.

The same applies when you prepare for aerobatic flying especially if you are going to do any negative-G manoeuvres like flying upside down. You squash and shrink yourself down as far as you can and then pull the straps as tight as you can. Not very comfortable but, even so, as soon as you turn upside down you still find yourself hanging in your harness with your bum off the seat and all the dirt from the floor in your face.

The only way to get airborne this day was to aim into the strong wind, push the power up to full and blast off. If there is a strong enough wind over your wings, you don't need much ground run before you can fly. We were airborne within twenty metres.

Off we go into the wild brown smelly yonder – the smell of a big bush fire up close is something you never forget. I was flying on instruments to get to the assigned area even though there wasn't a cloud in the sky, just smoke. It was already getting rough. I was used to turbulence, it sort of comes with the territory flying in Australia in summer, but this was something else. When we got to the fires we tried to find something worth reporting, but with no GPS we couldn't be sure exactly where we were. I could find clear air behind the fires but there were lots of clouds of smoke with rocks in them. A strong rule for instrument flying is to assume every cloud, even a smoke cloud, has a mountain or rocks in it. Don't go into it unless you know it's empty. It was challenging but I was having a ball. These were fast-moving fires and, from what I could see, that meant not everything in their path got destroyed, well, not instantly anyway. Some houses were burnt but the fire just parted and went around others – weird.

Fast moving is an understatement. You cannot outrun or out drive one of these gum tree fires, they have a special secret weapon – eucalyptus oil. These Australian eucalypts let the oil evaporate above them forming a gas or mist. The Blue Mountains west of Sydney are so named because that's what the eucalyptus cloud looks like from a distance. This evaporated oil is flammable and goes off like a ... I'll resist a bordello reference here and just go with ... a firecracker in a furnace. Ignite the gas, blow it sideways at a hundred klicks and you have the classic 'crowning' that Aussie fires are renowned for.

The flames just shoot across and through the tops of the trees, scary as shit but incredible to see from a light aircraft even though your eyeballs are starting to bounce. I tried to measure the speed and I reckon one demon I saw was travelling over my estimated mile in about a minute – one hundred klicks or sixty miles an hour. Try driving through the bush at that speed – I could in my new Subaru Outback if I wanted too. (My grown-up kids still refer to me as the 'Coulda Woulda Shoulda' – whatever that means.)

The poor fireman beside me had been vomiting for a while. I'd almost run out of sick bags and was getting worried about dehydration – and not just him. No way could I hold a bottle up to my mouth and fly. We headed back and I discovered why these blokes had turned up with ambulances. There had been a steady stream of very sick firemen arriving back at the airport. These guys were all volunteers, the professionals were elsewhere.

Back to home base, using all sorts of instrument navigation skills I found the airport. I lined up on final approach for the runway, but not like normal. I was approaching the ten-metre-wide sealed strip at ninety degrees. That's the way I and the few other crazies were doing it – straight into the raging wind at high speed to actually get to the airport. I got near the really short, but really incredibly wide, runway and slowed up. I touched down with so little ground speed that we almost stopped on the hard bit. I pulled up still facing into the hot wind right next to an ambulance. I wasn't in a 707 so all this was not only possible but fun.

The plane didn't need refuelling but I was glad to get about two litres of water into me, which I did standing outside the aircraft watching the ambos help the firies – Aussie slang for ambulance crews and firefighters. I was just glad to have a break from the thumping. My next passenger, already looking as white as his overalls, was being strapped in when the ambo turned to me. 'I can help you now,' he said. I wondered what he was on about and told him, 'It's okay. I'm the pilot.' He just pointed at my shoulders. I'd rubbed them raw under the shoulder straps and there were two small red patches on my nice white overalls. I never wore brand-new scratchy overalls again. A couple of bandages and some padding and I set off back to the fires. The take-off was just straight ahead across the grass for about twenty metres and zoom up almost like a helicopter. All this was unusual and as much fun as a young bloke could get – well almost.

Back over our operations area and we – my new mate was another young bloke – were seeing more burnt-out houses but we could also see groups of fire fighters, most of them on foot. One group of fifty or so blokes was in a valley, busily trying to clear a firebreak. I couldn't see whether they were able to use the 'back-burning' technique. This is where they set small fires to create a fire break. Sound iffy to you? On a day like this, it would take a pretty brave Fire Captain to order any new sources of ignition. The fires were raging through the trees and moving fast, these guys were not going to stop anything.

We could see a big fire front crowning towards them. It was going to hit them in a minute or two and they didn't have the Subarus to outrun it. There were enough gum trees in the valley for the crowning to sweep straight down it and over the fighters. I flew as low as I could down the valley, trying to remember all the instruction I'd been given about low flying. I knew strong winds and low flying don't go well together. I went over the top of the firefighters rolling my wings violently from side to side – a lot of vomiting beside me – as I tried desperately to alert these blokes to what was coming at them. At the end of the valley, just before the fire front, I did a gentle 'wing over', that is I climbed, washed off speed, rolled and yawed the aircraft around so that it was going back the way it came, dived back down to get the speed back and set off to see what was happening on the ground.

The firefighters had disappeared. In their place was a whole mob of bright silver rectangles laid out all over the ground. The firies had unrolled the space blankets that they carried on their belts, flattened themselves on the ground and put these magic heat reflectors over themselves. The fire front would blast over them with all its radiant heat and, while setting off a lot of fires around them, would do little or no damage to them. Once the main front had gone, they could jump up and run to the safer bits of ground around them – you know, the bits that aren't on fire. I didn't see the front hit and couldn't see much of what happened after for obvious smoky reasons. All I know is that no firefighters were killed that day. That was enough for me.

The following day I was still working in the area and kept an eye out for the Barrel Restaurant – a big building shaped like a wine barrel tipped on its side. My parents were planning to celebrate their twenty-fifth wedding anniversary there and I was able to tell them that, while other buildings all around had been flattened, amazingly, it was still standing. We all drove up through the smoking ruins and had a good night out – that was Australia in the sixties. Being Australia in the sixties also meant that a TV cameraman was able to bribe his way onto my aircraft on the second day. Film from that flight was shown on BBC television in the UK and the ABC network in the US. The video journalist got three times my yearly salary for his one flight and I got diddly squat. I wasn't the bloke he bribed.

I've had a lot of time to reflect on these flights that took place over several days. I am a lifetime regular donor to the bush firefighters for obvious reasons but I also know now why young people are sent off to war. They can handle harsh conditions and have less fear. I had turned twenty the day before I was sent out on this little mission. I witnessed the almost total chaos that accompanies such events and the real problems that inadequate command and control can bring. I'm very impressed with how the modern services handle things these days but, of course, things can still go pear shaped. The same area that I had been fire spotting in went up again about forty years later with one hundred and forty dead and five hundred houses destroyed. These fires won't be denied.*

Just over twenty-five years after my bushfire flying, my wife and I were allowed through a roadblock so that we could check on our little holiday home in the Blue Mountains. You know, the ones made blue by eucalyptus oil. The mountains had decided it was their turn to burn. Our house was actually in a town but there was enough bush and grass around to put it under threat. We were going up with hoses and grass-clearing equipment. There were escape routes and an Olympic-size swimming pool near our place so it wasn't our safety that we were worried about.

It was late at night and the huge fire front could be seen in the distance just lining the ridges for kilometre after kilometre. The amount of equipment and the number of people that had been mobilised was impressive. About seven thousand fighters with a huge number of trucks were lined up along the highway just waiting to go. These were the reserves. The only way you knew that this wasn't a huge army about to attack was that the men and women were in yellow uniforms and the trucks were bright red instead of camouflage. Hold on there, the fighters and machines were in fact perfectly camouflaged for fighting a fire.

---

*Early 2020 and the worst bushfires ever were still burning around south eastern Australia, they'd been burning for months. Firefighters were using big numbers of aircraft of various sizes and types to watch or to drop either water or fire retardant on the flames. On 23 January, a large C130 Hercules water bomber was flying low in strong winds – it's a high risk thing to do and on that day the aircraft crashed killing the crew of three. Respect and gratitude to the three Americans who gave their lives.

As we were motoring up the highway, a refrigerated blood delivery vehicle with its siren blaring passed us like we were standing still – we hoped that there weren't casualties up ahead. A few minutes later we passed the van driver on the side of the road, among about five bush fire trucks and their milling crews. There he was with the blood fridge door open distributing soft drinks. These blokes weren't letting any chances go by.

VERTIGO

Work as a flying instructor was pretty varied. There were always little one-off flights that took me over fires or oceans. Certainly not much chance of being bored by it all. I could find myself 'streamer cutting' one day and landing on a farmer's dirt landing strip the next.

Streamer cutting was where you tossed an unfurling toilet roll out of the side window and then threw the little Cessna around so you could cut the now vertical strip of paper with your propeller. I would act as the safety pilot as private pilots competed against each other – a fun workday. The following day involved a flight taking a Government aviation official down to a sheep property for a meeting with a farmer. To land on the dirt strip, I first had to buzz the strip a couple of times to scare the sheep off it. After landing, while waiting for the farmer, I asked the Government bloke what business he was on. I'm sure there was more than a hint of a smile as he told me, 'I'm investigating complaints about pilots buzzing sheep on the landing strip.'

One day, a fellow instructor and I were selected for a trial by the regulator. Because we had more training on instruments than the average junior instructor and were moderately experienced at instructing, we fitted their criteria for the new rules being tested. We were to train private pilots in what was then a new concept in Australian aviation – *Night VMC*. This was just day VMC with the lights off. VMC is short for Visual Met Conditions, meaning private pilots, who can't fly on instruments, have to keep away from clouds and mist. They have to stay *visual* and, up till then, had had to get home before dark. If one of these blokes got stuck away from his farm, or his hometown, as the sun went down, too bad.

The Regulator decided that, with some extra training in night landings, night navigation and some basic instrument training, they could upgrade their licence which would enable them to get home after dark. It was extra flying for my mate and me, so we were up for it – see my earlier comments about being young and making wrong decisions.

We were both instrument qualified, of course. Qantas had sent us out into the big bad world to get experience with pretty good survival skills. For instance, just before we left the sheltered workshop, the chief flying instructor of cadets called us in for a lecture. He started off by warning us that, under no circumstances, would we ever be allowed to *low fly*. We might be out in the bush or interstate but we were still their boys, and it was dangerous. There had been a nasty incident with some more senior cadets just prior to this. Having berated us into submission on this point for five minutes, he then proceeded to give us an hour's lecture on how to *low fly* safely – this ex-fighter pilot was a realist.

Well, it wasn't low flying my mate and I had to be checked out on. They decided to make sure we could fly small aircraft at night with limited IFR instruments. Instrument Flight Rules meant you didn't need any visibility. The aircraft we were going to be permitted to fly around in the dark were basically designed for daytime stuff. During the day, you could see outside and note whether the houses were getting bigger or not. At night, at least some reliance on instruments is useful because, if the houses have their lights off, how can you see how big they are?

The night check flight was in a four-seater that had the minimum complement of instruments needed. The flight also had the minimum complement of gung-ho pilots on board – namely me and a pilot inspector from the Government. This gung-ho guy was straight out of Vietnam where flying was ... well you can imagine. I'm not saying he was in it for the adrenalin rush but it sure looked like it to me. I think the expression 'gung-ho' probably comes from some wartime flying exploits. 'There we were over Korea, upside- down and diving towards the Gung Ho River and that's when we went supersonic.' You know the sort of thing. This check pilot fitted the mould. He wasn't interested in whether I could teach private pilots to land, or navigate at night, he just wanted to have some fun.

When you learn to fly on instruments you are taught to believe your instruments.

Well, not always, because sometimes they topple over and lie. Some of them just spin around in panic when the going gets tough and others fill themselves up with ice or insects and refuse to budge. But you must believe them or you die. Just make sure you believe the ones that are telling the truth. Why wouldn't you believe them? After all, the emphasis throughout the training was to follow what the instruments are telling you and not to go with something else.

That 'something else' – and it has been telling mostly the truth for millions of years – is the human balance system, the little circular tubes in the inner ear with fluid and tiny nerve hairs and all that. Tip your head forward and fluid swirls. The tiny hairs pick up the movement and tell the brain that you have just planted your face in the soup, or the mammoth stew. We humans have evolved this ability for good reasons and we have learned not to dismiss what the system is telling us. Of course, our ancestors didn't have aircraft which have the ability to screw with this sense of balance. They had a simpler life. They might have had to walk to London or Perth, but things were more simple.

On a passenger jet, the aircraft banks to about twenty degrees to go around a corner. Unless the passenger pulls up the window shade and looks out they won't know this is happening. The only sensation might be a slight increase in weight, and even that is not there if the pilot lets the aircraft drop altitude a bit in the turn. What you need to do to see the turn is to look out the window or to see it through your instruments. When you are in cloud, looking at your instruments is the only option. If your balance system is being fooled into thinking that nothing is happening but you really are descending in a turn, then you better learn to take on board the limitation of your middle ear and actually believe your instruments. Pilots have to do this and Captain Gung Ho was about to test my ability to overcome evolution.

We took off in the four-seater and went straight up to a safe altitude to do some aerobatics. As we were climbing, the check pilot decided to make it harder for me. He covered some instruments leaving me with just a few basic ones. In pilot speak this is called *limited panel*. I then had the big Instrument Flying Shade put over my head. This is like a baseball cap with a huge curved peak made out of white plastic which prevents you from seeing outside while looking at the instruments. I was now in simulated cloud. 'Taking over. Close your eyes,' said Gung Ho as he started throwing the aircraft around trying to dodge those Viet Cong bullets.

I don't know what he did – I had my eyes closed, remember – but he was deliberately inducing a severe case of *vertigo*. He was getting my head spinning and doing a good job of it. After a minute or so of this he yelled, 'Handing over,' and I took control.

All I knew was that he had handed over to me while he was flipping us onto our back by tipping the aircraft backwards very rapidly. I resisted pushing forward and took in the information from the few instruments that were still available to me. I could see that, while I was obviously zooming up into the sky, somehow the altitude was going down quite fast and also the airspeed was increasing. The fact that both indications were backing each other up confirmed that maybe I was wrong and we were in fact going downhill, not up.

My training kicked in and I did the right thing. Over the next hour of dodging Viet Cong rockets, I managed to convince the bloke that I could easily overcome the severest case of vertigo I had ever experienced. I was now one of the first two Night VMC instructors ever – see earlier references to being young and stupid.

Recently, while in the Alaskan tall pine trees, my wife suffered a severe case of vertigo. We were zip-lining and, while the rest of us were having a ball, she was terrified. I knew what this disorientation was like and made sure I was there for her. When she thanked me later, I explained that, forty-something years earlier, I had learned all about vertigo and would never take it lightly – millions of years of evolution can be a powerful thing. My wife has the *I survived the Alaskan Zip-line* fridge magnet proudly displayed and I'm pretty sure it may still be there forty years from now.

EARTH SHADOW

After years of study, learning to fly and then advancing your qualifications and experience as an instructor, you get your chance to be trained on the mighty Boeing 707. After further months of study, learning to fly the big jet – both in the simulator and the aircraft itself – you are then qualified for absolutely nothing. You have to do your *Line* training. That is, you go off up the line as a trainee on regular flights until a line Captain signs you off. The line is just another way of saying 'the route structure that your airline operates'. After sign-off, you are allowed to sit in the back of the flight deck but not touch anything, even though, by then, you are actually qualified to do so. That was, and is, the system.

I was hoping to get to this stage of not touching anything by demonstrating that I could, in fact, touch everything on the 707 with considerable skill. I was now a Pilot Under Initial Training with, wait for it, one stripe on my shoulders. As a PUIT I was as happy as I could be. Surely only a few years more and I would be a Senior Captain. I've always been a dreamer. By the way, Qantas was one of very few airlines that used this rank with only one stripe. A mate of mine, who was wearing his one day, was fronted by an American pilot somewhere who asked very loudly, 'Wow, what did you do to get busted down to one stripe?' It's hard to always wear happy pants when you're junior.

Wearing a real uniform with a cap and everything – including the stripe – I was up for my last line training trip, the big checkout one up to London and back. The Qantas line went all round the world back then and to a lot of airports. Of course, I didn't know any line Captains, I was too new, but the one assigned to check me out was a doozy. He was an Englishman who had been in the British Royal Air Force during the war working as a mathematician. I found this out over the course of the next twelve days big time. He took on the task of polishing my knowledge and testing what I knew with a zeal. He was signing me off and, if I didn't measure up to Zealot Standard, I'd fail and have to continue training with a black mark against me.

The training on this trip was a saga in itself and I may talk about it later – I'm still traumatised forty-seven years after the event. I will talk about the space-related aspects of this flight to London and back because that aspect of the trip will outlast, in my mind, even the trauma.

The Captain tested me a bit to see where my maths was at by making up little scenarios concerning various energy states of aircraft. He was right to do this, managing energy is what pilots do. Sometimes they don't use those words but this Captain did. Just on this energy thing, it is not insignificant amounts of the stuff we are talking about. If you take the world's biggest aircraft carrier going flat out at thirty knots you have less total energy than a Jumbo going at five hundred knots. Kinetic energy is all about the square of the speed. The Jumbo has huge amounts of potential energy from its altitude as well that I haven't bothered to add. Fast, high-flying aircraft are just full of energy.

I had found out from the other crew members by now that this Captain was a bit of a legend. In the early 60s, the Americans had got their space program up and running. Beginner steps in the early days, but they were getting people up into orbit in little capsules. The Gemini program was a series of flights that would go up, do a number of orbits and then splash down in the North Pacific somewhere. My Captain would do the maths, and then arrange his regular Qantas service to be in a position to observe the re-entry of these spacecraft. He also arranged to transmit his coverage, on the scratchy long-distance radio, to an American broadcast network – pretty cool. All this required plenty of detailed planning to achieve.

This was not the only maths-related pastime this bloke had. He was also building a lead balloon. Why would you build a lead balloon? Because it had never been done, of course. How is it done? Well, you just make the lead thin enough, fill it with hydrogen to inflate it and put the little white mouse in the basket and you have a winner. What was the Captain trying to win? A cover story in the *Scientific American* that's what. He told me they had even promised him a photo on the cover if he ever got the balloon flying.

We were now in Tehran, two-thirds of the way up to London, and the Captain and I were in the hotel dining room drawing all over their white tablecloths with a biro. We were working out the volumes of spheres of slightly different sizes, and I do mean slightly. The difference in radius between the two was the thickness of the lead. By subtraction, we now had a figure for the volume of lead and hence its weight. The pen marks on the tablecloth were getting embarrassing but we had nearly got the little mouse airborne. All we had to do was find out how big the balloon had to be to get it to float. The difference between the weight of hydrogen and air is the key to this and we were well into the calculation when he looked at his watch and called a halt.

The truth is he had been keeping a close eye on his watch the whole time and it had got me wondering. His watch was a beauty, obviously up to chronometer standard, which meant only a few seconds slow or fast a day. Remember, this was an era when clocks were still made with clockwork. They were the direct descendants of the original navigator clocks developed for the early seafarers. I loved going to see Harrison's timepieces at the Royal Observatory in Greenwich and not only because you could stand with one foot in either hemisphere while doing so. I knew about accurate clocks and longitude. The Captain's watch was worthy of the title 'a serious chronometer'. He needed to know accurate time because he had a celestial event scheduled for that dark and starry night.

I was off alcohol for a while due to illness and the Captain was a non-drinker – the rest of the 707 crew didn't have these handicaps. They were sitting around the pool outside in the dark. It was a beautiful warm night that obviously had to be celebrated with many vodka and limes. This was the standard drink for crews in Iran, but only in the hotel – it was Iran after all. The Captain and I walked out sober into my first crew party. They were having a ball.

We had come outside so that we could see a satellite. The Captain knew of a low- orbit one that was due to pass over the top of us. You can only see satellites in low orbit, so this was a great chance. They also had to be a reasonable size and shiny to be visible and this one was both. Google when the International Space Station is due over you one evening and have a viewing. You could do it in the early morning but having several vodka and limes at dawn isn't as acceptable as during happy hour.

So, in comes the Legend with his calculations. To see anything in low orbit, there must be some light on it – that means sunlight. If the sun is around the other side of the planet there is no sunlight to illuminate the satellite. This means to see satellites in orbit you have to be close to either sunrise or sunset, when the satellite above you is still in sunlight and you are down on the dark ground – remember the Earth is curvy. If the satellite you want to see is coming from the dark part of the sky where the sun doesn't shine, (careful), then it is coming out of the Earth's shadow into the lit-up area. The Captain had taken orbits, Earth shadows, latitude, longitude and entrusted his timepiece to come up with the answer.

Captain Frank Brown got his motley crew to look up into the heavens. He pointed out two prominent stars, told us to draw a line between them and keep a close eye on that point. He was looking at his watch and called, 'Now!' What looked like a large star appeared out of nowhere and proceeded to march across the night sky. I was impressed. The satellite was big and shiny. It was amazing. I'd never seen anything like it.

I looked down to see how the rest of the crew had taken it. To a man and woman, they had dropped to their knees, bowing before the Captain and chanting, 'Oh, Bwana, please make the bad sky god go way.' A great space experience for me but I seriously wondered just who these Qantas crews were and what sort of job I'd got myself into.

10
EARLY DAYS

I did my early airline flying in the mighty Boeing 707. This first-generation jetliner wasn't very sophisticated compared to today's wonders but it was a big step up from the piston engine clunkers that came before it. I enjoyed flying on it and actually flying it – even us lowly Second Officers were trained to fly and land these Kings, or Queens, of the sky. On that point I don't think aircraft have ever really achieved gender status. I was always told that 'it' not 'she' or 'he' would respond to whatever you were doing with the controls. Maybe the female gender is used sometimes but only by people I would be wary of.

To go onto the biggest four-engine jet around straight from flying little 'bug smashers' is bloody hard. A bug smasher is a small aircraft that flies in the lower bits of the sky where all the bugs are. Things happen a lot faster in a jet and, not surprisingly, it's way heavier with what that implies for inertia. It was a steep learning curve for anybody and I was no exception. The challenge of flying was there in spades and that challenge, as I have said, was a big factor in making the job worthwhile for me. There is a real sense of achievement when difficulties are finally overcome and qualifications gained. No flying qualifications are given to you; they must be earned by reaching the standard. It's stressful but ultimately rewarding. I got my 707 endorsement and the world awaited.

These great state-of-the-art machines took me on, literally, the adventures of my lifetime. I travelled to tropical islands, developing Asian cities and freezing snowbound destinations. I saw Middle East trouble spots, war zones, major world capitals and bewildering peoples and cultures. I saw ancient city ruins, modern cities with new emerging lifestyles and, in all these places, for a young suburban boy from Melbourne, there was a great education in how different people were. Some of these people, for instance, had never even heard of Australian Rules Football.

It was a fully escorted tour of the world with English-speaking mates and 'beer money' supplied when you got to your fully paid-for hotels in these world-standard destinations. The meal allowance given in those days was not only referred to as beer money but also 'beer tokens' or 'fun tickets'. I'm beginning to realise why I went into this job in the first place. But wait, there's more! This airline I worked for, and rubbish quite a bit every now and then, would put money into my bank account while I was away on these adventures. I'll try not to rubbish my 'Golden Goose' too much – very easy to become the entitled dropkick I see so often in others.

The only drawback to all this, and it was a big one, was you had to go away on these adventures when the airline wanted you to and you left your loved ones at home – mostly, anyway. Being newly married, this was not fun. The longest trip I could do was nineteen days, a great South Pacific and Caribbean holiday, but I dreaded the calls assigning that one to me. There was no Skype, email, messaging, phone, mail or carrier pigeon available and I would just lose touch with my gorgeous red-head for nearly three weeks. Mind you, the homecomings were something else. On one of my first trips, an older pilot told me, 'The second bang you hear when I get home is the suit case hitting the floor.' I have no idea what he meant.

I do know that, after one of these nineteen-day South Pacific marathons, I emerged from the Sydney customs hall out of the little crew exit. The passengers were emerging from the main door about twenty meters away. My wife had decided to surprise me by being there for this early 6:00 am arrival. Not too hard really because she was on her way home from a student party, but even so ... This absolutely beautiful, long red-haired goddess with her hotpants, knee-length white boots and tight top spots me from where she was waiting with about three hundred other welcomers. Hey, it was the early seventies and her outfit wasn't that strange, just unusual at dawn. She let out a yelp just to attract my attention but succeeded in getting everyone else around her interested as well.

She did the running thing, arms outstretched and swaying in welcome, big red hair streaming, appropriate parts undulating and then she leaped at me. She did it well, not straight into me but slightly to one side, locking her arms about my neck as she hit. At least two full rotations around me with the white boots way off the ground – true Hollywood spectacular. I was impressed and so, apparently, were three hundred other people who gave her a standing ovation.

I won't go on about the places I've been and seen. Enough brilliant travel writers make a living doing this. Read anything by Bill Bryson and you'll see what I mean. I have seen a lot of the world and its people have seen me. I know, for instance, that I have been the first white person that at least two groups of people and several individuals have seen in the flesh. You have to get yourself into some pretty out of the way places to achieve this. No deliberate travel stories. I may stray from this commitment to make a point, so please forgive me if you find yourself reading something about me being alone on a cliff overlooking Victoria Falls in Africa with one mean looking warthog. The surprise on this tusked monster's face meant I was probably the first white man he had seen. He was certainly my first tusked monster.

Just a bit more on this 'first white person' experience. It's one thing to have a group of people follow you around to see how the strange creature bargains in the local market. It's another thing altogether to have them sit in a line outside your tent in an effort to see what white people look like without clothes.

The 707s went everywhere Qantas went back in those days – and then some. Charter flights could see you going to places the regular flights bypassed. One charter flight I could have done without was one into Madras in India. It was a while back – that city has been called Chennai for quite a while now. The mission was to deliver three hundred and sixty-five pregnant ewes to India. It had to be a Government aid thing as the expense must have been horrendous.

We soon found out what pregnant ewes do. They piss a lot and the piss smell is so strong that it sets off aircraft smoke detectors – continuously. When you are the S/O on such a flight, you are the 'first responder' and have to get ready to fight a fire every time the alarm triggers. We've all heard the story of the boy who called 'wolf', well this trip was a nightmare about the alarm that called 'sheep'. That's how this flight conditioned me.

Towards the end, the alarm would go off and instead of thinking 'fire', I was thinking 'sheep'. Pavlov would have been proud. The subcontinental heat and the smell on unloading are burned in my memory – the job's not so fancy now is it, shepherd boy?

Some charters were at the other end of the spectrum. The early seventies was a different world and one night I got the call – the following morning I would be crewing the Prime Minister's flight to the USA. Up to Honolulu, the first stop, anyway. No security checks, no briefings, just be there and do your job. I suppose the spooks did have some idea who was who, but this was a time when we didn't even have ID cards with all the checks they entail.

The flight was just a normal Sydney to Honolulu jaunt and wasn't weird in any way. If there was any security, I don't remember it and we just did our job. Prime Minister Whitlam was the bloke who had become an RAAF navigator at the same time as my dad was becoming an RAAF pilot. They never met but I had met Gough once before he became the PM. On a flight to London he had visited us pilots on the flight deck as we flew over the Mediterranean. Apart from being a navigator, this bloke had become a lawyer and was interested in all sorts of things – and he knew a shitload about a lot of them.

You always know when you meet someone way smarter than yourself, or at least you should. So, while he was looking out for the remnants of the Minoan civilisation down below, he noticed me sitting in the flight engineer's seat. Gough knew rank markings and was right onto me. 'You're not the engineer, son,' in his big booming voice. 'You haven't got the purple between your stripes.' He was right, of course. Then he asked me if I knew why engineers wore the purple. 'No, sir.' Nobody had ever told me and the internet wasn't even a dream. He went on to explain that purple was the colour of mourning and that the self-sacrificing engineers on the *Titanic* had earnt the right to be immortalised with the purple between the gold stripes. Google my arse, I got it from Gough Whitlam.

So, a normal flight to Honolulu with the Prime Minister and his party in the first class section with the press and staff down the back. Mrs Whitlam, an equally daunting intellect, was also on board.

Come out of the flight deck on the 707 and you have two toilets on the left as you go down the only aisle, followed by a galley. On your right, you have the front door and then an overhead storage cupboard. This cupboard had a couple of cushioned benches underneath it with very little headroom. The storage was called the 'overhead storage'. It should have been called the 'near-head storage' especially for anybody over six foot sitting on those benches. I was squashed into this Crew Rest having a break. I had the curtains open watching the 'galley slaves'. Aviation is full of such plays on words, you see they worked in a galley and they were workers and galley slaves work in a ... you get the drift.

I was playing catch-up in these years, I was not only reading great science-fiction, I was actually into all sorts of literature. The STEM background can turn you into a nerd if you're not careful. I was reading my copy of *Island* by Aldous Huxley and taking in the clever ideas. Margaret Whitlam obviously spotted the title and the next thing I knew the Prime Minister's wife was asking me if she could join me and talk about the book.

Margaret was way over six foot. She had represented Australia in swimming – she was an Amazon with a brain to match. She took an interest in a young bloke and not only discussed Huxley's ideas but directed me towards other worthwhile books. My first-ever book club was held in this weird little space with both people touching their heads on the ceiling.

I will never forget her kind interest in me and regret not having said hello when I last saw her walking into a play at the Sydney Opera House shortly before she died. I was torn between saying hello and respecting her privacy. Legends like her must dread being accosted. She had demonstrated to me many years earlier that she didn't need adulation to feel worthy.

While sitting in the little crew rest cave on a trip a while earlier I became quite interested in the goings-on across the aisle in the galley. This was a first for me because a pilot mate had just become a galley slave. He was the brand-new junior flight steward working the ovens. He and a lot of other Qantas pilots had just been retrenched – during a period of lots of pilot recruiting and training everything had suddenly ground to halt as the airline had a conniption. For 'conniption' read 'panic' as circumstances changed.

Management, and I use the term very loosely for what existed back then, downsized and pulled back as if Hannibal had just appeared out of the mountains with his elephants. The government had kept its rural rump happy by gaining beef exports to the US in return for more US airline access to Australian routes. Airline jobs were traded for cowboy jobs.

Australia has always tried to deskill its workforce – well, hey, you don't have to spend as much on education then do you?

So my mate with lots of expensive education and training was pouring coffee and pulling meals out of ovens. A doctor friend in Melbourne told me that his professors had told his group of medical students that a lot of money was spent on their training, second only to the amount spent on training pilots. One expensively trained flight attendant was having his first go in the galley and I was watching him like a hawk in case he messed up and I could have a go at him. He would have done the same if roles had been reversed – such is the duty of mateship.

Everything proceeded perfectly through the white tablecloth and silver service, right up until the grand finale when the coffee and tea cart went out down the aisle. Very shortly, the cart returned with a very perturbed chief steward, who had had his presentation ruined. 'Garry, something's wrong with this cream,' he said in what had devolved into a very camp accent. He took the lid off the little silver pourer and had a taste with his finger. 'Garry, it's MAYONNAISE!' A lot of frantic emptying and refilling and he departed with his cart. Garry looked across and eyeballed me, 'One word, Austen, and you're fucking dead.' What could I do but feign total ignorance of what had just gone on? After all, we were mates and I would never say anything anyway.

A short time later, when the meal service had finished and I was standing in the back of the flight deck between the navigator's table and the engineer's position, Garry rang up and asked the Captain for any drink orders. The Captain with a very nonchalant voice said, 'Yes there are orders, the F/O would like a tea with some mustard please and could I have a coffee with a little horseradish if possible.' Garry came through the door a split second later and crash-tackled me to the floor. I remember being totally helpless under his knees as he biffed me around the head in a manner the Captain later described as vicious. I was as weak as a kitten in defending myself – uncontrollable laughter will take the fight out of anybody. He didn't hurt me of course, we were mates.

This mate went onto a pilot internet forum when I retired and, while congratulating me on my career, posted this story for all to see. It might have taken thirty-seven years but he could finally see the funny side as well. By the way, he only spent a short time as a flight attendant and went on to become a highly respected Qantas Captain. The retrenchment proved to be just a minor speed bump on his career path.

11

GUNS, DIAMONDS AND CASH

When I checked out as a Second Officer, I had been trained to a high standard in the flying, navigating and operation of the biggest, fastest passenger jet around – the mighty Boeing 707. So, with a licence to prove this was so and a uniform to show this was so, I set off on my first flights, and discovered the truth. I would not fly, navigate or operate anything. I was to be an airborne clerk with all sorts of paperwork and other duties entailing responsibilities that had nothing to do with my licence or uniform because neither of these bits of pilot paraphernalia entitled me to carry a gun.

On one of my very first trips, I was to be the S/O on a flight from Sydney to Honolulu with a one-hour stopover in Fiji. This meant an overnight flight of two sectors and an early morning arrival past Pearl Harbor onto Honolulu's airport. You could look down into Pearl as you passed by it and imagine what the Japanese pilots saw about thirty years earlier. You certainly had time to look down and do this imagining if you were the S/O sitting in the back of the flight deck and not actually doing the flying. My father used to explain to people that my seat in the aircraft's flight deck was actually the doorknob of the flight deck door. I might not have been flying the aircraft but I did have other duties and, on this particular flight, I was in a bit of an anxious state over one of them.

I was still finding out exactly what I had to do on these flights and, prior to leaving Sydney, was in the back of the flight deck doing some of the navigational paperwork when two Qantas security dudes arrived in uniforms that did mean they could carry guns. They didn't have them drawn at this stage because they were too busy carrying a large package between them. It was wrapped in brown paper and I soon learned it contained five hundred thousand US dollars in cash. In 1970, that amount was actually worth half a million U.S. dollars. Now it's worth just a week's pay to some airline CEOs. So, these guys with guns were looking to get rid of a lump of money equivalent to thirty or forty times my yearly salary by handing it over for 'safe hand' transportation to the United States. By the way, don't do the sums vis-a-vis a CEO's yearly salary versus a pilot's – it's just too depressing on all sorts of levels.

As a new pilot, I had been issued with a padlock. One of those small flimsy ones you might use to secure a locker at the gym. It was fit for purpose – it was meant to lock a thin metal locker. This one wasn't in a gym but was inside the door of the forward cargo hold of the aircraft. Basically, a tin box, it had the impressive title 'Dip Locker' – short for Diplomatic Locker – and was there to carry 'safe hand' stuff. From the name, diplomatic material on its way to some embassy somewhere was what you might expect to find in it but in all the time that I was the safe hand bloke, I never once saw any government papers. Someone in government was smart enough not to put their sensitive material into a flimsy tin box.

Those two men with guns turned up with the US Treasury reserves, got my signature and departed. This meant a young sprog Second Officer was now sitting in the back of the flight deck with a fortune and a padlock – not at all what I thought flying for a living would be like. I'd been told I might have to sign for things. 'Just make sure you get a receipt when you hand over whatever it is and keep the receipt! Keep the receipt!'

Down I went with what was now my package and deposited it in the gym locker. Baggage handlers are very aware of someone in their area and eyes were on me. Did these guys weigh up the possibility of waiting until the young bloke in a pilot's uniform went back upstairs before they took out a screwdriver and broke the toy padlock, just to see what the kid had put into the stupidly positioned locker? Of course, they did. These guys have been known to pilfer gorilla suits out of passenger bags and drive around on their little tractors in them. Mind you, why wouldn't you?

After landing at Nadi (pronounced Nandee) for the one-hour stopover, I was now worried. Had the boys in Sydney yielded to temptation? Were they, at this very moment, actually buying gorilla suits of their own with my money? Or had they just done their job and gone home? I could see from the flight deck warning lights that the Fijian baggage handlers had opened the forward hold door. Down I went. Lots of huge blokes hanging around an open cargo door and my little brass lock clearly visible just inside it. Any of these blokes looked strong enough to just reach in and wrench the whole locker door off. As far as I could see, the only function the lock served was to provide a convenient handhold for such wrenching. What should I do? Draw attention to something of value by taking it out and going upstairs or just leave it there? Mind you, I had already drawn attention to myself by going down to the apron in the first place but, then again, they would have seen the padlock. I didn't know about this stuff. I was supposed to be a pilot.

I left and just hoped it would remain there. Luck, or the fact that organised crime hadn't actually got organised that night, meant that I did safe hand it on and got my receipt, which went straight to the bottom of my pilot's flight bag. Every year or so I would do a big clean-up of these little tear-off stubs. US currency wasn't the only valuable stuff placed in my safe hands and the next big fortune I was entrusted with did go missing. This crime, or fuckup – I'll never know which – happened a long time ago and was either a non-event or was covered up – again I will never know. Nobody ever contacted me about it after it was all over, I was a small bit player and quite happy to remain one.

South Africa produces a lot of diamonds, a fact that is brought home if you ever find yourself on a particular street in downtown Johannesburg. From this vantage point, you can see the DeBeers headquarters, a glass skyscraper with facets cut into it just like a diamond – pretty cool. But the real attraction of this scenic vantage point was that you were outside a witch doctors' supply emporium. You could turn from the view of one of the twentieth century's most innovative buildings, duck your head and enter another realm entirely. This stinking, and I do mean stinking, shop was where you could buy, for whatever purpose, any dead African animal you wanted, and I do mean any. The carcasses of these beasts were hung up and dried somewhere else and, at a certain stage of putrefaction, would be brought to the shop for sale. Literally hundreds of smelly bags of hide and bones were on display hanging from the ceiling awaiting the discerning purchasers. If you didn't duck your head, you got a face full of something you would never ever want your face in contact with.

I first found this shop back in the day when a few of us pilots on a stopover hired ourselves some bodyguards from Soweto and visited, not only Soweto, but also other no-go areas around downtown Johannesburg – areas that white people didn't really visit alone.

When my daughter heard about Soweto at school and asked to come on one of my trips to see this symbol of South Africa's struggle, I again hired bodyguards and repeated the earlier tour. I had some fun backing her into the store entrance while distracting her with the diamond building view. She didn't get a face full of dead zebra but I'm not sure she's fully trusted me ever since.

Why would she trust me? I was at one stage the prime suspect in what may well be Australia's biggest diamond heist. The safe hand shipments to and from South Africa sometimes involved little packages of these gems. I have never been able to understand why humankind has put such huge value on these little sparkly beads. Making a potion out of a dead zebra may at least give some sick African tribesman a little placebo relief but what use is a diamond? These thoughts didn't stop me carrying little boxes of diamonds around: each box worth more than fifty modest houses – my unit of value back then. Large transportable wealth is of course attractive to various players and someone did something one day and the shipment I was helping to carry around went missing.

I had just got home from a South African trip when the phone rang. The gruff Qantas security minion established who I was and then just went for it. 'You were the last person to handle shipment so and so and we would like to talk to you.' I knew shipment so and so was a box of diamonds being returned to South Africa. I had handed them over to someone on arrival in Jo-burg and got the little paper receipt, which had been dumped into the bottom of my flight bag and forgotten – like all the rest of the little slips of paper down there.

By this stage, I knew about the security department. They were pretty useless. When you think about it, the diamonds would have disappeared nearly a week earlier and, if the prime suspect was sneaking back into his home city with them, you might make an effort and actually grab him as he came through customs with the loot in the bottom of his flight bag. Not these blokes. True to form, they gave the suspect a ring at home to warn him and give him time to hide the loot before they got there – pretty smart.

I was, of course, a bit taken aback so, while this bloke was accusing me of being the last person to handle the diamonds, I was frantically scrummaging through the bottom of my flight bag. Lots of little bits of paper – SYD to SIN – no that's not it. TYO to SYD – not that one either. The bloke on the phone was still banging on about me being the last with the loot when I found the right one – what relief! I took great delight in reading out the name and date under the handover signature. The phone call ended pretty quickly after that. No time, it would appear, to offer any apology or, indeed, to utter any civil words at all but, then again, I didn't really expect any of these things. It was security I was talking to after all.

Was there a robbery? Did security ring the bloke in Jo-burg only to discover he wasn't there but on his new private yacht anchored off Monte Carlo instead? Or was he there sitting in his office with the diamonds in his safe waiting for DeBeers to come and collect them? The old quandary of whether to go with the conspiracy or just accept another fuckup was in play. It's very rarely the conspiracy. Thinking about it later, I was so very glad to have documentary proof of my innocence. I could see how things could get real bad real soon if other people needed a fall guy to cover their own arses. I was certainly getting a few life lessons.

The short flight from Mauritius to Jo-burg and back was a good day out. All daylight and a couple of hours to grab a cab from the airport in Jo-burg to get to the favourite grog shop to pick up enough wine for the beachside barbeques back in Mauritius. The little Indian Ocean island of Mauritius was a great place to relax and, indeed, had a few resorts just starting up. Quite a few African heads of state must have thought one of these resorts was a good place to have a meeting because that's what they did. To start their journey home, they chose the Qantas flight that I thought was really just a grog run.

These presidents and prime ministers all had bodyguards – serious security killers – and they all had guns. Let's face it, how many peaceful transitions of power from one African head of state to the next have there ever been – ever? There is a rule, of course, that no guns can be carried on board an aircraft, so the airport officials had collected all the handguns and put them into a medium-sized carryall. Of course, they gave the bag full of guns to me. I was in charge of safe hand. I looked inside to see a dozen or so weapons and then wondered about what to do with them. If I put them downstairs in the locker, it would take some time to get them back up after arrival and I knew heads of state, and therefore their minders, weren't going to want any delays. So, I put them under the navigator's table in the flight deck. We made sure the flight deck door was kept locked – amazingly, that wasn't the norm back then – and I kept an eye on the carryall, ready to get the guns back to their owners as soon as I could. In Jo-burg, I came out of the flight deck ready to hand over the bag to someone who would distribute the guns to their owners. Nobody wanted the bag. The VIPs and minders had all gone and I was naively wondering how the

PMs and presidents were being protected. It slowly dawned on me. The bodyguards had given me their throwaway guns and kept the real ones on them at all times. Nobody wanted a bag of old guns that probably didn't even fire. This was a bag that was never going to be collected. I did eventually get some airport official to take the bag and I made sure I got a signature – the last thing I needed was to be classified as a gun runner as well as a diamond thief.**

**I said at the beginning of the book that all my lifelong flying mates have their stories. In talking about this chapter to one such mate, he told me about how the diamonds that he was accused of pilfering were found on a diplomat's mantelpiece and that he'd actually got into trouble for carrying a bag of guns on the flight deck. Why can't he get his own stories?

12

ON THE CHANGING TIMES

So far in this story about aviation, women haven't got much of a mention. The newspaper ad for the cadetship didn't explicitly exclude women applying but it may as well have and, in those times, that would have been totally unremarkable. It was the sixties. The times they were a changing but even in the Dylan song it was still 'How many times can a MAN turn his head and pretend that HE just doesn't see?' The women's movement was just spluttering to life and us blokes weren't even noticing.

The major change I witnessed over my years in flying was the acceptance, at last, of women pilots. I grew up in a household with two capable, accomplished women and, as I have said, went to a school where there was no difference in smarts between the sexes. I was surprised by the attitudes I found after I left home. I started to realise that half the population was pushing it uphill big time.

My childhood mum just got on and did things. If a netball club needed organising, then it got done. If the high school Parents and Citizens Association needed a president, then she was it. If the YMCA needed an organiser in the community to help form a youth club, then they had one in her. This mum of mine had been selected as a teenager to work with the US Army in Australia during the Second World War. She had work and people skills beyond her years.

Mum has told of how huge US military policemen would salute her and then take her to interview the girls in the brothels the Americans used for R and R. The Yanks had given her a little badge that meant she had officer status. Her job was to make sure those working girls with German ancestry weren't a security threat. She would also take notes when the same military police 'interviewed' suspects in rape or racist incidents. She would wield the pen while the MPs wielded the batons. There were huge divisions of US troops under the control of the headquarters she was attached to.

She grew up quickly and learnt a lot about the big bad world the war had brought about. For instance, a couple of years after finishing school, she found herself sharing the tram to work with an old school mate, one she had already interviewed in the course of her brothel-checking duties. These experiences made her a pretty practical woman, one who wouldn't take any bullshit from her sons when it came to the role women played in life. Mind you, with the role models on display, neither my brother nor I had any issue with the equality concept.

My sister had her own problems with the sexist downdrafts. She had a mathematical brain and had scored a high-level computer programming job on one of Australia's few big computers. Because this profession was so new, a popular TV show about lying featured her as one of its truth tellers. Three men pretended to be Lyn Austen. They, and my sister, then answered questions from a celebrity panel about the job of a computer coder and what this new exciting profession was all about. When it came to, 'Would the real Lyn Austen please stand up,' only one of the panel had picked her as the real programmer, and the studio audience all gasped in surprise – obviously it was a man's job. Thinking about it a few years later, after I'd had my eyes opened to inequality in the workplace, gave a new dimension to that interesting night out I'd had as a schoolboy.

So, no women on my cadet course. What would be the point? There were no women pilots in the Air Force or any of the airlines. There may have been a few enthusiastic amateur women pilots but very few professionals. This was the late sixties after all. As a flying instructor in those times, I found a few women flying light aircraft but then quite a few started to learn to fly. Nineteen sixty-eight was when all sorts of things started to change and women pilots was just one small example.

I taught a few women basic flying and, while not expecting them to be any harder to teach than blokes, I actually found in some ways they were easier. For a start, they were less gung-ho and reckless than a lot of the younger blokes – they were more mature. Sometimes a little too cautious but is that such a bad thing when leaving the Earth's surface? By the time I was flying on the line with Qantas I was a believer – well not just a believer, because I had enough empirical data, I actually *knew* that there was absolutely no reason there shouldn't be women airline or Air Force pilots. I did find one of my female students hard to teach but that was because she was one ravishing redhead and I found her distracting, to say the least.

In the early seventies, I would say things that would get me into trouble with some of the old troglodytes inhabiting positions of power – I have this egalitarian streak that just will not fade. Actually, it wasn't only in those days. This tendency to upset authority continued throughout my career – egalitarianism is just part of the good fight and that never stops.

Back then, if you said controversial stuff, people would notice. I got into the lift at work one day in about 1973, this was before ID cards with names on them, and the senior Captain who got in with me confirmed how I was indeed being noticed. I knew this Captain was about to be made Chief Pilot and I nodded the appropriate greeting. He just looked me up and down and said, 'Second Officer Austen.' Oh, oh. I'd never met him but he knew me. He watched this realisation dawn on me, then nodded back. Well, what could I expect? I wasn't the only boat-rocker, but I was one of the better ones – couldn't help it.

A few months later, this new Chief Pilot had to transfer from the 707 to the new 747 'Jumbo jet' to have any credibility in his new job. As fate would have it, I was on his fifteen-day check-out flight up to Rome and back. This switched-on Captain just didn't get along with the stodgy old Captain assigned to check him out and, as result, I found myself sharing the front seats with the new 747 pilot whenever he was on the flight deck. He got me to tell him all about operating a 747 and my old flying instructor skills got a workout. When we were in the stopover cities, this bloke preferred the company of the young flight engineer and myself for meals and drinks as well – he really couldn't stand the old checkie.

So, over too many late-night red wines in the cafes of the squares of Rome, he found out that, while I was a stirrer, there was usually a bit of logic floating around in my less-than-polite conversations. These late-night piazzas in Rome could get pretty crazy. Around this time, an F/O tried to auction my wife off to a table of lesbians after they had sent over a single rose to the gorgeous redhead sitting next to me – yes, the same one from the flying school. Anyway, if there was ever a place where there is *veritas in vino* then Rome is it and by the time I got back to Sydney the new Chief Pilot knew me and I'd found him to be a progressive and modern thinker.

What happened not long after didn't surprise me but it did irk the Captain I was flying with up to San Francisco and back. The new Chief Pilot had been to the States for a meeting of Chief Pilots and was on his way home on our aircraft. After dinner, he sent word that he would like to visit the flight deck and our Captain prepared us for the visit by making us put our ties on. When the boss came in he, a little embarrassingly, virtually ignored everyone except me. The conversation was about how he had just discovered that United Airlines had, for the first time ever, put a number of women pilots into their training school. He was obviously chuffed and knew he had a receptive audience in me. This man was instrumental in starting to crack one glass ceiling. I don't think I had anything to do with his ideas, they were his own and all power to him.

A few years later, now an F/O, I entered the breakfast room in the London crew hotel and noticed several tables with crew but only one with a young woman sitting with them. Luckily, I resisted the urge to ask who she was with, because I soon found out she was a new S/O under training and was on her last check-out flight before qualifying. She and another woman pilot were, naturally, the talk of all the bars and flight decks around the Qantas world at this time – women pilots were at last joining Qantas. The first woman in the world to become an Airline Captain was the American, Emily Warner, who started in 1973. Australia was slow in taking on women. The first to fly for a major airline was Deborah Lawrie, then Wardley, who had an incredible fight to get into the domestic airline she joined. Helped by new antidiscrimination laws, she was at last taken on in 1979.

Back in London, the talk about the new women pilots continued. Later that night, the Captain about to sign off on the new woman pilot and I were enjoying a quiet beer in the bar. I asked how he was finding her operational abilities. Apparently, she was very good, knew her stuff, had excellent book knowledge, was a good listener – no problems really. Well, except one. How could he, the Captain, sign her off when he knew that, because she wasn't a man, she would never be able to give anybody an order or stick up for herself if the going got tough.

I spent several beers pointing out to this guy that she was probably tougher than either of us. She'd done her years out in general aviation and that meant she'd already had her share of sticking up for herself with engineers, refuelers, passengers and anybody else taking a less than compliant view of her pilot-in-command decisions. This Captain must have ticked the box, however, because it was only a week or so later I flew with her on her first- ever operational sector, a twelve-and-a-half-hour flight from Bangkok to Athens.

Virtually no women airline pilots, especially in Asia, meant that at the immigration sign-out at Bangkok airport she was subject to the unabashed stares of Japan Airline's large cabin crew – every one of them female. Their Chief Purser saw me standing a little apart from the Qantas crew and approached with a question. This woman wanted to know if we had a woman flight engineer on our crew. The unspoken assumption was that, while flight engineers could have relatively low qualifications – not the case in Qantas by the way – it would take way more qualifications to be a pilot. That was why they assumed a woman in a dark-blue uniform with two stripes must be an engineer. When I told her no, the woman she was staring at was indeed a pilot, her surprise was obvious. She went straight over to her crew and announced in a loud voice

'Pairotto, pairotto!' Our new S/O saw all this and, as you might imagine, she was totally embarrassed.

This long flight to Athens was teaching me just what these women were up against. As the junior pilot on duty, she was responsible for the radio calls during the cruise. As we flew over the various control centres in Asia, India, the Middle East and the Mediterranean, her job was to establish comms and give position, altitude and estimated times to the controllers – again almost always men in those times and places. The Greek controllers had a particularly bad reputation. They had really poor microphone technique and, instead of making clear, loud transmissions by having their microphones close to, but not directly in front of, their mouth, they somehow managed to get a weak garbled sound that seemed like it was produced by putting the said microphone in a bucket and then yelling at it from the other side of the room. Contacting the Greeks was going to be fun.

They wouldn't answer her. After several calls she was asking me what she had done wrong – incorrect frequency, non-standard wording? What was she doing that needed changing? Nothing wrong. Have another go. Still no reply. I picked up the report and keyed my microphone. Maybe the radio was cactus. Not at all. There was an instant reply to my transmission and our clearance into Greek airspace was given, just not to that uppity woman on the radio who should be at home making the baklava.

Back in Bangkok, at dinner on the way home, there was me, the ex-NZ-Air Force male S/O, the new female S/O and a handful of male flight attendants. Cue one outspoken, drunk flight attendant who took it upon himself to tell us all how wrong it was to have women pilots. I was just about to rip this character to shreds when the NZ S/O did it for me – after all, New

Zealand women were the first in the world to have the right to vote. The most senior flight attendant, to his credit, just leant forward and pointed to the loudmouth and said, 'Don't worry, Bill, he's T A T P.' When I looked a bit nonplussed, he shrugged and said, 'Thick As Two Planks.' That was the first time I had heard that expression but I've used it many times since. That dinner and another nasty incident on the same stopover, which I won't go into, made me fully aware of just how tough these women were doing it. Fast forward many years and again I'm in the Bangkok bar and I'm talking to the check Captain friend who had just awarded the first command to a Qantas woman pilot.

He'd done this earlier in the day after the female Captain candidate and he had fought their way through afternoon storms to land in Bangkok. More correctly, she had fought the storms while he watched and assessed. As I said earlier, he was a friend but I was, after all, a male Captain and, until this particular afternoon, there had never been a female Captain in the airline's seventy-something year history, so when I, just out of interest, asked how it had all gone on the check flight I got a surprise. He turned and went for me. 'She's as good as you and me, Bill,' is how he forcefully, and rather defensively, put it. Suddenly I realised just how much scrutiny and pressure he would have been under – a lot of prejudiced people were watching. If he was under so much pressure, just how much had the new woman Captain overcome?

The world was changing for women but the steps were many and the journey long.

About twenty-five years later and I have just seen a news report from Saudi Arabia. They are now letting women learn to drive cars but at the same time they have jailed the main women activists fighting for this change. It makes for a slow journey when for every step forward there can sometimes be two backwards.

As fate would have it, a few years after the first women checked out as Qantas Captains, the S/O I had flown with on her first flight was now a Jumbo Captain flying into a very wet and stormy night for a landing into Bangkok. Her decision not to land her aircraft onto the wet and slippery runway is well known in Qantas and is an example to all pilots of how to make the right decision. This was the same woman the Captain in London was worried would not be able to stick up for herself or give any orders.

13

ON SPACE AND STUFF

Every young pilot back in the sixties dreamed of being an astronaut. I did anyway. Flying an aircraft is a step along the way to flying a spaceship – that's how I saw it. Space flights were all the go and the media was full of the adventures of the people going up THERE and doing incredible stuff. I pity the current crop of space explorers. They have to compete with funny cat videos and whatever celebrity has posted the most outrageous tweet.

Pilots were all astronauts in training, and we knew it. When the first moon landing happened, I was still a flying instructor. One of the boys had got hold of a small black-and-white TV – as they all were back then – and set it up in the instructors' room in the flying school. There wasn't going to be any flying that day. We had rung as many of the students as we could and told them so. Those that didn't understand went down in our estimation as just not having the right attitude.

My mother and grandfather watched the landing at home on a slightly larger TV. A measure of the immense change that culminated in this magnificent feat in such a short space of time was on show in that lounge room. My grandfather had grown up in the bush with no electricity or running water and had been an actual bullock team driver. He would attach a huge wagon of wool bales to half a dozen or so bullocks and off to market he would go. He was now a witness to this unfolding piece of history and was seeing it live.

Well, not quite. After touchdown, the two astronauts were taking their time checking everything but what really slowed them down was getting the moon lander's flimsy little door open. The astronauts were having trouble pulling it in against a little bit of residual cabin pressure caused by a sticky relief valve. Quite correctly, they were hesitant to pull on the door too hard. They didn't want to break it and leave themselves in a permanent vacuum while down on the moon's surface. (I talk about aircraft doors and cabin pressure later in the book.) Anyway, I could have designed a much better, stronger lander – it just would have been 15 tons heavier.

My grandfather sat and watched and when asked what he thought of it all, he said that, while it was a good story, it took too long for anything to actually happen. He liked the cop shows way better. He had watched but I don't think he really grasped the concept of a live transmission – let alone one from the moon. A bloody lot had happened since he was a young bloke – and not just to the price of wool.

I read all the books, *The Right Stuff* and *Space*, as well as a million science-fiction space stories. I'm still reading them in the hope that one day I will get my chance. One night, about nine years after the first moon landing, flying with about ninety percent of the earth's atmosphere below me, sitting in a control cabin about the size of a moon lander and separated from a hostile-to-life environment by a thin layer of aluminium, I was as close to being an astronaut as I would ever be. A couple of hours out from Honolulu on the way to Sydney on the flight deck of a Boeing 747, I was the Second Officer relieving the Flight Engineer so he could get some sleep.

The Captain and F/O were up the front. I was sitting at the Engineer's panel and our intergalactic time warp journey was proceeding well. You think I jest about time warping? How do you account for the fact that we would land twenty-nine hours after we took off and yet it was only a nine-hour flight? Okay, the International Date Line might have been a factor, but only for less wannabee astronauts.

On this flight there was a fifty-six-year-old American. He had been in his business office when a phone call from the Royal Melbourne Golf Club had given him his big chance to come Down Under. He had been offered a gig as the club's mystery guest speaker – *The man who has driven a golf ball further than any other man*. Alan Shepard was, and still is, the record holder for the longest golf drive. He took a golf iron and a couple of balls up with him to the moon and belted the life out of the second little bugger; which means he managed to hit it – no mean feat when you are hampered by a space suit. Having connected with it, the moon's reduced gravity and lack of atmosphere did the rest. The ball just soared off into the distance. Exactly how far it went doesn't really matter. We just know it was the best golf shot ever.

This ex-US Navy test pilot was NASA's first astronaut and one of the last Apollo Mission Commanders to the moon. He visited us in the flight deck – good old days, remember – to meet some 'fellow aviators'. Yes, he was a pilot, but he'd gone where others fear to tread and, by calling us 'fellow', he'd won me. Alan wasn't a big bloke but for his age he looked incredibly fit. The chatting went on for hours. He was totally willing to go over stuff he would have talked about a zillion times before.

He told us of his first space flight in a very small capsule on top of a relatively small rocket. This mission was a face-saving US reaction to Yuri Gagarin's first orbiting space flight a little earlier. Looks good in the papers but he pointed out just how inferior it was to the Russians. His capsule, with him in it, weighed about a ton and didn't go into orbit. Gagarin's was many times heavier and did get into orbit. Alan was telling us how much more *Throw Weight* the Russians had compared to the Yanks at this time. Not good for strategic war plans.

I had read the books and asked whether it was true what he had supposedly said about being perched on top of a huge rocket made from two million parts, every one of which was produced by the lowest bidder. He said the expression came from some publicity department but it did actually reflect exactly what you thought just before lift-off.

On that flight down to Sydney, Alan looked out of the 747's front windscreen at a nearly full moon and said with some nostalgia, 'Eight years since I was up there.' Wish I could say that. Going up to the moon when he did made him by far the oldest man to do so – he was forty-seven. For those who aren't into space flight in the way that a lot of us could- a-beens are, I will try to provide some essential background for the best space story I have ever heard.

Here is a quick course on going to the moon. Just as, elsewhere in the book, I've tried to keep the explanations of the flying stuff as simple as possible, I'll try to do the same with the space stuff. Those who already know all about space science can skip to the stories down below but I would appreciate them keeping quiet so as not to distract those who are paying attention.

First off, a space capsule, once up in space, does not need to keep its engine running. Not everybody knows this, because it doesn't make sense. Everything else from a bullock cart to a jet fighter needs a constant source of energy to keep moving. That's our experience of the world so spacecraft must be the same. But because there's no air, there's no drag, so there's nothing to slow you down. Science-fiction films showing Empire Cruisers with constantly glowing engines don't help people see through this misapprehension. Don't start me off about how these same films have space battles with sound. Without air to cause drag, or to transmit sound, space is a different place.

A retired maths professor mate gets upset at the disrespectful way filmmakers treat angular momentum in these films. Another mathematician mate told me in a discussion about the Romans that they wouldn't have got to the moon as their maths was limited.

They didn't have the Arab/Indian concept of zero and consequently would never have finished the countdown. We won't speak of these gentlemen again. By the way, you can't get to the moon without computers and for them you do need ones and zeros – just saying.

Before heading off to the moon, the moon shots went into Earth orbit. Orbiting can be explained by the cannonball. Fire one horizontally and, while going a long way towards your enemy, it will also fall down. Gravity makes no exception for ordnance. If it goes fast enough, the ball will find that the ground is curving away from it because the Earth is a sphere, and it takes longer to fall all the way down. Faster still, about 28,000 klicks, and the ball will never hit the ground. The ball wants to fall down and hit the ground but the Earth is too curvy. The cannonball has no choice but to keep flying. Now take the ball up above the atmosphere so that the air can't slow it down, hollow it out and stick a really small astronaut in it and you have a Manned Space Capsule in orbit. See how easy that was.

A couple of points to note here. The cannonball capsule hasn't got an engine. It doesn't need one because the ball got the required energy to get up there from the gunpowder. If you have ever seen a photo of the very first Sputnik, you will see that the Russians thought of this cannonball theory of space flight a while back. The next point is a question. How does the Flat Earth Society explain horizons and still keep a straight face?

Alan made sure we understood that, once he and his mates got to the moon, they could zoom around it without engine power. They could do this at a way slower speed because the falling bit was dependant on a much-reduced gravity and a much smaller sphere. They could also do this at a very low altitude because there is no air up there to get in the way.

Let's get Alan and his mates to the moon. The Saturn V rocket was a monster. Tip a 747 on its tail, fill it up with fuel, knock the wings off, put the astronauts on the flight deck and light the wick. Very simple. Well, not quite. It's better to make the rocket out of some detachable *stages* so that, when you don't need them anymore, like when all the fuel has gone out of one, you can jettison that section, making the rest easier to lift. That is what they did with the Saturn.

Reminds me of the time my wife and I trekked way up into the Himalayas. For the two of us we had a team of nine Nepalese guiding us and carrying our tents and food. As we 'ate' one of the 'boys', their words not ours, he would walk back down alone. We had our own Nepalese-designed lifting system that jettisoned one fuel section once it was consumed.

The Apollo 14 mission Saturn V rocket was in low-level orbit around the Earth. A couple of stages of the rocket had been used up, but there is still some left. Gagarin would have been impressed – that is if he had survived the small jet crash that had killed him by this time. Remember all these guys were military test pilots.

Back on the flight to Sydney Alan Shepard, one of the most famous men on the planet and of course one of my heroes, turns to me and says, 'You should know. How much extra energy does it take to get a body from orbit up away from the Earth's gravity compared to how much it takes to get it into orbit in the first place?' Luckily, I had read this and was inspired by the equation. The answer is exactly the same amount as it took to get into orbit in the first place. Escape energy is double orbit energy. That equation is up there with $E=mc^2$ as far as I'm concerned – just magic. The last big stage of the Saturn had the fuel to impart this energy to a, by now, much reduced weight (it's actually a much-reduced *mass* but we'll save that for Sunday – sorry).

Still on this sidetrack before Alan's greatest ever story on the moon. One unused Saturn V moon rocket was turned into America's first space station, Skylab. All they had to do was get it into orbit without the last stage filled with fuel. They now had a big cylindrical spacecraft section that was an orbiting space station instead of a fuel tank. There was plenty of volume in Skylab to do experiments and it even had a running track around the inside skin for the long-term health of the crew.

To get some running in, the astronauts would float, freefalling remember, onto this track, then scramble along it and, as they progressed around the inside circumference of Skylab, would give themselves a little apparent weight. We've all filled a bucket with water and swung it around our heads with a length of rope and seen how the water doesn't spill out. Actually, I've never done it either but I have swung the billy can vertically around with my arm, which is an equally stupid thing to do, even if it does keep the boiling tea in. Anyway, the faster they crawled the more apparent weight. Fast enough, and they could get up and run achieving a 'wall of death' status, you know like motorbikes zooming around the inside of spherical cages. If the motorbikes stop suddenly, they fall down. If the astronauts stop, they just float off.

Alan told us all this as part of the second-best space story I have ever heard. He told us how, when he was still at NASA, the Skylab crew of three called everybody into the control room. 'Houston, we have something for you. Switch on the TV monitors. We're sending down some video.' When the picture came on there were three heads rotating around the screen at a fair rate and all at 120 degrees to each other. Spinning the camera? No, it's all relative remember. These guys had set up the camera looking down the length of Skylab and had then managed to all get on the running track. Alan said they had the greatest grins of satisfaction on their faces as they looked at the camera while running in vertical circles. The boss thought that these blokes might need to have their workload upped a bit.

If it wasn't for the little bit of atmosphere up where Skylab was, it would still be there but a little drag over time degraded its orbit and down it came. They knew it would come down in the Southern Hemisphere within a certain time window. How do they know this stuff? Anyway, it went into the Indian Ocean, sans crew by the way. They were back home trying to run up the walls.

It was just as well it didn't hit Australia, well some bits did hit Western Australia but there's about a square kilometre for every person over there so no worries. The comic genius Spike Milligan, whose parents lived in Woy Woy on the east coast, had warned that he would declare war on the USA if it landed on them. Even today's International Space Station is falling out of the sky. It has to burn fuel to lift it the seventy or so metres it falls per day.

Every now and then, when the sun does its thing and spews a whole lot of energetic particles at us, the Earth's atmosphere expands a little and gives the station a bit more drag. One day, a couple of years ago, it fell about one and a half kilometres during one of these events – Woy Woy, here we come. It's a pity Spike is no longer around to declare war. I love his tombstone inscription, it reads, *I told you I was sick.*

At last Alan Shepard and his team have got to the moon and are orbiting around it. He and Ed Mitchell have left Stuart Roosa up in the spacecraft they will all travel home in. It's in a higher orbit waiting for Al and Ed to come back up from the surface. Clever when you think about it. A really small ship with only two blokes in it will use a lot less energy to get into moon orbit. The bigger craft can stay in moon orbit with the fuel needed to escape back to Earth. Have I mentioned there are some really smart people around?

As the lander goes zooming around the moon, Alan is flying feet first – yes, feet first. It's not like that in the movies. Feet first because that's where the lander's rocket engines are – at the base of the craft. As you approach the landing spot you fire up the rockets and they slow you down, which allows the moon's gravity to pull you down for the landing. The rate of fall is only about one-sixth of that on Earth but you still need the main landing rocket and the little control thrusters, with the diminishing quantity of gas in the tank, to prevent you becoming just another moon crater. Hey, they are Americans and they have actually got to the moon so, if they want to say *gas* instead of *fuel*, they can.

Now it gets interesting. Alan says everything went okay up to this stage of the landing. It's all relative remember. This crew had had some real problems a little earlier when a short circuit in an *abort* switch threatened to ruin their day by blasting their lander back into orbit. NASA got the computer nerd in Massachusetts out of bed and he was able to get the crew to hack the lander's main computer and negate the faulty switch. Alan didn't bother to explain this, he had an even better story to tell.

The moon lander is on semi-autopilot. A computer controls most of the descent but the astronauts still have some manual control so they can avoid craters and boulders on the surface. With only 120 seconds of gas left, the lander is now vertical enough for Alan to get a visual on the selected landing area. What does he see? Well, in his words, 'Nothing but 30- foot boulders.'

He had two minutes of gas left to find a flat spot and land. 'After 100 seconds of searching, I know I'm running out of gas. The guy beside me is telling me I'm running out of gas. Houston is telling me I'm running out of gas. I KNOW I'm running out of gas.'

Right on two minutes he finds a suitable spot and touches down on the moon. As it turned out, after checking the gas tank, there may have been about ten seconds endurance left. If it had been ten seconds the other way, this story would never have been told. Finally, Alan is on the moon after a landing he can not only walk away from but he can also go and play golf if he wants to – and that's exactly what this forty-seven-year-old did.

And now for the best bit. Alan complained to us how, every time he visited NASA, they broke out the tape of what he said after that touchdown. 'Did I come up with a profound, "One small step for a man", like Armstrong did? Not at all. The tape, you know, the secret one that the public never hears, just has me saying, "I'm getting too fucking old for this."

PROBLEM PASSENGERS

One evening in the early 70s at Heathrow Airport in London, we were loading a full contingent of passengers and our ETD (estimated time of departure) was approaching. A delay can have serious consequences for our departure. Busy airports like Heathrow have *slots* – times they have reserved for your departure. Miss your slot and you might end up with a big delay waiting for another slot to open up. As the S/O, I was the one at the back of the flight deck messing with paperwork. The Captain was already belted in but he was getting time stressed so he ordered me out of the flight deck to go and find out what the hold-up was.

Outside the flight deck door on a 707 is the main aisle running straight down the cabin. To the right, facing down the aircraft, is the main door and to the left, a couple of toilets and the forward galley. Just inside the main entrance door, in full view of the passengers looking up the aisle, mayhem was breaking loose. This was a full flight and there was a huge amount of hand-held luggage coming on board. That is not a just a twenty-first century phenomenon – things were just as bad back then. The handling agents were taking the bigger bags off passengers at the door, tagging them and sending them down to the hold, but it was taking time and people were getting upset.

The chief steward, as they were called then, was an interesting bloke. Being independently wealthy, he was really only flying for the fun of it. But, even so, he was a dedicated professional. He was out to have a good time, and especially to meet a lot of young men – that is if he wasn't flying with the Queen Mother on Royal flights. He told me she would ask for him specifically because she liked the way he prepared her gin and tonics. Chris, or as we knew him, Crystal, was directing the passenger-loading process and was doing his level best to keep everyone happy. Just before I came out to investigate the delay in boarding, a big suitcase had been taken off a middle-aged woman and she was not happy. She grabbed her handbag off the top of the confiscated bag and promptly spilled the contents of the smaller bag all over the floor outside the flight deck door.

Chris, being the helpful soul that he was, got down on his knees and started retrieving passports, make-up and the rest. Unfortunately, this left an angry woman with a weapon in her hand. She wasn't going to let the opportunity go by and, just as I opened the flight deck door, started hitting Chris over the head with her handbag. I took in the scene very quickly – a woman whacking away, Chris politely asking her to stop and uttering the occasional 'Ow!' as the handbag connected. All down the aisle startled passengers were staring in disbelief at the scene but what really flummoxed me was what was happening in the galley. Up against the back wall, out of the line of sight of the passengers, the hostie was sliding down the wall – literally legless with laughter. Other staff were rushing in to help Chris, so I instantly stepped back through the flight deck door and slammed it shut behind me – I'm not stupid.

The Captain notices my sudden return and asks, 'What?' I tell him, 'They're fighting outside. I'm not going out there.' All this time I'm watching the end of the fight through the little peephole in the door. This was a very different time. Now, police would arrive, statements would be taken, handcuffs would appear and, in some parts of the world, guns would be drawn. But this was the early seventies, so the passenger just took her seat and we departed pretty much on time.

Later in the flight, Chris came up to the flight deck to show the Captain the report he was preparing about the incident. He told us that the woman was still mouthing off about the injustice of it all and really upsetting the people around her. Chris felt that he would have to go down and confront her himself. The Captain responded, 'See that second officer there. He didn't come out to help you before so he can go down now and sort it.' Off I went as ordered. Great. She was still holding forth. The gist of what she seemed to be saying was – I'm the victim and I know it and I'm going to tell everyone.

The conversation between us was being closely monitored by about twenty interested passengers. I couldn't tell her the real reason we take the big heavy hand luggage off people is actually safety related, that is if 'safety related' is the right term for what happens when a big unsecured bag smashes into the back of the head of someone sitting in the rows in front. This would happen if the aircraft suddenly stopped, like up against a fence if you ran off the runway. The bag wouldn't actually fly forward it would just keep going at about 200 klicks, it would actually be the aircraft and the back of the passenger's head stopping really quickly that would make the bag appear to fly forward and break a neck or two. It's all relative.

The conversation could not include these crash scenarios so that limited my ability to shut her up. So, I relied on a technique I've used a lot since – I let the angry person just say stuff. Eventually angry people say something wrong, ridiculous or just something that gives you a chance. She was telling me all about her husband working for the New South Wales Government and, when that didn't seem to impress me that much, she made her mistake and gave me my chance – never let a chance go by.

She told me, and the audience, that she wasn't going to fly Qantas ever again. I went for it. I told her that was a good decision because, in fact, her name was going to go onto the list of people who are never to be allowed to fly with us again. Furthermore, her name would probably end up on the list shared by all airlines of people who would not be allowed to fly on any airline.

There was stunned silence for about the time it took the audience to realise a clear winner had emerged. After this silence, a decent round of applause erupted – their preferred combatant had won. One victorious S/O exited stage left. Back in the flight deck the Captain asked how I'd got on. I told him about the round of applause and why I got it. If, in the middle of an argument, you can come up with the concept of the first *No Fly* list you certainly deserve some applause.

The next time a Captain sent me out of the flight deck of a 707 to sort out a passenger problem, the circumstances were totally different. For a start, it was in New York and I was outside trying to help, not hiding in the flight deck. Same scenario, something was holding up the closing of the main door and time was a-ticking. I quickly found the problem. A young male passenger had come back up from his seat and was trying to get off the aircraft. He was telling some story about how he couldn't leave her – whoever she was.

This was a time when hijackings were happening all over the place, security systems were primitive and all sorts of people were having a go. The east coast of the States was the favourite area for hijackings to Cuba and the Americans were trying everything to stop the practice. One of the handling agents helping to board the flight had obviously pushed the secret button because, as we were gently trying to get this bloke to tell us exactly what the problem was, all communication suddenly ceased. Four big blokes in suits came running down the aerobridge. New York was the centre of the universe at the time and its airport had aerobridges. The four suits didn't say anything, just grabbed one corner of the young bloke each, ran back up the finger with him held high in the air and disappeared.

Losing one of your passengers before the door is even closed is not good, especially if you don't know why. The G-Men, as these FBI blokes would have been called back then, may, or may not, have been finding out why in some backroom somewhere, but we weren't going to get any information. The FBI had their own priorities and Qantas wasn't one of them.

So, we couldn't go anywhere and, before we could, we had to find out quite a lot. This was a time before computers so information was much harder to come by. Did the disappeared have a bag in the hold and if so where was it? Easy, just put his name into the system. Whoops. There is no system – you get what I mean? We were going to be delayed, and we were – three hours in the end.

An aircraft can't go anywhere carrying a bag whose owner is not on board. A sensible way of saying if you blow up the aircraft, you go too. The arduous task of taking all the bags out of the cargo hold and lining them up on the apron near the aircraft began. Once they were all lined up, the passengers got off the aircraft, filed past and picked out theirs. I kid you not; this is what you had to do back then. The bag left over was, of course, the one belonging to the young bloke. Nobody went near that one.

Before the bags were ready for inspection, the passengers had to wait on board. We had no idea whether it was a real security scare with bombs and guns on board or just a *scared of flying* incident. There was one empty seat on the aircraft, the one the passenger had left to try and deplane. The Captain decided the seat had to be searched but with as little provocation to panic as possible. As the most junior officer the S/O is the obvious choice for such a task.

Down I went with strict instructions not to scare the punters. Luckily, it was an aisle seat and I could get to it easily. I asked all the people around whether they had seen the bloke with any hand luggage or anything else. I sat in his seat and spoke to the young woman next to me, all the while surreptitiously feeling the seat cushions for any hard bits – I'd already crawled around the floor looking for any possible 'hand luggage' he may have stowed under the seat.

I noticed that the young woman was quite agitated and I tried to calm her. It didn't work as suddenly she broke into tears and said that it was all her fault and asked me if she would lose her job. The day was already stressful enough but now it was getting downright confusing. She told me she was a junior Qantas staff member and it was her fault because, 'Look. I offered him this paperback to read.' The book she showed me had one word on the cover, HIJACK.

We didn't find anything suspicious and I didn't dob on the young woman. What was the point? Eventually, we left for San Francisco but I still have a mental image of the lone suit case sitting on the apron – I wonder whether it's still there. We didn't find out the story of what happened to our passenger or why he wanted off – communications remained broken.

The next time I saw a passenger being held high above policemen's heads and being run through a terminal happened thirty years later. It was the day after the 9/11 attacks and the aviation world was on tenterhooks. I flew a 747-400 from Sydney to Auckland on this day and, like all Qantas Captains, provided special briefings to the cabin crew assuring them that security was as strong as possible and that it would all be good. What did we know?

The other part of the briefing was to make them aware that our passengers would be nervous about things and may well say or do stupid things. They might even make jokes about bombs and how they didn't have one today – ha, ha. Watch out for that and use discretion when handling these situations.

We made it to Auckland without incident and were walking through the arrival terminal when suddenly a passenger off another airline was seen flying through the terminal about seven feet off the ground. It didn't take four G-Men this time, just two Maori coppers. They breed them big in New Zealand, so don't joke about bombs anywhere near them.

15

VIETNAM FLYING

In the early 1970s, Vietnam was a war zone. Indeed, in the mid-60s they were going at it for all it was worth as well. As I have said, to get past a threesome of interviewers to get into Qantas back then I had to pretend I was all on board with the weird concept that if South Vietnam fell to the Northern Commies then Australia would be next. The prevailing Domino Theory had to be quoted along with the threat of the Yellow Peril if you wanted to be seen as acceptable pilot material. The few of us with more progressive ideas had to be careful about what we said.

Flying as a junior 707 Second Officer in those years meant flying near or over what shouldn't have been flown near or over. On the Hong Kong flights from Sydney, it was common to see the USAF (US Air Force) B52s flying between their Philippine and Guam bases and their targets in either North or South Vietnam. They were usually in formations of three, crossing at about right angles to the civilian aircraft tracks going north/south.

The young USAF pilots were bomber crews, not safety-conscious professional airline people. I have no idea how close the Qantas aircraft and these bomber formations ever got to each other but on a clear day you could see them returning after a mission. At this stage, they would usually be higher than the 707s but in a very undisciplined loose group of three aircraft in a line.

These guys would celebrate having survived the day by relaxing and playing their version of leapfrog. This involved the B52s, big eight-engine jets, forming a line astern formation – that is they were following each other at the same altitude. The first in line would then suddenly drop a hundred feet or so and slow down a bit, probably only about 10 or 15 knots – about 20 klicks. It would then let the other two pass over its head before popping up to be the last in line. The new leader would then drop down. These manoeuvres may well have to do with inspecting each other for battle damage but I like to think it was just their version of leapfrog.

Two issues concerned me at the time. How much lower were these aircraft flying on their way to their targets with their extra weight of bombs and fuel and how would any separation with us civilians be guaranteed? Our altitudes were not kept secret but I have no idea how good communications with the USAF were back then. Would they be aware that we were flying in the line of clouds they were about to fly through? The sophisticated TCAS (Traffic Collision Alert System) radar transponders were still decades away. A lot fewer aircraft and a big empty sky made up for a lot of deficiencies in the system in those days.

An incident a few years later in the same part of the world illustrates the dangers of the less than ideal communication systems. As the S/O on a 747 on the same Hong Kong route, I was the radio man – the bloke responsible for reporting position and altitude to the various Air Traffic Control centres. After leaving the Australian region, you eventually entered the Philippine area of control. I forget whether the Americans or Indonesians had control of the airspace before the handover. All I knew was that the Comms were shit that day with the really second-rate HF (high frequency) radios virtually useless. That system used a frequency range that allowed the radio waves to bend around the earth by bouncing off the ionosphere. Some days the ionosphere just wasn't there to bounce off. VHF (very high frequency) radio allowed much clearer, stronger signals but only in a straight line – 'line of sight' they called it. Hence much shorter range and it was dependent on how high you were.

Having had no comms with Manila Control via the HF, or anybody else for a long while, I was concerned to contact them ASAP and certainly before entering their airspace, our track joined with another converging track at the boundary and we had no information as to what was on that airway. I called on the VHF frequency hoping Manila might hear me as we were right on max range. They didn't hear me but a Flying Tiger cargo aircraft did and *relayed* my position report and altitude to Manila. He was able to do that because he was much closer to them. By the way, in those days every pilot *relayed* quite often for other airlines or other Qantas mates.

In those older aircraft, the radios had a circuit that would eliminate weak background signals and the static due to the airflow over the aircraft. It stopped a lot of background *hash*, and made life easier. This circuit, called *squelch*, could be shut off in just these circumstances if you wanted to listen to everything the poor little radio was picking up. I listened to the Tiger give my report with the squelch shut-off button pushed. I heard a very weak but urgent reply, 'Tell Qantas, climb immediately, climb immediately to 34 zero.'

This could mean only one thing, there was another aircraft converging on the other track and the bastard was at the same altitude. Remember how I was concerned about the B52s being lower when they were heavier? Well, that is indeed how jets do their thing. As the weight reduces with fuel burn you go up to your new 'optimum' altitude. That is the altitude for best efficiency. Planes can go higher than their optimum just not to the stage where it gets dangerous. They call the dangerous height and speed *Coffin Corner* for good reason. So, we were at 32 zero and were told to get out of there fast. I yelled at the F/O sitting next to me that we had to climb now. I got the auto pilot climbing straight away and pushed the thrust levers up – good old days, so there was no auto throttle.

Now the Flight Engineer was sitting behind us doing his monitoring thing, planning ahead for the next climb in about an hour. He was surprised to see the S/O push the power up and zoom into a climb. He put his hand on the thrust levers to pull them back with the words, 'We're a bit heavy to climb.' Strong language was heard as I grabbed his hand and stopped him. I then told him to look out of the window. There was the Philippine Airlines DC10 slipping underneath us.

After we had climbed to our new level, I was able to see the other aircraft as well as watch it on the weather radar by tilting the antenna way down. It was a couple of miles ahead. How much speed, and therefore distance, we lost in that climb I'll never know.

Less than perfect radio communication, poor coordination between Air Traffic Regions and rampant military activity were part and parcel of the job in those days. As a young bloke, I tended to accept that that was just how things were. With the wisdom of hindsight, I can see that things weren't as good as they could have been.

One of the main Qantas routes to London was via Hong Kong. There was no overflying of Mainland China then. Nixon and Whitlam hadn't started the process of opening up the relationship with Mao and Western airlines were just not welcome over the mainland. The track to London, or more correctly to Bangkok or some city in India, was back down into South East Asia and, believe it or not, across South Vietnam and then west. Again, as Radio Man, the S/O would get the job of reporting in with the Americans before we passed over Vietnam. Luckily, this was done with their very good network of VHF stations.

At least we could get our message across accurately and in a timely manner so that they knew who we were and, hopefully, didn't feel inclined to put a missile up our tail pipe.

We knew that the B52 was an aircraft similar to us in terms of speed, cruising altitude and size. We were also flying in the same region they were operating in. Did the North Vietnamese have us on their SAM2 radars? The SAM2 is a Russian Surface to Air Missile. Were we ever in range? I don't know. Were there any MIGs zipping over the border to have a go at anything? I don't know. I do know that a Cathay Pacific aircraft blew up over Vietnam at the time. A bomb on board was blamed and, of course, I believe everything the authorities tell me.

I discovered transiting over a war zone had another little quirk. When the Americans were using their artillery, they had a system in place to warn aircraft that there were shells about to go into the air. They would come onto a special frequency and give a position, usually a radio beacon, and then give two radials (compass directions) from that point. This would give an area on a map. My job was to quickly find said position and define the area described by the radials. This defined an area you didn't want to be in. If the artillery officers ever used their guns' ability to shoot a very high trajectory you might get a really big explosive shell pop up through your wing.

I still remember the young-sounding US Army radio guys. They were probably younger than I was and had a particular way of ending their warning calls. They would give the position and directions and then tell us pilots to, 'Pick it out.' That was my job, to pick it out ASAP and then scream at the Captain if necessary. That's how it would have come out, I can tell you, if we were in a fire zone and a very loud scream it would have been, too. I wonder how many passengers knew what was going on. Did they realise that their main problem was not the chardonnay being a touch warm?

Again, good communications were being relied on when we were doing these Vietnam overflights. Did the Yanks get the info from all their big gun teams in the country? Were the people in charge of getting the warnings out stoned that day? It was the Vietnam War. All I know is that, decades later, the Russians, or their puppets, did indeed shoot down a civilian aircraft over a war zone, probably inadvertently due to poor intelligence. It was a Malaysian aircraft that really should not have been there. I was pleased to note at the time that Qantas hadn't tried to save fuel and was going around instead of flying over this particular war zone.

Flying past and over Vietnam at this time was one thing. Flying into it was another thing altogether. As a new S/O in 1970 and 1971 I went where I was told. I had escaped the conscription call-up for military service literally by being born on the right day. My birthday was not one of those drawn out of the barrel. However, being a S/O on the line meant I was sent up there on troop charters. My number came up and off we went to pick up a troop contingent from Townsville. These blokes had done their jungle training near Townsville and were off to war. I can still remember one young digger getting to the top of the stairs into the 707, where I was supervising the orderly loading, he turned around and said, 'Well that's Townsville, next stop Vietnam.' He was on an adventure.

Flying into Saigon's (Ho Chi Minh City) Tan Son Nhat airport was not to be taken lightly. The arrival was different to coming into a regular airport. For a start, I was given challenge and response code words to memorise before leaving Sydney. These were to be used if we suspected the Viet Cong were giving false radio instructions. Again, bloody iffy communications but I still remember those codes 47 years later – Re-tread, Redbrick. It would appear you never forget stuff your life depends on.

We made our approach, really steep, close and tight over the moonscape. The moonscape craters were the result of American bombing and shelling to clear any vegetation from around what was then the busiest airport in the world. No Viet Cong hiding places left, thank you.

On the ground, past small concrete hangars, which were still there 40 years later, across super-busy taxiways where fighter bombers would scream past on their way to a mission somewhere, we found our parking spot out on the open spaces. Around us other transports were arranged. The big new shiny, silver C141s were from the US of A. They were four-engine high-winged transports, probably a bit bigger than the 707. They were new and, if you saw the pilots through the cockpit window, they had really cool helmets that were painted with the stars and stripes. On the smaller taxiways, however, you could see World War II vintage piston-engine transports, obviously doing the runs up country. They were probably supplying artillery shells. These aircraft were dull green, had blokes, usually black, hanging out open doors and roof flaps keeping cool and watching for fighters roaring past. The airport was like nothing I'd seen before – or since.

After our load of Aussie soldiers got off, it was time for some other Aussies to unload both the cargo holds and whatever extra stuff had been carried in the cabin. Not all the seats had been used by soldiers but they were all full – a lot of mail arrived with us. It hadn't occurred to me that, of course, we wouldn't have the usual Qantas loaders, engineers, refuelers or caterers. Anyway, these shirtless soldiers came on board at a run and just went flat out, emptying the cabin in no time. Impressive on what was the hottest most humid day I had ever experienced. The F/O and I then took a very tentative trip outside, being careful not to silhouette ourselves in the doorway or to hang around out in the open to make ourselves a sniper target. A Pan American crew member had become a sniper target a while earlier – this was a dangerous place.

On departure, the cabin crew would always try to make things special for the blokes going home if they could – the beer would flow and the relief laughter would start. At the time, pre-digital days remember, you could buy a little plastic box in Hong Kong that you wound up to get the little baby record in it to spin and scratch up against a little needle.

Result, a few seconds of maniacal laughter that the cabin crew would play over the PA just on lift-off. I remember that weird laughter occurring just before 150 soldiers broke into cheering and applause. I often wonder whether the young infantryman from Townsville cheered when he came home at the end of his tour.

The other thing about the take-off from Saigon was that, to keep away from any little nasties, the procedure was as steep as possible on a departure track as unpredictable and expeditious as possible – this was just logical. We got some impressive performance from a now relatively lightly loaded 707. We didn't have much cargo and weren't full of fuel. Aircrew who flew these flights into Saigon were awarded the Australian War Service Medal and the Vietnam Logistic Support Medal, oh, and a mention on a Government website among civilian aircrew in Vietnam.

The Qantas Aircrew who did these charters also became instant members of the 'Skippy Squadron', which was eventually invited to join the Anzac Day march and I did, indeed, start to go along with a few pilot mates and quite a few cabin crew mates from those times. The impetus to join the march came from my daughter, Hannah, who by then had become the Australian Air Force Cadet Warrant Officer in charge of organising the banner carriers for all Air Force squadrons in the Sydney march. She had hundreds of cadets under her command.

One of the proudest moments in my life was to see Hannah arrive specially to lead the Skippy Squadron in the march. She had organised her duties around that moment. The Skippy Squadron is named after the popular TV character Skippy, the Bush Kangaroo.

Qantas also had a kangaroo on its aircraft tails by then. The Squadron had another nick name, the Red Tail Rats, because apparently not everybody in Vietnam knew about kangaroos, but they certainly knew about rats. There is a nice little tribute in the Australian War Memorial in Canberra.

16

REFUGEES

From the mid-seventies well into the eighties, Australia took large numbers of refugees from South East Asia. The aftermath of the Vietnam war and other smaller regional troubles ensured a never-ending supply of desperate people for the camps in neighbouring Thailand. It was not unusual to find the normal Jumbo service out of Bangkok filled with the usual passengers on their way to Australia but also a sizable number of refugees being taken to their new country as well.

I was co-pilot one night on such a flight out of Bangkok to Melbourne, arriving on a wintery morning just before dawn. All of the passengers including the refugee families, for that's what they were, families, got off in Melbourne before the aircraft continued up to Sydney without passengers. There were about 100 refugees on the flight.

The flight down over Australia had been smooth, and if you can call 300 tonnes of metal, fuel and people hurtling through the upper atmosphere at 1000 klicks peaceful, then it was peaceful as well. The cabin had been quiet and dark anyway. Even so the refugees may not have slept a wink despite their near total exhaustion. They had packed up their lives in the camp, said goodbye forever to the close friends with whom they had endured the last years of horror and deprivation. They then travelled over rough roads through storms and mud, crammed into the back of canvas covered trucks with their new travel companions; all this would have been just be the beginning of an unimaginable journey to a strange and distant land.

They would have arrived at Bangkok's Don Muang airport, just as the sun was setting, and been *processed* onto a huge aircraft it is likely none of them had ever seen before. A Jumbo jet was not the usual thing you found in South East Asian villages. They probably had no idea of what to expect from the flight either as the likelihood of any of these people having flown before would be small. They would have found themselves sharing the flight with a large number of white people, again probably seeing big numbers of foreigners would have been a new experience for these people.

They had to deal with a flight that would feel to them like it just went on and on, how could this big machine stay up for so long, just how far away is this new country, Australia, anyway? As I said it took until an hour before dawn to get to Melbourne. They weren't allowed off the aircraft before the other people of course, the paying passengers had priority and besides the system was well oiled by this stage, the authorities had it all worked out.

The families were allowed to grab their meagre belongings and when the aircraft was clear they were made to disembark and line up out in the passage way immediately outside the aircraft. I knew this because by this time the whole Qantas crew had already found some chairs out in this passage way so that we could kill some time while the cabin cleaners did their thing before the flight up to Sydney.

Now I grew up in Melbourne and I'm not sure I was ever out of bed at this time of the morning. Four AM in a Melbourne winter is dark and cold. The airport back then didn't have heating out in the passage ways and where we were seated there was not the tropical heat and humidity we had been in about eight hours earlier in Bangkok; in fact, it was edging on being dangerous for brass monkeys.

The immigration officials were all men and were dressed in dark brown police type uniforms complete with a peaked cap. They looked like military coppers to me and to the refugees they must have looked like huge nine foot tall soldiers. Most refugees have learned to fear uniforms and these white 'soldiers' in their brown uniforms were so big they didn't even need guns it would seem.

I looked and what I saw were defeated, frightened and now shivering people. Shivering may well have been a totally new terrifying experience in itself. The kids weren't crying; they were too scared I think, or just too tired. These people had very little and if you took the time to look it was clear they had no warm clothes for the dark, freezing world they had been transported into.

The Qantas crew - pilots and cabin crew - had gone quiet. I presumed they were watching and contemplating like I was. My thoughts were complicated, I was seeing the results of a war, a war I had been a small player in as a transport pilot, and it wasn't pretty at all. What I definitely wasn't seeing in front of me was a group of cunning sneaks getting into our country with huge amounts of gold hidden somewhere on their bodies, people intent on stealing our jobs, even though their plan was to actually just live on welfare. I didn't see this in front of me but the male flight attendant sitting next to me did. He let all around him know just how wrong it was to let these rich dole bludgers into Australia. This was an attitude that I knew a few non-thinkers had towards refugees, I was just a bit surprised to hear a non-thinker say it out loud.

To digress for a moment, a little while earlier my wife and I had trekked way up into the Himalayas. Not into snow territory but into mountainous areas that still had some small villages, places where people still hadn't seen white people. I can remember our chief guide stopping us on the trail one morning as we were approaching some people coming in the opposite direction and he was very wary. He had sent a runner ahead and knew that these people hadn't seen white people before and he was concerned at what their reaction might be. This astute guide made sure everybody paused their journey as delicate warnings were given.

I had raided a few Qantas passenger supplies before taking this holiday and had come on this trek with a reasonable quantity of little Qantas give-away kangaroo pins. The little golden kangaroos were mounted on a little printed cardboard rectangle. When we stopped on this mountain track I produced a few of these little presents and had our guide send them up to the travellers up the hill. They were now warily viewing us from a distance. The runner went up to them with the gifts and a little while later a half dozen or so men and women approached us for a closer look. They would have seen a woman with RED hair and her companion possibly the world's biggest human. We greeted them warmly but respectfully and had to be very careful of how we reacted to the fact that they had all put their kangaroo pins onto their chests with the cardboard backing still attached.

In the cold airport refugee staging area I stared at the opinionated flight attendant. I must have given him one hell of a look because he suddenly went quiet and looked decidedly uncomfortable. I kept the stare going as I pointed to the aircraft door and told him that since he knew where they would be, he would now go on board and collect all the little kangaroo pins on the aircraft and give them to me. Nobody watching minded that I didn't make this request very polite.

Armed with the pins I then joined the other nine foot tall uniformed white men. I, however, didn't throw any orders around putting smaller brown people into straight lines. I just walked along the lines smiling - I hadn't seen one smile all morning - and distributed the pins to every kid I could see. I had been emboldened by the loudmouth and I was angry, no brown uniform was going to stop me and maybe the look on my face prevented them from even contemplating doing so. Up close the look of defeat and desperation in the faces of the parents was even more obvious, those expressions haunt me still. The one saving grace was that when some of the adults realised what I was doing, the looks of relief and gratitude they gave me have stayed with me over the years as well.

So, a hundred or so South East Asians did enter Australia carrying gold that morning, well little bits of brass anyway. I like to imagine that round about now, a fifty-year-old Vietnamese Australian has just returned from his daughter's university graduation. I like to think as he puts his tie pin back in his trinkets box, he sees a little brass kangaroo pin and wonders for the umpteenth time why his father made him promise to always keep it and never throw it away.

17
LOS ANGELES RIOTS

When departing from Saigon during the Vietnam war the steep, high-powered climb was a lesson to a young bloke. I filed this 'combat departure' away and actually applied it many years later in Los Angeles on one of the worst nights of rioting that city has ever experienced. Rodney King was a large black man who became famous, although I'm not sure he wanted to be, when some LA coppers gave him a beating after a car chase. Unfortunately for the police, they were subject to one of the first 'caught on video' exposés. For the first time in history, law keepers could be seen by a mass audience carrying out their duties, in this case, in a way too enthusiastic manner.

A year or so later, the white cops involved went to trial and, by chance, I was due to fly a Boeing 767 from LA to Honolulu on the evening the verdict was handed down. While packing my bag in my room an hour or so before pick-up, I was watching what I thought was some courtroom channel on LA TV. You get all sorts of stuff on TV in the states. My cultural bias showed up as there were a lot of black and white Americans in that courtroom and I found myself wondering what the black guys were accused of and whether they were guilty. By the way I didn't realise it at the time but the presiding judge handing down the verdicts was indeed none other than John Davies, one of only two Australian men's Olympic breaststroke gold medalists.

When the first white cop was found innocent I had my little eyes opened as to what was going on and who these blokes really were. The TV channel flipped to a black social club somewhere in LA for a comment and there was, to say the least, a less than positive response. Back to the courtroom – more acquittals. Flip to the black club for a reaction. The atmosphere there was getting darker and darker – no pun intended. I was now on the edge of my seat and starting to think that this might be a good time to get out of LA.

Down in the hotel foyer early and the transport driver was already planning a safer route out to the airport. His dispatcher was really on the ball and had good information as to where trouble was breaking out and which way we could go to avoid it. The other pilots and all the cabin crew except one were early and ready to go. The last flight attendant was one of those blokes who wasn't going to be hurried – twenty past was pick up and he'd be ready at twenty past. I told him that was fine but we were off. He could stay in LA and fend for himself in the riots that were breaking out everywhere. He was on the bus in no time.

At LAX there were National Guard troopers everywhere as well as LA's finest. I often wonder, when these guys were fighting the riots over the next day or so, whether they reflected on the causes. We were directed straight to the aircraft because, luckily, it was only a domestic flight and we didn't have to go through immigration. As I got off the bus, the dispatching engineer came straight up and told me he'd put fifty tons of gas on, he hoped it was enough because he was going home to protect his family. It was plenty. The aircraft was lightly loaded because only half the passengers had managed to get to the airport and I don't think anyone was bothering with cargo. Lighter aircraft use less fuel.

Now the runways at LAX head straight out to sea because that's the prevailing wind direction; 90 to 95% of my departures from LAX were in that direction, especially at night. That night, Murphy was enforcing his Law and there was a strong easterly wind, meaning we had no choice, we had to take off in the opposite direction over the now riot-torn city. Fortunately, we were in a relatively lightly loaded two-engine aircraft. This is an important factor for performance reasons. Four engines have lots of power, but two engines have way more power-to-weight and therefore more get up and go. The 767 was a sports car compared to the 747 bus. Why is this so? Well, if an engine goes bang on climb, and they do, you have to be able to maintain about a 1% climb gradient. To do this a four-engine aircraft needs 75% of its full power – that is three engines –this is incorporated into the aircraft's design. The 767 with two engines only needs 50% of its maximum power to climb out – just one engine. Keep all engines going and the 767 has 100% extra power for climbing while the Jumbo has only 33% extra – 767 sports car.

On take-off I got the F/O to tell LAX tower we would be doing a steep climb with an early turn back towards the ocean. The unspoken words were that we were trying to avoid any stray, or not so stray, bullets that may come our way. Now, with a long runway, light load, a cool night and a strong headwind as we had that night, you can reduce your take-off thrust to save the engines quite a bit of stress. Instead, we used full power for the take-off – my lessons from Vietnam came into play. After a fast acceleration and steep take-off, I looked out over the nose to see, not LA, but what looked like a European city in flames straight after it had been bombed back in 1943 – not big fires, but plenty of them. As you might expect, that image is ingrained on my brain forever. A quick, steepish turn back and we were on our way to the beautifully peaceful islands of Hawaii.

Ironically, given all the trouble bad radio reception has caused me over 40 years, that night we were able to pick up a strong signal from a commercial AM radio station in LA. Their frequencies sometimes allow great range but usually only at night, when there is a bit of that ionospheric reflection, and usually only if the station is high-powered. We listened to the breaking news for the next four or five hours down to Honolulu. At last a radio was doing what I wanted.

In fairness, I should point out that when the old HF radios worked they could work very well. I was on a flight with Prince Charles on board in the late 70s when I managed to contact British Airways in London from our position off the coast of India. I was able to receive and pass on the message that he had become an uncle: his sister, Anne, had just had her first child. By the way, you have to feel for Charles. He's a little older than me and is still waiting to start his main job.

My First World problems with radio reception pale in comparison to what the previous generation of pilots had to put up with. My father spent quite a bit of World War II transporting valuable personnel and cargo from the southern Australian states to Darwin, way up in the north. He was a desert-flying expert. In fact, he scored a job in the new Trans Australia Airlines after the war on the strength of his experience. (TAA changed its name to Australian Airlines and later became part of Qantas.)

Darwin had been bombed badly, by the same blokes who had done the number on Pearl Harbour a couple of months earlier. The Japanese continued to make raids all over the north for quite a while. My dad was in and out of Darwin over a long period – wet season or dry. One wet, he was carrying a US General and his staff, including bodyguards, into a stormy Darwin. With bad weather and Japanese raiders in mind, some emergency airstrips had been built a bit out of Darwin to the south. Batchelor was one of them. The DC3 Dad was flying had to land there to avoid the huge thunderstorm in the way.

HF radio was the main comm system at the time and, while voice radios were available, using Morse code keys was the most frequently used method. Radio aerial technology wasn't that far advanced and using HF radios while flying required the pilots to wind out a trailing aerial. This was a wire with a little cup on the end to help drag it out from the little winder. You let it out a certain distance, ideally, half the wavelength of the frequency you wanted to use, and then you tuned it by winding it in and out until you got good reception. I learnt to use this set-up in the late 60s.

What with all the hard flying, military-coded Morse and huge electrical discharges from said thunderstorms, no message had been sent to Darwin about the VIP making an unscheduled stop. Dad had two vivid memories of what occurred after landing on the gravel emergency strip: the look of fear on the faces of the young Aussie airport guards as two huge US Army bodyguards jumped out of the aircraft with their Thompson submachine guns at the ready; and what happened when he tried to get a message through to Darwin.

The message could only go via HF radio of course, the same bloody comm system that gave me the irrits for years but at least I had voice coms and the aerials had become solid state. So, Dad jumps out in the rain and drags the trailing aerial out from the tail to get the appropriate distance for the thing to work. The American General is now sitting in the DC3's doorway watching this, and is probably not surprised when the next big electrical discharge finds a convenient way to earth using a handy length of wire being stretched out by an obliging Australian pilot.

Dad remembers being flattened by the lightning. It may well have hit the wire and ground near him. He doesn't think he was knocked out because he remembers the General falling out of the aircraft laughing his head off and telling him to get back in the plane and forget the radio. One young Aussie pilot was very happy to follow this American order, especially since he had noticed by this time his uniform was steaming from the passage of about a billion volts through it. Just as well it was wet. I don't think I'll complain about radios so much.

Since we're on the theme of the destruction of cities and radio frequencies – hopefully the two things aren't connected – Darwin was destroyed again 32 years after the WWII bombing, this time by Cyclone Tracy, and I heard evidence of it on my old friend the HF radio. Over Christmas Eve and into Christmas Day 1974, the cyclone moved over Darwin and destroyed most buildings and 50 or more people were killed. That night I was a crew member on a Jumbo flying across the Tasman to New Zealand and back from Melbourne.

Being the S/O I was of course on the radio, which meant using the HF to give position reports. To do this, I would have to listen out on the very scratchy, hash-polluted frequencies allocated to the station I was trying to communicate with. Electronic hash that is, not the other stuff that was around in the seventies. By this time, a system had come into use where, if you gave the controllers your *SELCAL* code you could hang up on them when you were finished and they would use the code to *Selectively Call* you when they wanted to talk to you. A chime would go off in the cockpit and you would see which HF radio selector had lit up and you would then pick up the call. Bliss! It saved you listening continuously to the cacophony of what was on those frequencies – hash, multiple voices from near and far and, in those days, Morse beeps from who knew where.

When you had to make a report, you started listening out on the frequency, waited for a break and then in you went with your transmission. There was no point trying to transmit over the top of another strong signal, both would just end up garbled and listeners would get pissed at the dropkick doing it. Listening out that night, I heard very unusual transmissions from Australian stations and others. These contact requests were on all sorts of frequencies, a lot of them not registered as Darwin frequencies, and they were all directed at the big receivers in Darwin. There was no reply. Quite understandable when you realised later that the 200 kph plus winds had blown the huge antennae, along with any power sources, halfway to Alice Springs. I can remember informing the other pilots, 'Something's up in Darwin,' not realising that the whole town was up – good old HF had done it again.

One night about thirty years later, I flew a 767 from Singapore to Darwin and then on to Cairns. On approach into Darwin there were plenty of heavy clouds with lots of electrical activity as there was another cyclone in the area. Our weather radar was picking the 'cells' out for us quite nicely and then, there it was, a classic spiral swirl with the blank eye in the middle. We'd found the little bastard and kept well away. That night the cyclone was passing Darwin by. The city was dodging the bullet. But, when you see how chance plays with peoples' lives like this, it does tend to make you lean towards fatalism. Not sure you can give any deities the credit for the miss. Where were they on Christmas Eve 1974?

18

MELBOURNE BALLOON

Flying the Boeing 767 in the mid-1990s meant that I quite often found myself down on the Melbourne Airport apron doing the pre-flight inspection before flying to Sydney and back and then again flying to Sydney and back. Four sectors in the day and then you were woken up by the alarm in the hotel the next morning so that you could go and do it all again and the next day you would do it all again. The poor bastards allocated to this pattern of flying called it 'Ground Hog Day' for obvious Hollywood movie reasons.

Pretty boring stuff. One early morning 'walk around', as these aircraft inspections were called, was just like the previous one and the one before that. If everything is good and there are no problems then this situation repeating itself is okay. Actually, it's the way things should be. I'm told that aviation, like being in a war, is ninety-nine percent boredom and ten percent terror. (Terror makes the one percent seem longer.) I found the actual figures for aviation to be even more boring than that. One flight out of a hundred creating sheer terror would be totally unacceptable. Luckily, even quiet, no-drama flights weren't that boring.

The routine on one of these 'ground hog days' was to get out of bed at dawn in the high-rise hotel we pilots stayed in and take it from there. The first thing I'd do was open the internal window shutters and feast on the view. If you have to be up at dawn at least you should try to enjoy it. Melbourne provided some great misty sunrises and on a lot of mornings you could spot the hot air balloons on their early morning joyrides. I was interested in these contraptions – well what do you call something that has a wicker basket hanging from it? Answer, a contraption. I was interested in these lighter than air conveyances having taken a ride in one up in the Hunter Valley just north of Sydney. My wife and I had spent a birthday celebration weekend there, the highlight being the ride. It must have been my wife's birthday because I can't see me agreeing to get up before dawn on my birthday – pilots get enough early wake-ups thank you.

Regardless of wake-up time, the balloon ride was a great experience. Standing in the basket with the other passengers and the pilot with his gas tanks and burners was the only option – no business class upgrades here, it's all one class in wicker. The reason balloons do their thing just after dawn is because of the light winds at that time of the day. Just after sunset is good for the same reason. Dawn is better because you can see where you're going and actually enjoy the scenery – of course dawn is better. What got me was the silence, between the roaring gas burns that is. Quiet flight was a surprise to me – noisy engines had accompanied me on every other flight I'd ever taken. The balloon also flew pretty low this day and really only gained and lost altitude to find winds with slightly different directions and strength.

After a really interesting flight in the light winds, I watched with some admiration as the pilot drifted down to a paddock where his ground collection crew waited. More admiration was earned when these guys and the pilot teamed up and the wicker basket, with all its passengers and the pilot, was lowered onto the slowly moving trailer. Not bad when you remember that a balloon only goes where the wind does. Airships with engines and propellers can move through the air, not just with it, but they do need fuel to achieve this. A balloon needs fuel too, but only to heat the air inside the balloon to make it less dense so that the whole thing can float. There's no propulsion system it just goes where the wind goes. The Hunter Valley flight was so nice and gentle. I knew that balloons didn't like strong winds but if you stick with the dawn whispers I had just found out that you could land on the trailer and not even have to lift the basket onto it after landing.

Out on the Melbourne Airport apron under the 767, the tyres passed muster. The amount of tread was way above minimum and was still on the tyres and not coating the touchdown area of various runways around the world. That's where the rubber goes, abraded off the tyres on touchdown as the wheels spin up. Sitting at the holding point of any runway watching the blue-white smoke under the aircraft landing in front of us was always interesting and, if the wind was right, you got the fumes coming into your aircraft and you understood the whole 'I love the smell of burning rubber in the morning' thing.

Other parts of the undercarriage that got abraded pretty quickly were the brake pads. These pads were slammed onto the multiple brake discs by a three thousand PSI hydraulic system. This basic method of converting the energy of the landing aircraft to heat was effective but things got worn down. Brake pad wear could be monitored by checking little metal rods on each wheel. As the brake pads wore down the metal rod got smaller and at a certain point you told the ground engineers.

While I was checking these vital undercarriage components of the thumping great all-metal monster that was a modern heavier than air flying machine, a lightweight contraption stopped Melbourne airport in its tracks. Behind the 767 I was inspecting was a *runway threshold* – that is the touchdown bit. Something made me look up just in time to see a sightseeing tourist balloon, with its people-filled wicker basket, making what looked like a normal aircraft approach to the runway. It was not travelling like a balloon should in that it was herbing along quite fast and descending pretty quickly at the same time. It was going to hit hard and at speed. This was not good.

The balloon came over the fence at what I reckon was about ten to fifteen knots and, if it hit the ground, there were no wheels with shock absorbers to take the landing thump and, with no wheels, the wicker was going to have to stand in for rubber and brake pads. This retardation of the bottom front of the basket was going to do one thing – the laws of physics will not be denied. The basket was going to tip forward. Well, it's all relative. The top of the basket would not actually tip forward but the bottom of the basket would be dragged back by the ground making the top look like it was tipping forward. The big wind- driven balloon was also going to make things worse in this situation. It was attached to the top of the basket and so it would drag the top of the basket forward as well. Whoever was in this out of control flying machine was in real danger of being banged onto the ground at speed as the basket tipped right over. The people inside were likely to be of a certain age and they wouldn't be used to being thrown about much, let alone being thrown on their faces with gas tanks and burners being flung about. This was definitely not good.

I watched this slow motion train wreck unfold in front of me; bang, drag, tip, tip, some more drag but, incredibly, the basket didn't quite fall right over onto its side but came to rest still upright on the grass beside the runway about a hundred metres into the airport. A big gust of wind could still push the balloon and tip the people out. They were still in real danger.

Near me was a baggage handler sitting on a little tractor. I pointed to the balloon, jumped on beside him and we were off. The first people there could hold things upright, pull people out of danger and generally be of use. As it turned out, I and my new mate, the baggage handler, were the first ones there. On arrival, I leapt down and braced the top front of the basket and checked out what was going on inside. One group of very scared individuals was standing there frozen in a state of shock. As predicted, to a man and a woman they were all older than me by far with the exception of the pilot. He was a much younger man but looked just as scared as his passengers. I checked as much as I could. The gas bottles seemed secured and burners were certainly switched off. The pilot had by now dumped as much of the hot air out of his balloon as he could to drop the buoyancy. He was still working hard which meant trying to contact the air traffic and airport controllers. He had a handheld VHF radio transceiver and was frantically dialling up frequencies. This was where I produced my only real contribution to the situation. He looked at me and, obviously recognising an airline captain when he saw one in uniform, asked what the Melbourne Airport ground control frequency was. Ground hog days meant I knew all the control frequencies off by heart so I told him and he got busy.

Other people began arriving in official-looking vans and utes so I was no longer really needed and my status reverted to bystander. I was soon on my way back to a big metal thing that could actually fight a little bit of wind if necessary. On the way back, I reflected on just how lucky my wife and I had been to have had a balloon flight in perfect balloon-flight conditions. I also wondered how much wicker was abraded off the basket during the landing I had just witnessed and whether it was now mixed in with those runway rubber deposits.

19

I ONLY FIGHT WOMEN PASSENGERS – ALMOST

In many ways, long-haul flying is different to flying short sectors. This is obvious when you think of the vagaries of weather forecasting, fuel usage, navigation and all those other operational details. What isn't so obvious is how the passengers affect the flight and vice versa. It is always nice to think that a passenger getting on a flight for fourteen hours is going to walk off happy at the end of it.

Unfortunately, things happen to passengers on long flights that can cause serious problems. Medical conditions can be exacerbated by the on-board environment – reduced oxygen, dry air, stress, fatigue, separation from medicines and a lot of minor complications. In an attempt to thwart such problems, the only thing to do, in obvious cases, is to not take the problem on board in the first place. I could give numerous examples of passengers being refused boarding. People are never happy with this but sometimes it has to be done.

Preparing in the terminal in Hong Kong for the flight to London one night, I was lamenting with my technical crew about the appalling Russian weather. The snow and ice would all be below us but you can't just pretend that you will never have to actually go down into it with your 747 and four hundred passengers and land. This would have to be done on a snow-covered ice strip using iffy electronics and communications. If you think you'll never have to do this they don't give you the required number of stripes to go and fly a Jumbo. So, you prepare for the worst and accept the problem-free flight to London when it happens.

This night we had a problem but, luckily, it was before we started. The acting CSM, the customer service manager, had been thrown into the job when her superior went sick. She came to me in the flight deck before the doors were closed and handed the problem on to me. She was unsure of her powers and quite rightly passed the buck upstairs – literally in this case.

On the inbound service of this Jumbo into Hong Kong, a European woman of about forty had slumped unconscious in her seat. She had come to reasonably quickly but was still a bit groggy an hour or so later. Qantas had brought paramedics on board to assess her for further flying. They had investigated things like previous medical history of diabetes, epilepsy and whatever else they could think of. Had she stowed some vital medication in her main bag in the hold? No reason for losing consciousness could be found so there was a problem. If they had found something, it might well have been fixable. As it stood, they would have to take her off in Hong Kong and have her properly assessed. Well, she didn't want to get off. Understandably, she just wanted to get home. The flight attendant needed the Captain to do his thing so down I went to explain things. The passenger was sitting in a premium seat and I made sure I got down lower than her so the uniform wouldn't be too confronting and explained our problem. I didn't talk about risking four hundred lives if I had to land in Russia,

I just emphasised that Qantas would sort hotels, doctors, transport, the works and get her home as soon as. 'No way,' she said. 'I'll take full responsibility.' Well, I wish that could happen but it's not how these things work.

The last stripe they give you to put on your shoulder actually means you shoulder all the responsibility. It is one heavy stripe. I explained that, unfortunately, she couldn't take the responsibility away from me and I was now going to have to insist she go with our ground staff. She didn't continue her fight to stay. I was pleased she was seeing reason and I got up to go back upstairs. It was then I noticed the two mean-looking Communist Chinese paramilitary soldiers with their automatic weapons and their helmets standing behind me. They had come into the cabin without me knowing and I'll never know whether it was my calm logic or her fear that made her leave.

Of course, you can't prevent all the problems, some just happen. Murphy and his law come into it of course, and when things went bad on another night it was at the worst time and therefore place. We had left LAX many hours earlier and were well on our way to Sydney. Thousands of kilometres to the nearest main airport and that meant hospitals as well. The woman downstairs was screaming in pain and the cabin crew were doing their best to help her. They didn't know for sure what was happening but an American nurse was saying it looked like a bad urinary tract problem. The medical kit had been opened and the strongest painkiller allowed without a doctor's permission administered. If we could find a doctor, a diagnosis and stronger drugs would be available to one very distraught woman.

We were virtually the same distance from Honolulu and Tahiti, and, if we didn't get better information to work with, we would have to seriously consider diverting to one of these islands to get her medical help. The CSM, the man in charge down there, told me the drugs he had given her were doing nothing to help. I asked if he had found a doctor on board and was told there was one but he had declined to get involved. I don't criticise the doctor for this. The unknown legal status is only one reason he may not have wanted anything to do with the situation. He may have been an ear nose and throat specialist who had never encountered a case like this. But we needed to find out what help he could give.

Meanwhile, we were in contact with what was a fairly new service that airlines were using around the world at this time. MedLink was a service provided over satellite phones for problems just like ours. A doctor could talk to us on the flight deck from his base in Phoenix, Arizona. A special question and answer sheet had been filled out and we had passed details of the symptoms and medical history to him over the phone. This doctor couldn't authorise the use of the heavy drugs without a doctor on board concurring with him. We needed our reluctant doctor to become helpful and fast. I got the CSM to bring the doctor into the CSM's little office under the stairs. I would meet them there.

When the doctor came in, I asked him if he knew who I was. He knew I was the Captain and I pointed out that meant I had responsibility for everyone on board. (See my earlier gripe about the Captain's stripe.) This responsibility meant there would be no legal comeback on him in regard to anything I ordered. He was happy with that and became cooperative instantly. So, he talked to the doc in the states and they came up with a plan involving heavier drugs and monitoring and we were able to continue the flight to Sydney with a much relieved patient.

Not all of these sorts of cases have been as easy to handle. This is where the fighting comes in. Actually, I shouldn't make light of it. When these things happen, they are definitely not funny. The first time I had to intervene in the cabin with some violence was in the mid-seventies – an almost full Jumbo on its way eventually to London but an hour inbound to Bombay. It had the English cricket team on board and, being the good old days, they were down the back in economy. There was a set of four toilets quite close to where they were sitting and they had been given the seats on the exit rows so they could have the extra legroom – some of them were pretty tall. The first we knew of a problem was when a flight attendant arrived on the flight deck to tell us they had a woman who had become very disturbed and locked herself in a toilet.

They couldn't get her out by pushing the door in as she was now lying on the floor screaming. The fact that she weighed about 130 kilos wasn't helping with the door going in either. The cabin crew wanted someone to come down and take the door off and help calm her down. I still remember how it came down to me. The Captain said he couldn't go down. He was the Captain. The F/O, not being slow, said he couldn't go down because he was the deputy Captain. Guess who that left? The flight engineer would come down with his screwdriver set, take off the door hinges and then leave it to me, the trusty young S/O, and the cabin crew. In all fairness, he was needed back on the flight deck to prepare for the descent.

We thought we were ready. We had amassed our forces. There was the chief steward, the woman's husband – strangely, a fairly small bloke – two doctors and me. Doctors, as I've said, were usually always on board even back then – a very handy fact on long-haul operations. The two doctors, one older and one very young, had prepared a Valium injection ready to put into a vein to render our now really screaming woman unconscious. We had one backup – a female flight attendant who had been a nurse who turned out to be the best of us all.

The door came off and one wild woman came out. Within a couple of seconds, the poor husband is out of the fight – she just decked him. The rest of us blokes weren't getting it much easier. She was not holding back. There was blood and plenty of other bodily excretions to slip around in. This was not a polite affair with rules but lots of, mostly, wrestling later, we had her pinned down and I looked around and took stock.

The two doctors were slumped on the floor. The chief steward had taken a couple of heavy thumps but was still functioning. The husband was still out of it – conscious but obviously seeing stars. So, five blokes and one woman were all in a big pile just outside a really filthy toilet. The woman was still struggling and I was only just managing to hold her as she was slippery all over – this was not a clean fight, I can tell you.

I watched the doctors preparing to get the knockout injection into her. The older doc had the needle but he was shaking so much with the adrenalin rush that he handed it over to the young one – wise move I thought. The young bloke had to find a vein to inject the drug into. In later years, all you had to do was get it into a muscle – way easier. One huge arm was not going to allow any veins to be found and this is where the ex-nurse hostie won me over.

She took one look at the situation and took charge. She turned to the audience, namely several rows of English cricketers, and zeroed in on one of them. He was wearing one of the old earphone sets. They were actually two thin plastic tubes joined together that you stuck into your ears while the other end plugged into two holes near the armrest. Magic sound came out and you could watch the movie up on the wall. The nurse just eyeballed the cricketer and grabbed his earphones off him hard enough to dislodge them from both his ears and the armrest plugs in one swoop. Instant tourniquet, and brilliantly done. She applied it professionally, up came the vein and the young doc did his thing.

When the poor woman had become docile and was just about out to it, we tried to get her up and onto a row of seats. I cleared three cricketers off a row, put the armrests up and proceeded to try and lift her. The other blokes were of little help. The docs were either cactus or helping the husband. Passengers weren't going to help. They could see the mess I was in and weren't coming anywhere near me or my charge. I managed, but only just. My work there was done and the aircraft was about to descend. I should be upstairs – not that the Captain wanted me anywhere near the flight deck. He took one look at me and sent me into the toilet to wash away as much evidence of the fight as possible. The woman, who had been given enough Valium to knock someone out for eight hours was coming round an hour later as they took her off the aircraft.

You could call that a fair fight, if six against one is fair. Well, it is fair if you are one of the six – winners write the history, remember. The next fight I had with a woman was about the same odds but I wasn't too positive about coming out a winner. She was one tough customer.

It's not actually true that I only had altercations with women. Over the years, I had been called back into the cabin to sort out problems with blokes but they seemed more prone to being affected by alcohol or drugs. On one occasion, I had to help with a passenger who fitted that 'should never have been on board' category. This bloke, aged in his late seventies, had slipped in the Bangkok terminal, bumped his head badly and then got on the flight. He had shown strong indications of hypoxia early in the flight and the cabin crew had administered oxygen. This was not unusual on long flights – probably fifty percent of flights had at least one passenger needing oxygen.

This elderly gentleman was a bit wonky even with the oxygen and the all-female cabin crew were having trouble getting him to keep the mask on his face. They thought he might respond better to a male authority figure. I had just hopped out of my seat for a break so I was it. The old fella looked blue, the classic symptom of hypoxia – blue lips and blue areas around his fingernails. He didn't respond to my requests and kept pulling the mask off. An undignified struggle ensued between a younger man and a dignified old gentleman who was not hurting anyone. At least, that was how I could see the situation viewed through the eyes of the surrounding passengers.

The most galling part was that he was winning. It is amazing how strong people are when they think they are fighting for their lives. I had a strong grip on his very thin wrists but could only just keep his hands away from the mask. We needed to get some oxygen into him. I got him to calm down a bit – probably he just got tired – but I was concerned that he was using up more oxygen in the wrestle than we were getting into him. My presence wasn't helping so I left – defeated. I mean, I made a tactical retreat. He did settle down and we made our destination with a couple of oxygen tanks that needed refilling and one elderly gent, the undefeated champion, who was able to walk off the aircraft.

Now to the flight between Singapore and Adelaide where I thought we may well lose the fight to a significantly smaller force; namely, one little old lady. This flight was the last sector of a service all the way from London. These last sectors into Australia were where a lot of problems arose and, if you think about the stress of the flight on passengers, we were probably lucky not to have more.

Imagine the new grandparents in the midlands of the UK. Their first big trip out of their hometown and it's to Australia to see the son or daughter plus the new arrival – exciting in the extreme. The stress of getting a passport, organising travel arrangements, getting packed and ready to leave home all adds up. They are what we now call *stressors*. But the stressors don't stop there. Dorothy and Joe have to get themselves down to Heathrow for the evening departure with all their bags and papers. 'Oh, did we cancel the newspapers, Dot?'

On it goes, train rides, huge busy airport, through immigration and security, into their economy seats. 'Did I switch off the iron, Joe?' The couple are now exhausted. All the excitement and lack of sleep on top of the stress has ensured this. Now for a nice cup of tea, an episode of *East Enders* and bed. Well, no – the trip to Australia is just beginning. Bumpy air, noise, strange people all round – not all of them Australians – mean no sleep in this uncomfortable seat with airline food being offered four hours after dinner time.

I've used this scenario of what a happy trip to Australia can be like for decades now to encourage people to consider stopovers along the way. Most people don't, and certainly didn't twenty-five or thirty years ago. Fares are much cheaper now but stopovers are an added cost. It is little wonder that, on the last sector into Australia, a lot of older passengers have problems. Long-haul flying can be fun, but not always.

We were halfway between Singapore and Adelaide. It was as very quiet and as black as can be outside. It felt like we could be in outer space. There were the stars above and only the occasional light below us from some station homestead in the desert. In fact, we were probably near a famous waypoint.

Twenty-odd years earlier, all positions that aircraft flew over had local names, but you can imagine the difficulty foreigners had trying to pronounce these local names. New Zealand's 'Whykickamoocow' (you say Waipukurau fast without it coming out mildly obscene) and Australia's Woy Woy or Wagga Wagga were just the easy ones. You should have heard the American trying to report at Cunnamulla. So, some clever people came up with a simple worldwide solution – generate thousands of five letter words and stick them all over the maps. They didn't even have to be stuck over towns or features and therefore you could fly in a straight line. Pretty nifty since aircraft didn't have to actually fly over towns or radio beacons anymore. We were flying near the GAFFA waypoint which was right in the middle of the dessert. Nothing around, so some wag had named it after the *Great Australian Fuck All*.

As we were sitting in our little space capsule the S/O and I got a phone call from the back galley. 'Just letting you know, Captain, that we have a problem. A little old lady has just floored two female flight attendants who were trying to stop her opening one of the rear exit doors.' I wasn't worried about someone trying to open a door. The flight attendants were my concern. The Cabin Service Manager assured me the young women were okay and were now well away from the action. As I said, I wasn't worried about a door being opened because that's just not going to happen. The door is really a plug at this stage of the flight and the old woman would need to pull it in to swing it out. This would be against a pressure of several tonnes. Because we speak American in these matters, you have to multiply the area of the door in square inches by the differential pressure from the inside of the aircraft to the outside of it. In *cruise* the differential is about eight pounds per square inch. A lot of pressure either in tonnes or tons; modern aircraft are indeed pressurised.

The CSM, a little sheepishly, then added a bit more detail. Having witnessed the two young women being slapped out of the way he told me, in his words, 'I grabbed both her wrists but, before I knew it, she had grabbed my sleeves, tugged me forward and kneed me in the balls so hard I went down like a bag of spuds.' What was going on back there? The CSM said the female flight attendants had been replaced by another flight attendant who was doing the *verbal judo* bit and was establishing a friendship with her. Verbal judo is taught so that crew know how to talk people around rather than just resorting to force, and, since force was clearly not working, it seemed a pretty good thing to do. I was to be kept informed.

A while later more information came through, although it didn't help matters. This diminutive woman in her eighties wanted to leave the hotel before the bombing started. Okay, she has come all the way from London and has obviously lost it on this, the last sector down to Adelaide to visit her family, and, guess what, it's her first trip out of the UK. My warning scenario about the imaginary Dot and Joe is gaining credibility. Negotiations continued. By this time there were two big young male doctors – they must live on aircraft – hiding in the galley with the knockout needle ready to stick into an arm if necessary. A while latter I'm told they can't convince her to stay in the hotel or that there would be no Blitz tonight. In her mind, she is in London during the war.

Now I get involved. The doctors want the red overcoat she is wearing removed before trying to stick a needle into her arm. She is saying she will only remove it if ordered to by a senior policeman. 'Do you have a senior policeman up there, Captain?' hinted the CSM. I looked around. Unfortunately, I didn't find the legendary Second Officer known as *The Passenger Pacifier.* When you shook hands with this six-and-a-half foot monster, your hand disappeared into a huge paw and you just hoped he didn't crush your fingers accidently while being friendly. He'd got the nickname when a young bloke had lost it on a flight and barricaded himself in a galley with meal and drink trolleys. The big friendly S/O was sent down and, being big and friendly, offered to shake the young bloke's hand. Stupidly, the bloke put his hand into the huge paw that proceeded to crush said hand and render one out-of-control individual very much under control – extremely rapidly.

All I had in the flight deck next to me was the skinniest, youngest female S/O I had flown with. She was as fit as could be – she ran marathons for fun. I should send her but her father was a pilot I had gone through the cadet course with. He would kill me if she suffered the same fate as the female flight attendants. The F/O arrived back from his break and, rather than try to bring him up to speed – who would have believed what I was saying anyway? – I got him to take control of the aircraft and I put on my 'senior policeman' coat and hat. Down the back I was surprised at just how small and old this fireball was. But it was obvious that she still saw people singing 'There'll be bluebirds over the white cliffs of Dover' all around her.

She asked me if I was indeed a policeman and I told her I was a very senior one, pointing to the last stripe on my sleeve, which was now coming in handy, and I was ordering her to, please, take off her overcoat as it was very hot in the hotel. She would if I was willing to put the order in writing. Of course, I would, just take the coat off first. I'm not proud of my sneakiness in negotiations.

One bare-armed octogenarian, three big blokes armed with a needle and it was on.

Get in close, shut down her swinging and kicking room and we had her. As two monsters held her the other stuck a needle in her arm. She gently abused us. 'You pigs!' she said. Then a little while after that heavy serve she added, 'Now see what you've made me do.' Apparently, we made her be slightly impolite to the three thugs who had attacked her. This was one classy lady.

As she was going under, we gently lowered her onto a crew seat near the door. Her final comment was telling. 'At least I haven't said anything.' She was glad that the interrogation hadn't forced any secrets out of her. I had already come to the conclusion that she was one highly trained individual, this just provided more evidence. The door-side seat was not appropriate and she had to be moved. A rear passenger row was empty and, just to emphasise how fair this fight had been, I leant over, picked her up in my arms and carried her there myself.

The woman didn't have her boarding pass on her and it took a while to find her husband in the dark cabin. The one good thing about this whole incident, if you could say anything was good about it, was that no passengers saw anything. Mind you, it was a different world back then. There was no chance of our bullying attack turning up on Facebook or Twitter and going viral. Could you imagine the slow-motion, worldwide news vision of a 'senior policeman' in a pilot's uniform, going at the frail old lady as soon as she removed her red overcoat. The backstory of her abilities would not be anywhere to be seen – way too much information for the modern world.

We found her equally old and not too big husband and explained what had happened. He was, understandably, quite bewildered. I asked where he had met his wife. He told me that he had been the unarmed combat instructor at the World War II spy school where his wife was trained. The war had come back to visit us and it wasn't very pleasant.

I would love to say there was a happy ending but all I saw after we arrived in Adelaide was the woman, strapped to an ambulance gurney, being accompanied off the aircraft by two big coppers. Her husband had all the hand luggage and papers. She kept telling the police to get that old man away from her. I really hope things got better – the sadness follows me to this day.

20
MARS

I have never lost my interest in aerospace matters. I was like a little kid in my excitement at touring the Smithsonian Air and Space Museum in Washington DC recently. Aerospace is the word that says it all and for me. The difference between aviation and space-related matters is just too small to worry about. The Viking Mars lander in the museum was inspiring. Look up at that planetary red dot one night and know that we advanced monkeys have put more than one robot onto the surface of that dot and we made them crawl around taking photos and doing other things for us. Mars has always been there for me.

The planet has even made me a legend in my own lunchtime. That is a polite way of saying that maybe I have exaggerated my own importance in the scheme of things a bit. I will let you be the judge.

In August of 2003, one of my regular flights was to go from Auckland, New Zealand, along a great circle route to Los Angeles. It was a service that took off at sunset and flew over the shortened night arriving in the US at dawn. The time-warping ability of this flight meant you arrived before you took off. As I've said previously, some people still put this down to crossing the International Date Line but I know better. The

International Date Line means we have winter in Australia while Americans have summer; the young woman giving me a hire car in Honolulu once was quite adamant on this point – who was I to argue?

For a month or so, I had been watching Mars from the flight deck at night and from my back lane at home while putting the bins out. It was getting brighter and redder as the big moment approached. That 'big moment' was on the 27th at the exact time of 0951 UTC, it would come as close to its neighbouring planet Earth as it had been for 60,000 years. Modern humans had never experienced such proximity and it was exciting for us stargazers. UTC (Co-ordinated Universal Time) is the same as GMT. Pilots know it as *Zulu*, as in *0951 Zulu*, or, when written, as *0951Z*.

I had been a stargazer ever since we had to learn a bit about the stars, planets, moon and sun when learning how to navigate by them. They were no longer a mystery and became interesting to read about. All my mates knew from *astro nav* the names of some of the main stars and where to look for them. They also knew interesting facts like you can only see Venus just before dawn or just after sunset because it is closer to the Sun than we are. You have to be looking close to the sun to see it. Half of its 584 day cycle it is the *evening star* the other half it's the *morning star*. Satellites are only visible just before dawn or just after sunset as well but for a different reason. As trained navigators, new Second Officers were supposed to be able to identify some of the brighter stars to make selections for *astro* shots easier.

Some of the old Captains back then were always pointing out how little we really knew. One Captain, who had been a senior WWII Air Force pilot, was famous for his put-downs. One night, in pointing out to one of my mates how deficient his star identification was, he stated that his fifteen-year-old daughter was better at it than this newbie S/O. My mate still doesn't know what made him say it but he replied, 'Well, Captain, maybe I don't spend as much time lying on my back as she does looking up at them.' Having realised what he had just said made him freeze and wait for the Captain to go ballistic. The Captain just looked him up and down and said, 'Good comeback, son. Good comeback.'

When I realised that I would be flying at the time of this encounter I took out my trusty Palm Pilot. This was a great little device we used just before smartphones arrived on the scene. It had the equivalent of 'apps,' one of which was a useful star map. I set up the date and time, found Mars, put it directly above the observer and noted where this observer was on the Earth's surface. The spot just north of Tahiti was easy to find using this new technology. Who would have thought you could find out all this information without hours of calculations using charts and logarithms and clockwork chronometers?

Captain Frank Brown and, especially, Captain James Cook would be amazed by such a device. They would also freak had they known that you could make yourself a watch that used a quartz crystal, vibrated at a known frequency by a tiny electric current, to measure time really accurately. The end of clockwork had arrived. You could still buy the twenty- thousand-dollar Swiss watch or you could opt for the more accurate fifty dollar Japanese quartz one – your choice.

I had the information I was after and I'd won the jackpot. By pure chance, at the time in question, I would be above that exact spot on the Earth's surface. If the Jumbo left Auckland on time and followed its normal routing, it would arrive under Mars just as the planet was the closest to us since humans were grunting in fear about the bad sky gods. I'm not talking about vodka-soaked Qantas crews here – I'm talking ancient nomads in animal skins.

Whoop-de-doo! What to do? Aviation being what it is, you never count your chickens until you are actually sitting on the flight deck under the red planet. I did get my artist wife to do an illustration though and, being an ex-science teacher, she made a simple and easy-to-understand diagram of it all. A certificate was produced and I got 400 printed – it was going to be a full flight.

The certificate looked really cool. It had me congratulating the passengers on choosing, at no extra cost, to be on board this particular history-making flight. This would be something to tell their grandchildren. I went on as if I was becoming a legend. Apart from all that, it had the diagram and underneath it, my signature – how official could you get?

The flight left on time and went as planned. I didn't have to adjust times of departure or anything to reach our destination at the right time: the destination was, in truth, probably a few hundred square miles but that is a pinpoint when you take in the distances involved. It certainly looked right when we got there.

We were ten kilometres above the ocean, right under Mars. We were now the closest modern humans to Mars – ever! We were even closer than Alan Shepard and the other astronauts and cosmonauts had been. Mars had moved much closer than just the distance from the Earth to the moon. It looked really close, like a red Venus. There was, however, one small problem. Only us pilots on the flight deck could see it. The roof was in the way for everybody else.

I had, by this time, organised the cabin crew to distribute the certificates as they collected the dinner trays. Perfect timing again because, as dinner had finished just as zero hour approached, nobody had settled down to sleep yet. All this was going like a battery- driven watch. I had put the spare pilot – we always carry a spare – into the Captain's seat and was standing behind the pilots. I used the PA to explain things and do the countdown to the moment. It was a beautiful clear night with no moon or clouds to cut down visibility – again fortuitous.

Right at the exact time, I had the F/O do a fairly steep turn both ways. With the aircraft in a 30 degree bank the passengers at the windows could look up and see the bright red planet directly above them. They could see what I was on about and they were happy – but now could we go to sleep, please?

Most passengers did then get into watching movies or slip into the land of nod but a few got enthusiastic. There were a few requests for my non-photocopied signature and even one request for a certificate to prove that a particular passenger was indeed on board this night. A few thankyou notes arrived on the flight deck but then came the note that made the night for me. We had a NASA scientist on board and he had a question. Was the time, 0951 UTC, the time that Mars was closest to us or the time the light got to us after leaving Mars as it hit the closest point? He even added a quick calculation of distance and speed of light, no less, to point out that there was in fact a three-minute difference. Bloody hell! All I could say was that I'd got most of the information off the NASA website, so, take it up with them. Scientists!

This bloke was actually very nice. I met him in the baggage hall at LAX and had a good chat. He was married to a United Airlines pilot. I often wonder, though, whether she picks her trips with the longest time away from home that she can get.

Now, on a point of personal glory. Aircraft usually cruise slightly nose up – about a degree or two. They do this for angle of attack reasons and to piss off cabin crew who have to push meal trolleys up the aisle from the rear galley. 'Angle of attack' sounds cool; all it means is the angle at which the airflow hits your wings. I was happy about this situation that night because it meant I could be higher than anybody else on board. Because the aircraft was tilted nose up and the flight deck is at the front of the upper deck on a 747 then we pilots were highest of all the crew and passengers. Me, I was standing behind the other two pilots, and therefore I was higher than them. They are to be known from now on as 'the lower order'. Ipso facto, QED, I am *the* modern human who has been closest to Mars.

The fact that there were a couple of Russian cosmonauts crewing the International Space Station that particular night should be discounted, I will argue until I turn blue that they were on the other side of the Earth and therefore not in the competition. If you think about it, that would make them the two humans furthest from Mars. Also, the fact that I actually have no idea where the Space Station was should also be discounted because that would prevent me from becoming a legend in my own lunchtime, and we can't have that.

This is all very interesting – to me, at least – but I actually know from all this *astro* training and stargazing one really cool fact. If you are under a clear blue sky on a sunny day you can sometimes see the moon. Neil Armstrong said once that he was one of the few kids at his high school who ever noticed this. This is not, however, the coolest fact that I have amazed people with over the years.

The coolest fact, which I demonstrate every now and then by pointing out a little bright spot in a clear blue sky, is the fact that you can also see Venus during the day. It is always near the sun and you really need to know where it is in relation to the sun to find it easily. This is all the more amazing because what you are looking at is a planet that goes through phases just like the moon. If you ever see me standing with a group of friends looking up into the sky through a cardboard tube, you'll know I'm boring the crap out of another group of innocents.

TYPE WARS AND AIR SHOWS

From the mid-eighties, for about fifteen years, I flew the Boeing 767, a great twin-engine, twin-aisled foretaste of what most jets now are. They carried two hundred and thirty passengers. These aircraft came with big fuel tanks and were starting to take over from the old Jumbos on a lot of the routes we flew. The regulators around the world were quite rightly making these new boys on the block prove their safety when it came to flying over oceans. For the first years, if they had an engine failure, they had to get to an airport somewhere close by. Complicated rules about how many electric generators and hydraulic systems these aircraft needed were incorporated into their design and a trial period was set where they were not allowed to fly more than an hour away from a *funk hole* – that's pilot talk for an airport.

Having been checked out as an F/O on these aircraft as they came onto the *line*, I found it quite annoying to fly around Asia always having to be close enough to an airport to satisfy this rule. One night on a flight into Darwin from Singapore, we found ourselves closely following an old 'classic' Qantas Jumbo on a special flight with a whole mob of cruise ship passengers on board.

A friendly rivalry had developed between the 767 and 747 crews and it was on display this night. On the chatter radio frequency, it was busy. The 747 blokes were giving us a hard time. 'Stay close to land there, little brother,' or 'How's the light twin going tonight?' We would come back, quick as flash with sparkling responses like, 'Ah, get stuffed.' Pilots are, if anything, so quick-witted. For example, in response to their next jibe, 'Watch out, you might lose an engine down there,' I came up with a beauty – a real winner. 'Yeah, well, half as much to go wrong, my friend, half as much to go wrong.'

Both aircraft landed at Darwin and were both due off again in about an hour to continue our journeys south. We were parked pretty close together and I was watching the big four-engine dinosaur being refueled from our flight deck. When our ground engineer came in to sign our paperwork, he casually mentioned the 747 had an issue with one of its engines. The white-shirted flash that passed him a split second later was me on my way across the apron to get some points up in the 'type wars' of the mid-eighties. First off, I stopped under the wing with the 747's flight engineer to look up at the cactus engine. The engineer had the good grace to look at me and say, 'Twice as much to go wrong.' One point to us.

I ran up the Jumbo's stairs – no aerobridges at the time in Darwin. I was having a ball. At the flight deck door, I looked in at the old technology instrument panels with all the dials and gauges – not a computer screen to be seen. What type of throwbacks flew these antiques? I soon found out. The Captain had seen me arriving and ordered one of his many crew members to, 'Charge that bastard an admission fee.'

This was just another little battle in the 'type war'– I was in full combat mode. I took his comment on board and went for it. 'Sorry, Captain, didn't realise they were charging to let people into museums now.' Score – two nil and counting. I had become a 767 warrior and I was good at it. I had been a 747 fossil only a couple of months earlier and, back then, those 767 upstarts needed sorting. Now I'd seen the light – fickle yes, but fun was were you made it.

A few years later and I was now a Captain on one of these EROPS (Extended Range Operation) flights. Boy what a quick throwaway line. Becoming a Captain doesn't just happen overnight. What I should have said is that, after a twenty-year apprenticeship, I got the chance to go for a command and, like all pilots who get that opportunity, my world got really stressful and busy for the six or seven months it takes to jump through all the hoops to get the extra stripe. It's very hard to describe what command training means, even to other pilots who are not yet Captains, let alone to non-pilots. The flying tests and simulator checks are really just the start. The real difference between a Captain and a more junior pilot is the mindset. There are books written about what it takes to be in command and I won't even pretend to know everything – or even close to it.

The ability to manage situations and people in circumstances where lives are in peril is obviously something that needs proper assessment. Leadership and the ability to command are qualities that are both natural and learned. A command trainee is always being trained and assessed. Qantas prides itself on having the toughest standards and we Captain candidates had to walk the talk. It's demanding, and Qantas was totally uncompromising, as you would expect. There was a significant failure rate for F/Os upgrading to Captain and this was with some of the highest standard F/Os in the world. The accident-free record didn't get there by accident. (Oh, no. I'm so sorry. A serious subject and a pun still falls out of my head!)

Captains have to learn the rules and, obviously, have to follow them – that's a given. Indeed, as Captain of a 767 EROPS flight a few years after my glorious 'type war' victories, I had occasion to follow some. EROPs flights, as I have said, had extra rules as to what systems had to be working. Specifically, there were many restrictions some of which concerned how many electrical sources had to be available at any given time during the flight. There was battery power, but only for about half an hour's duration, and you didn't want to get down to that if you could avoid it. So, we had left Melbourne for an EROPS flight over the Tasman Sea and had all these extra rules to follow.

When an engine-driven electrical generator gave up the ghost and the Auxiliary Power Unit (APU) wouldn't stay alight, we had the classic double failure of two essential items. Redundancy is the name of the game and, if the backup doesn't work, then action must be taken and rules followed. The APU is actually a small jet engine we keep in the boot to supply electricity and high-pressure air. During this incident, I wanted only the electricity its generator could give me. When no amount of changing speed, flight levels and electrical loads helped in keeping our little friend going, we had to follow the rules and go back to Melbourne.

Back where we started. While I tried to personally explain to our passengers the complexities of EROPS, the engineers found and fixed the problems. You would expect that a main generator, with all its moving bits, could throw a wobbly somewhere and stop working. You wouldn't expect the problem to be in the little electronic box on top – but that's where it was.

You'd also expect a complex thing like a small jet engine to be capable of throwing a wobbly in all those areas that huff and puff and spin and burn where something might break. Well, no. Once again, it was the little electronic control box that had withdrawn cooperation. With two new controllers, we thought we'd be on our way, but first I had to check in with my boss, the 767-pilot manager. I told him where I was and he wasn't impressed – I wasn't where I should have been.

This was a problem for him because of EROPS. It was causing a lot of people grief this day, including the passengers who were by now about three hours late. The boss, however, had the concern of trying to keep the integrity of his fleet's EROPS history intact in order to convince regulators that everything was fine – I was messing with this. It got worse. I told him I was going to have to put in a report to the regulator.

He freaked, as you would expect, not only had I come back to Melbourne now I was going to tell everyone. He asked whether I was sure I couldn't just keep it a secret. He rang the safety department to see if they had a way out. They just backed up my thoughts and said, yes, I had landed at an airport that I wasn't supposed to – instant report needed. I promised to downplay EROPS participation in my report as much as I could and I was then allowed to fly to New Zealand. I had to follow my boss's orders, but a pilot also has the overriding government regulations to follow. The trick is knowing which authority to obey and how to keep the other one from getting too pissed at you.

I would like to think that the boss now thought that, while I was a pest, at least I would do the right thing when it came to the regulations and that was why he got me to do a couple of air show days for Qantas. It was much more likely that he got me to do these days because he couldn't find anyone else.

There is a big air show that happens every two years at Avalon airport, south of Melbourne. This is an airport where I have done a lot of training over the years, including learning how to fly my first aircraft without a propeller – the mighty

Boeing 707. By the early nineties, the airport still didn't have much going for it, so, when the air show came to town there wasn't much to disrupt. I got the call to passenger down from Sydney in the morning and bring the aircraft home late in the day. Some other Captain would fly me and about two hundred and fifty aviation tragics, who all worked for Qantas, down to the show. Not too many pilots were giving up their weekend to man – or woman – display booths and show people over aircraft like these staff were. Weekends are precious to aircrew.

At Avalon, I met my father who had driven down from Melbourne. We were going to make a day of it, especially since I wasn't needed until late in the arvo when I would take 'command' of the 767 and fly it home to Sydney. We had a great time with my Dad showing me the old 1930s aircraft he had flown. One old contraption, a de Havilland Dragon Rapide, made out of fabric and wood was actually a biplane: double wing, tail wheel, two old engines with wooden propellers – the Wright brothers would have been right at home. Dad showed the owner his old pilot's licence with this aircraft as one of his endorsements.

The bloke was impressed, so Dad told him his favourite story about this type of aircraft. He was flying one into Adelaide midway through the war and was still about thirty minutes from home when one of the engines nearly shook itself off the wing. Such was the vibration and shaking that Dad said he just managed to shut it down before real damage was done. He got home on one engine and handed it over to the ground engineer to see what he could do.

The next day, when Dad asked the engineer what the problem was, the response kept him amused for decades. The engineer said, 'Just like me on Saturday night, pissed 'n' broke.' Apparently, one of the pistons had broken. Dad always saw the funny side of scary moments. Most pilots have this black humour thing, it's a way of coping as well as a source of inappropriate jokes on occasion.

On this tack, an ex-RAF fighter pilot used to tell this shocking story with the humour up-front. You could tell he still needed to talk decades later and I'd heard the story a couple of times. Flying 1950s fighter jets in Germany during the early Cold War, British fighter pilots would sometimes fly down the big German rivers below the riverbanks so the Ruskies couldn't see them. Pretty low and dangerous, especially since these old jets had engines that would just go phut every now and then. If that happened, you had about a second to bail out, otherwise you were dead. In those days, bailing out meant letting an artillery shell blow you, and your seat, out of the top of the aircraft at a million miles an hour.

On the day my old mate spoke about, he was following his Squadron Leader down the river, below the banks. They were rolling their jets, at times over ninety degrees to get around bends and, on one of these turns, the Leader's engine blew. My mate described what happened next and included his thoughts on the matter. 'I saw the engine go. The aircraft was rolled right over. A second later the pilot banged out but straight into the riverbank. It was the funniest thing I ever saw, really shocking, but the funniest.'

I guess you had to be there to see the funny side but that's how this bloke was coping. Mind you, I can never watch those 'funniest home video' shows that have people falling off roofs or onto the sides of pools, or other solid concrete structures, all to the accompaniment of hilarious laughter. What do these shows say about us as humans? I do love, however, the Japanese shows where blokes have their pants filled with cockroaches and stuff – those shows are just classic.

The only disaster that I had on this air show day was in climbing in and out of these antique aircraft I managed to rip my uniform trousers down the side, luckily without revealing too much. Sixteen hundred hours and I was suddenly 'the man'. There was an official handover of the stationary display aircraft to me and it suddenly became an operational unit with a flight and passengers and everything – I told you these guys were tragics.

The F/O and I did our planning and flight-plan lodging and anything else we had to do. This was far more work than we had bargained on but we suddenly realised that we were not only the pilots but the logistic support team as well. Operations up in Sydney had forgotten about us. Either that or they couldn't have cared less. Operations never forget anything, so you get the picture about what had really happened.

I did the walk around outside and obviously had to make a really professional job of it. The aircraft had been overrun for many hours by thousands of spectators so I did the most thorough inspection possible. A teenage boy had asked to accompany me. I suspect he'd planned his move on me for a year or so and now I had to look after him as well.

Hundreds of spectators watched my every move and no doubt were all wondering why Qantas Captains had a huge rip in their left trouser leg. Nothing like a little bit of embarrassment to keep you grounded.

At last we were ready to start our engines, normally a routine operation, but this day we had an old DC3 right behind us and were concerned that, if we fired up the engines, the jet exhaust, even at idle speeds, would flip the glorious old fossil onto its back. Okay, no worries. As the aircraft in front of us moved forward a bit we could be towed forward ourselves and fire up when safe to do so. We moved forward and, of course, the DC3 followed. A ground engineer finally twigged to the fact that when we moved forward again it would be a really good idea if the DC3 did not follow blindly – it could all end badly. The engineer had probably noticed me going apoplectic over the intercom. This was a simple flight and we couldn't even get our engines started.

At least when we got up into the air, I could go for it. With only staff on board, I could implement the *no passenger* unofficial rules. We would overbank the aircraft on any turns and I would try to get permission for a low, fast pass over the adoring crowds. On our descent into Sydney I would demonstrate the diving capability of the 767, as if it had experienced an explosive depressurisation. Fun was going to be had. The tragics would love it and forever worship my name. We did at last start our engines without becoming the news story of the air show by blowing the DC3 back into the 1940s and the fun flight was on.

However, my dreams ended abruptly when a check pilot mate walked into the flight deck and announced that he had to do a snap inspection flight and we were it. I knew the score. He'd got himself down to the air show but had to work his way back. I had to do everything by the book and the most boring sector was achieved – just what he wanted. His only comment to me was, 'You haven't forgotten much.' Instead of hero, I had achieved grey man status and boxes were ticked.

The next time I was called up for an air show, the notice was given at the worst possible moment. I was in the *flare*, about to touch down in Wellington, New Zealand, when the little communication box between the pilots went 'ping'. Yep, pilots have machines that go ping, too. This box hardly ever went ping and one of the reasons for that is, if someone sends a message through it and it comes through during a critical manoeuvre, it might well distract the pilots – as it did this day. All the other times I had received messages on this box we had asked for some weather info or operational stuff to be sent while we were on the ground or in cruise. It had to be something important.

Pilots know Wellington airport for what it is: 'Windy Wellington'. Around this time, I became the Qantas pilot with the greatest number of landings at this notorious strip, which also meant I had experienced the greatest number of windshear events of any Qantas pilot. Pilots very rarely experience these sharp changes in wind – certainly not to the Wellington extent. Maybe a few times in a career, if you're smart enough to avoid places like Wellington. Me, I wasn't that smart, and I actually liked the challenge plus the nice hours a Sydney to Wellington return trip in a day gave me. Almost 9 to 5 with a good fish lunch on the other side of 'the Pond' – that is, the Tasman Sea. Qantas pilots called it the 'Pond' rather than the 'Ditch'. Pilots are very reluctant to call a body of water a ditch.

Windshear is exactly like it sounds, a rapid change in the wind for some reason: gusts or different wind speeds at different altitudes which affect the aircraft as it climbs or descends. If the wind change causes the airflow over the wing to reduce, the lift is reduced and the aircraft needs to increase its power and therefore its speed through the air to compensate. If you don't do that, you fall out of the sky and ruin your day. This is *Undershoot shear*. If the airflow increases over the wing there will be too much airspeed and power will have to be reduced to slow the aircraft or it will climb or be too fast for landing – *Overshoot shear*.

The briefing I gave the F/Os on the approach to Wellington had extra warnings about expected windshear and what we would do if we couldn't power out of it to get our approach stable in time. The Wellington shear occurred at a reasonably high level and, while the aircraft pitched and slewed like a drunken stallion, you could get it stable with copious amounts of power and control wheel waggling and control column pushing and pulling. I used to warn the passengers that we pilots were about to have some fun but it could get rough. If they thought we were enjoying the turbulence maybe they could just put up with the bumps without needing a change of underwear on the ground – that was the theory anyway.

When the wind is blowing during a landing, you just hope it's blowing straight down the runway. If not, then you have some crosswind component to cope with. The same controls needed to handle windshear come in handy plus the rudder gets a workout in a crosswind as well.

With a crosswind blowing you have to point the nose into the wind a bit so that the aircraft tracks down the extended centreline of the runway. Imagine a boat on a flowing river having to point its nose upstream so it can track straight across the river. The aircraft is doing the same thing but it makes the landing complicated because the nose has to be pointing straight down the runway on touchdown and it can be tricky getting that right.

During the landing, you have to flare the aircraft with the elevators while, at the same time, you have to keep the wings level with the ailerons and, just before touchdown, the nose has to be *yawed* around with the rudders to align the aircraft with the runway.

Timing is everything when doing this yawing. Do it too early and the wind pushes you off the runway centreline towards the downwind runway edge before you touch down: too late with the rudder input and you land with the wheels still pointing towards the upwind edge of the runway.

Neither of these scenarios is what you want but there is another complication.

Having eased the nose up for the landing you then have to push the rudder just enough to get the aircraft straight. The problem is, when you swing the aircraft, the upwind-wing swings forward and the downwind-wing swings back a bit – it's all relative, remember. Faster wing equals more lift, slower wing equals less, so the aircraft just wants to roll and you have to use the ailerons to keep the wingtip, or engines, from scraping along the runway. Just on this point, I'm pretty sure they put the engines under aircraft wings so that aircraft don't look silly. Pilots would not fly machines with engines sticking up out of the top of the wings – we do have some self-respect.

Wellington was always a challenge and really got the blood flowing on some days. Once, it was so rough I had senior cabin crew vomiting and that was before we even got to the landing. I just assumed that the poor passengers were faring even worse. During this landing, there was a strong nasty crosswind from the left and my crosswind technique was about to be tested. We had survived the shear and the rest should have been easy. It was at first, I had flared, pushed the nose around with the rudders so we were pointed down the runway and I was managing to keep the wings level with the ailerons.

A second or so before touchdown the aircraft just rolled over towards the downwind side of the runway. I instantly applied full opposite aileron to try and roll back level and my right hand was about to shove up the power – about a hundred thousand pounds of thrust by the way – and we would *go around* – that is go back up and have another go. The right wheel bogey touched down at this precise moment and the aircraft righted itself. I completed the landing which went on surprisingly smoothly. 'More arse than class' as they correctly say of these events.

On the ground is where the fun began. I was holding full aileron to keep the left wing down as the wind was desperately trying to blow over it and under it to lift it up – the *sweep* of the wing was definitely not helping here. The *sweep* presented the wing to the airflow at a right angle and therefore ideal for maximising lift. The *spoilers* had come up on top of the wing on touchdown to dump the lift but this was only partially successful.

Meanwhile, the crosswind was blowing on the vertical tail fin and, perversely, trying to turn the aircraft into the wind. This is actually its function. Without this huge vertical fin, the aircraft would just swish from side to side through the air. The rudder is attached to the back of the fin so you can yaw the aircraft around. The nose was going left even though I had applied full right rudder; that meant we were heading for the grass – not good.

Going off the hard bit onto the soft bit in an aircraft is like driving your car at speed off a sealed road straight onto some really soft sand. You stop really quickly and nasty stuff tends to happen, like snapping your long thin undercarriage off. Why you would have long thin struts with small wheels on your car I don't know but you can see what I was up against in this situation.

I was doing everything I could to counter this turning and was using every trick in the book; apart from full opposite rudder, the auto brakes – which were applying equal braking to both sides just after touchdown – had been kicked off when I applied hard toe pressure onto the rudder pedals. I was now applying full manual brake only on the side I wanted to turn towards. Two engines were giving me reverse thrust and, just as

I was about to release the reverse on the left engine and let the right engine help in pulling me straight, the nose came back to where I wanted. What I wouldn't have wanted during all this was a machine that went 'ping'.

The control tower congratulated me after the landing and the ground engineer, when he plugged in the intercom, did the same. The Qantas airport manager came into the flight deck and also said nice things. Apparently, all the staff would watch the landings on days like this and take bets as to whether the aircraft would actually make it in. Her comment that day about how, once they saw my name, they knew it would be in, still worries me – maybe I was doing way too many of these flights. Mind you, I was glad to be the 'old Wellington expert' a half an hour later. A brand-new Skipper arrived with another 767 from Melbourne and had an equally bad, if not worse, experience on his approach and landing. We had lunch together and I was able to point out that, while he may feel a bit shattered, the adrenalin was still making my hands shake a little even with my extensive Wellington experience. I think that made him feel a bit better, even though I noticed he didn't touch his fish.

So, the boss wanted to talk to me and he sent the ping. Luckily, during a relatively relaxed landing. When I called from the office a little later, he pointed out I was the only skipper with the following Saturday free – as I was senior I tried for weekends off, if possible. 'Too bad,' he said. 'Qantas wants a 767 on static display at an Air Force open day at a base just out of Sydney. So you're it.' My theory about being used as a last resort was holding up. The following Saturday, I turned up to take another 767 full of aviation enthusiasts across the city to the Richmond Air Force base. These tragics were all Qantas staff and they were going to do the same public relations job as the Avalon mob had done.

After the shortest flight I ever flew – only about ten minutes – we landed in a great spray of water. It had just stopped raining and our reverse thrust produced some great photos that people on the ground showed me afterwards. The day was a relaxed outing for me but I was aware that Qantas was doing all this to keep the Air Force happy. Qantas did then, and no doubt still does, a huge amount of engineering/maintenance work for the Air Force. I flew only about fifteen minutes that day but I was on duty for about ten hours. I knew my job was to be nice to any Air Force hierarchy and generally say good things about the Air Force, Qantas and anything else I could think of. Diplomacy is my forte.

For the whole day, the diplomat would have to overcome his instinct to tell the truth. As a result, when virtually all the young Air Force pilots I ran into asked about getting a job in Qantas, I kept my answers as general as possible. I'm glad I did because, just prior to our departure back to Sydney, the Officer in Charge of the show came up and thanked us but expressed the hope that I hadn't been on a recruiting run. I knew I was in 'bending the truth' mode, but I could honestly answer that recruiting was not what I had been doing.

I was pleased to get away from this diplomatic work and crew the aircraft back to Sydney Airport. Again, a short flight, but this time with the very new F/O doing the flying. It was fun to watch the flight display team do a formation take-off just before we did our solo one. I was a bit jealous of the machines and the flying these guys were into and couldn't quite understand why almost all wanted out. The approach back into Sydney was with a relatively light 767 – minimum fuel, no bags or cargo and only about a third of a load of tragics.

I had learned a long time earlier that aircraft landed differently if you varied the landing weight a lot. I seem to remember swearing expletives at the universe on my first solo flight because I hadn't taken the lack of the instructor's weight into account. The new 767 pilot sitting next to me had only done a few landings on the type and all at normal weights. We 'arrived' with enough force for me to know I wasn't about to become a hero to any of the staff on this air show flight either. My air show career was over and all I'd managed to do was to shatter the confidence of one brand-new F/O.

SEX (X-RATED)

What do pilots do on their stopovers in foreign ports? Some go on long walks, some get their mates and go sightseeing, some stay religiously on Australian time and don't do much at all. Some, well, some drink a bit and/or get up to mischief. Others do a combination of some or all of the above.

People may have the impression that pilots have a wild time every time they go to work. Well, some pilots like to talk the talk. Some pilots do indeed walk the walk. They were the ones that didn't talk about it – they were too busy to brag. Flight attendants did the same. A former beauty queen, married to a fellow pilot, tells of one such bragging episode. She worked as a flight attendant for a while and, on one trip, as she was walking through the open door into the Singapore hotel party room, and before she came into view of those inside, she stopped. She had heard her name mentioned. The male voice was telling a whole group of fellow flight attendants how she had gone back to his room in Bahrain a little while earlier and a great night (nudge, nudge) was had. She waited a few seconds and made the grand entrance: and she could do this, believe me, eyes flashing, fantastic smile and long blonde hair being tossed about. The bragger, of course, was the first to react. He offered the first hello and held out his hand. She took it, recognising the voice as he introduced himself. She held his hand tightly as she said, 'Hi.' (lengthy pause) 'My name is Such and Such.' To this day, she claims that his knees actually buckled under him.

My first brush with the risqué lifestyles of pilots away from home happened when I was still a senior cadet. My twenty-two-year-old sister, a tall good-looking blonde, was up in Sydney doing a computer course. My dad, who was a domestic airline Captain at the time, had an overnight stay and it was agreed that she and I would pick him up at his Kings Cross hotel and he could take us to dinner. We got into the lift on the top floor with him and down we went. One floor later we stopped and facing us were three of my father's workmates in their uniforms. There was instant recognition of Dad but, at the same time, my sister winked at me and made a big show of putting her arm through Dad's elbow and snuggling up to him. I took the hint and retreated to the rear of the lift. Who was this woman with the old guy in the suit anyway? It was a very quiet trip down to the foyer but one filled with smirks, I noticed. The three smirking pilots went over to the check-out desk and Dad turned to his daughter and son and said, 'I'm actually going to kill you two.'

So, in world of non-politically correct interactions, those good old days went on their merry way. Having witnessed the good bits, I also saw the bad. I won't dwell on the bad but I will point out I welcomed the anti-harassment laws as they came in. Fun is fun but only if everyone is having it. So 'the good old days' kind of fun is a lot rarer these days.

The scene was a huge basement in the Bombay hotel, so long ago it was still Bombay not Mumbai, and the big crew party was on. A couple of Qantas crews were there as were a lot of others, especially cabin crews from Britain and Europe. These parties were great and, on this occasion, our Captain, a former Royal Air Force fighter pilot, had organised a great food spread as well as plenty of grog – never mind the quality just look how much we've got.

On our crew on this trip there was a new pilot on his first overseas flight. His eyes were everywhere. Just as my Captain came over to check I was looking after him, this newbie noticed the prodigious number of pretty young women down in this basement with him. The Captain had come over to check I was 'looking after' him because there was an old tradition to be upheld if possible. New pilots should be initiated, and in a good way, not being sent down to the hardware store to buy a tin of striped paint or anything like that. So, the Captain eyeballed me. 'You are looking after him, I hope.' I knew an order when I heard one. When the newbie spotted a very pretty Pommie girl (this is all very old-days non-PC, and wait, it just gets worse). He looked at me and I tipped my head towards her in the universal bloke sign language for 'go for it'. He was a bit hesitant because she was in deep conversation with two British stewards and he didn't know how to break in. At least I could help him there. I just went over and told the two stewards that a young pilot wanted to talk to the hostie.

After the stewards left, the British woman looked at me and I just pointed at the new pilot and said two words, 'First trip.' She instantly looked at him with interest and, after about five seconds, looked back at me and nodded. She'd been around and welcomed that particular tradition. As she took his arm, our Captain walked by and said to her, 'If he's not a gentleman, put a note under my door.' It took me the rest of the trip to convince this new pilot that this may not happen on every stopover.

So, yes, there was opportunity, there were the means – all it took was the motive.

Flexible arrangements for some of the married crew took the form of marriage licences that seemed to be valid only until you crossed the coastline on leaving Australia. Other marriage certificates were even negated by the undercarriage coming up – you didn't even have to leave Australia. I saw all variations of flexible arrangements, including the classic, 'It's my dick and I'll wash it as hard as I like.' There's not much you can say to that one.

Flexible arrangements were thoroughly practised by some blokes. There was one pilot who nobody really liked and, as a result, he didn't garner much sympathy when, just after retiring, he was up on charges. He had two families, one in England and one in Sydney. Maybe he just didn't have time to make an effort to get on with workmates. Mind you, the best flexibility story was about 'double O six and a half'. He was a bloke who fancied himself as James Bond but we all knew he never quite got there. After he retired, so the story goes, he would get into his uniform and leave his wife at home on the Northern Beaches and disappear down towards the airport. He would return after a week or so. The other Qantas Northern Beaches wives were scandalised; how could the wife be treated so? At a Christmas party, she was taken aside by a group of the concerned and told that her husband was no longer a pilot. The other wives were shocked to hear Double O's wife say, 'I know, I know, please don't tell him though.'

Watching what was going on was unavoidable though, and one long nineteen-day Pacific/Caribbean tour of duty was an eyeopener. The whole crew was invited to the wedding reception in the Captain's room on arrival at the hotel in Tahiti, the first stopover out of Sydney. A very funny drunken pretend wedding was performed by the First Officer. The Captain and the only hostess had decided to become a couple, at least for the time being. They stayed together for about seventeen days, including while on trips to Bora Bora and other places away from the rest of us. They had a great time but not good enough it would seem because, in Tahiti on the way home, a very funny divorce was performed by the same First Officer and a great divorce party was held. This sort of stuff, no doubt, still happens but, I suspect, without the rest of the happy pair's workmates wishing the new couple well on their 'wedding' day and then commiserating with the now-shattered couple a couple of weeks later. Those parties were hilarious.

Tahiti featured a lot. In later years, I flew there often on Classic Jumbos and 767s. Lots of stopovers, lots of fun. One night, way after midnight, the skinny dip was on. We were at a beachside hotel and were all down in the warm water on the rocky sea front. If you swam around in the shallows with the naked Air New Zealand hosties, you had to be careful of the dangers. A lot of the rock pools contained black spikey sea urchins. Nature has given these sea creatures a formidable defensive system. The poison stings like hell if you manage to get a spine in your hand or foot and you'd better not sit on one.

A nice friendly, gentle, water experience was being had and everyone was mostly behaving themselves – the urchins were forcing this, to a degree. Imagine our surprise when most of us lying in the shallows suddenly looked up to see a naked hostie running flat out across the shallows in front of us. She was laughing hard and looking back at my Captain who was also laughing and running flat out as well. He had the same amount of clothes on as the hostie. I can remember thinking that these two were brave and, as I thought that, the Captain screamed and did the old double forward somersault with head plant. He had stepped squarely on a huge sea urchin.

So, it was back to the Captain's room with one Captain in a great deal of pain and a number of nasty looking black spines imbedded in his foot, lots of concerned crew, Qantas and Air NZ, all wearing beach towels by now – the fun was truly over. Tahiti didn't have twenty-four-hour ambulances of course, so I was out in the corridor trying to get advice from the concierge, the only staff member anywhere in the hotel. I was asking for some way to alleviate the Captain's pain; he was really feeling it. There were no drugs around and, by what the concierge was saying in his broad French accent, they wouldn't help anyway. He then got very sheepish and dropped his voice so that only I could hear. Apparently, the Tahitian locals did have a treatment. 'They would, you know, ah, urine on the skin.' Ah ha! I had something! I can still remember, for the next half hour, trying to convince two pretty New Zealand women to give my Captain the 'Golden Attention' he needed.

Now two of the best wardrobe stories you will ever hear: I heard one flight attendant tell the first and another told the second in response. The scene: Waikiki beach, specifically the Hilton Hotel grounds on a Sunday afternoon. The jazz club was in full swing and the Qantas crews were there in their usual big numbers. It was a great day out. A couple of the older, more senior flight attendants noticed a young F/A turn up for a few drinks with a young American woman. The old 'seniors' watched the younger couple get more amorous as the afternoon progressed. It was a judgement call, I was told, but at some point the two older blokes slipped away back to the crew hotel next door. Having got a spare key to the young F/A's room, they set the scene. Into his large wardrobe with the big sliding doors they went. Setting themselves up with a couple of suitcase stands for seats they put the young F/A's suitcase between them and proceeded to fill in the time playing cards on it. They were completely inside the wardrobe with the doors nearly closed.

They didn't have to wait long, the F/A told us. In through the hotel room door came the couple, crashing and banging against the walls as they tore at each other's clothes. They fell onto the big double bed only about two feet from the now closed wardrobe doors, and it was on. 'Very loud and vigorous' was how proceedings were described and everything was happening pretty quickly. In the teller's words, 'The grunting and yelps were getting closer together and, as the vinegar stroke approached, we suddenly slid the wardrobe doors open, looked at the couple about three feet away and said, 'Hey, can you keep the noise down a bit,' and, pointing to the cards, 'we're trying to win some money here.' That said, the two seniors just slid the doors shut again.

In response to this story, another F/A who was listening said, 'My wardrobe experience didn't go so well.' Everybody just stared at him in anticipation. His story was similar, a randy couple, two 'workmates', a rented room and, in this case, a big freestanding wardrobe with outward opening doors next to the single bed in the narrow room.

Downstairs, the Qantas Bat Cave in Singapore was in full lunchtime swing: I never knew its real name, but this place was dark and cool and Qantas bats would hang around inside recharging their batteries. The 'Bat Cave' catered to the crews for a late lunch and a couple of beers if they were leaving that night. The spring rolls were terrific and the Qantas soup was always great. Qantas soup was Chinese crab meat and corn soup – the only criteria being that there had to be more crab meat than corn. Put some of their really heavy soy sauce on these dishes and you could see why this place did a roaring trade with the crews.

So, amorous couple, with an unwise bit of pre-event bragging it would seem, because that's how the two 'mates' found out the young bloke had booked himself a short-stay room upstairs. Same scenario, two blokes snuck away and got themselves into the wardrobe, again with only a short wait. Clothes flung everywhere and similar grunting noises from the extremely close bed. The storyteller continued. 'The two of us are jammed into this wobbly wardrobe trying to open the doors a little so we could see what was going on. This was going okay until the other bloke in the wardrobe started to get a bit too involved. He opened his fly and started his own party. I was desperately trying to stop him but, in my efforts, I got the wardrobe wobbling too much and the bloody thing tipped forward onto the bed so that the doors were forced closed and we were stuck there. A lot of screaming from the bed and from inside the wardrobe as well. Yes, as I said, it did not go well.'

Typical nights out in Asian cities back then involved bars that catered mostly to visiting Westerners. That was us. Everybody knows about the Bangkok nightclubs but other cities had their share as well. I remember signing on for a Manila flight one morning to be told by another Captain that, since I was going up there, I should check out the new Mirrors Bar near the hotel. Sure enough, some other crew members had heard that this establishment was the 'new black' and off we went. We walked in, looked around and noticed a few mirrors on the walls – not such a big deal. It was only after sitting at the bar for a few minutes that we noticed that there was a line of mirrors at floor level behind the bar at about 45 degrees to the vertical. If you looked into those mirrors, you could see right up the pretty barmaids' miniskirts – miniskirts that didn't have any underwear underneath them of course. Mirrors.

Another Asian city that also had mirrors and could be fun was Jakarta. Again, another Captain recommended a certain bar but with a special instruction attached. I was to make sure to visit the boys' room, as the view from this high-rise toilet window was worth it. I had been set up, of course. When we got to this bar, we found it was more of a gay bar than a straight one. I did visit the men's room and did see the view out the window. There was a huge distraction, however. The big flat urinal was in fact a big flat mirror, angled perfectly to reflect the middle front regions straight back to the observers standing there.

Ah, life's rich tapestry!

23

DIFFERENCES

International flying is the way to see the world and to see how people live. Getting to stay in various climates was part of this experience. To show you what I mean, I'll try and contrast two countries, and two arrivals into them, that couldn't be more different if they tried.

Flying into Tahiti on the 767 in the nineties was always challenging. For a start, the flight got there just before midnight, which meant it was dark. Sorry, but I'm trying to say it was *very* dark with no city lights or their reflections off the clouds – what pilots call a *black hole*. A little island with a couple of smaller ones nearby was always hard to find. Luckily, by this time, navigation systems had progressed to a point that meant you were in no real danger of not finding them. I've just read a book on the history of Qantas during WW2. Qantas lost eight aircraft due to various actions or accidents caused by wartime conditions. One of those conditions was that navigation aids were pretty primitive, both on the aircraft and the ground. This meant that a mission to put a couple of meteorology officers onto the Cocos Islands, a similarly small, isolated island complex in the Indian Ocean, took several costly long flights, most of which failed miserably. Now, we just took for granted that we had the nav systems to cope and we didn't even need a dedicated navigator – pilots could operate the new systems.

Once found, Tahiti was still a black hole. Papeete has one main road and I'm not sure if there were even any streetlights. This small town did not shine like a beacon in the night. In fact, the airport beacon and runway lights were the only things visible from any distance. At the appropriate distance, depending on our altitude and wind conditions and, believe it or not, the aircraft's weight, we started the descent to the threshold of the runway. What this meant was that while hurtling through the upper atmosphere at nine hundred klicks, an atmosphere that was itself moving at sometimes up to three hundred klicks, we told ourselves that now was the time to dive so that we could magically arrive at the touchdown bit of the runway – pinpoint target that it was. During this dive, we would have to lose over ninety eight per cent of the aircraft's energy. This energy had the ingredients of height, speed and weight which meant that most of the equation we used to calculate the descent point had to do with the energy level of the aircraft. These dives were very easy to mess up, especially if the wind changed on us, and we were expecting the wind to vary all the way down.

This particular night's arrival wasn't too different to many others. We started down at the calculated distance, about one hundred nautical miles out, and virtually glided all the way. The engines were at idle. We were the equivalent of a car coasting down a hill in neutral with its engine still running. Theoretically, if there are no unforeseen wind changes, we could have just sat and watched the aircraft glide down perfectly to the touchdown point. As I said, winds do vary, and we had to adjust things to suit. As the headwind increased or decreased from what we expected, we took action.

If the headwind increased, away from expected, we *stretched* the glide by slowing a bit, this reduced the *drag* and would counteract the increased *drag* from the headwind.

Conversely, if a tailwind came in, we would dive a bit more steeply and increase our speed, which would increase our drag a bit to counteract the lessening drag effect due to the tailwind. We were constantly adjusting to stay on our *profile* or *vertical path*. We made a couple of radio calls to the friendly bloke in the tower and that was it and just flew down varying our speed as necessary. It was a relaxed approach with no other aircraft within cooee that we had to fit in with.

After landing on the very smooth runway – I wish my landing had been as smooth – we arrived at the lovely open-air terminal and instantly felt relaxed. Things just flowed, minimal customs and immigration and a quick ten-minute minibus ride to the beachside hotel. As I came through the airport, a lovely Tahitian girl had put a necklace of flowers around my neck and I wore them to the hotel. The crew beat any passengers to the hotel so check-in, at around midnight, was quick and painless as well – nobody else around. This was what we wanted because there was an important tradition to be upheld. We had to be out in the swimming pool within about five minutes of arriving at the pub. This pool was one of those infinity pools with the wall near the ocean having the gentle waterfall seeming to tip over it into the sea. The tradition also held that we had to have a beer can open in our hands and be ready to salute the aircraft we had just brought in as it departed along the coast in front of us. This was always a magnificent sight and a pool party was always the go at this midnight hour. A great start to the relaxing warm mini holiday on a tropical island.

Approaching into Frankfurt International in the middle of winter in an early model Jumbo was another experience altogether. As the first officer my job was to support the Captain during his approach and landing and on this early morning it was going to be hard work. You already know it's going to be bloody cold when even the upper atmosphere is twenty degrees Celsius colder than normal. The usual minus high forties in the last part of the cruise was now reading minus high sixties. Too much time spent at that temperature and the fuel could start to freeze. Years later, as a Captain, I had to increase the speed of a 747-400 quite markedly to get some extra friction heating out of the airflow to prevent my fuel just becoming thick sludge in the aircraft's tanks. I had to use extra fuel to increase the speed but the alternative of flying much lower in warmer air would have used extra as well.

We were preparing for our dive into FRA and, on this freezing early morning arrival, we were expecting the landing visibility to be reduced by mist, which could easily turn to fog, so we were watching the reports on the *split* very carefully. The split is the temperature difference between the wet bulb and the dry one, of course – thermometer bulbs that is. This difference gives an indication of the likelihood of fog. The other way this likelihood was conveyed to approaching aircraft was with a report on the current temperature with the *dew point* temperature also reported. No prizes for guessing what happens when the dew point is reached. Cloud forms on the ground and, instead of calling it 'ground cloud', we call it fog.

We had the complicated routing into the airport with all the height and speed restrictions needed by the ATC controllers.

They had us on radar and, while they could direct us, they mostly let us find the various *radio beacons* using our own navigation. 'Radio beacons', I hear you shout with derision. Well, it's a long time since I was an F/O and fancy TV screen maps driven by GPS weren't even a dream back then – radio beacons were it.

There were all sorts of height and speed restrictions to comply with and the Captain was working hard to get it right and I was there to make sure he got it right – the support pilot's job is to monitor everything.

We descended on the STAR (Standard Terminal Arrival Route) following all the routing, altitude restrictions and speed restrictions, no just doing our own thing on this approach. We had to comply strictly with the speeds and, if that meant we got high or low on our vertical path, then we had to use other means of adjustment other than the varying speed method I would use in the future on my approach into Tahiti. If we got high, the speed brakes were used. If we got low then some engine power was used.

We had got to the end of the STAR and to the beginning of the *letdown*. No, I don't mean the feeling you get at the end of some emotionally draining event, I mean the *FRA ILS 25R Cat 2b Autoland*. Translation – FRA (Frankfurt duh!) ILS (Instrument Landing System) 25R (the right-hand runway heading 250 magnetic) and we would be hooking up the autopilots and descending down to the minimums of Category 2, subsection b, with the automatic landing required with these low minimums. Minimums required a specified cloud base and visibility. This morning we were really just worried about the visibility, no low clouds had been reported.

As the ILS radio signals that gave us both our tracking and our glideslope were selected, the three autopilots came online.

Three means that, if two disagree, there is the third to check with. Hopefully, it would agree with the one doing the right thing and the two good ones would shut down the failing one. You could still land with one autopilot out but the minimums would have to be raised to take the less than ideal situation into account.

The aircraft was flying itself down the beams with the Captain and me watching like hawks – watching for any deviations away from the beams and for any unstable speed readings as well. The Captain was now starting to look outside to judge the visibility for the landing but his eyes kept flicking back inside to assure himself that everything was still okay. He was telling me what he could see outside just to assure me that things were okay out there as well. When I called, *'Rad Alt alive,'* the Captain checked his radio altimeter and confirmed his readout was working as well by saying, *'Checked,'* which meant the little radar system that looked straight down and told you how high above the ground you were was working properly. This was essential if the aircraft computers were to flare the aircraft for the landing and not just bang it on way too hard.

The Captain told me what he could see. 'A bit of ground between patches of mist – no clouds.' I replied, 'Tracking, glideslope and speed all good.' IAS is the indicated airspeed. We had groundspeed readouts as well but IAS is the important one at this stage. We were a team and had been trained to be a good one even though this was the first and last time we would ever do an *autoland* together. Standard operating procedures meant that I knew what he was doing and he knew what I was doing, including the sort of things we would say to each other. Many *autolands* in the simulators with me flying with other Captains and him flying with other F/Os meant we used the same procedures with whoever we were flying with and the operation was as good as it gets.

As we got nearer the ground, the boss was now almost exclusively *head free* – that is, looking outside for the required visibility as we got to the *minimum* height. If he could see the appropriate lights and could see far enough down the runway to know that it was both legal and safe to land, he would answer my call of, 'Minimum,' with the decision word, 'Landing.' I knew we were at 'decision' height, another way of saying 'minimum' height, because I had stayed *head down* – that is, my eyes were only on the instruments. Remember, no screens back then, just instruments. I was monitoring ILS readouts – speed, altitude, rate of descent, radio altitude plus a myriad of warning lights and warning/failure flags. If anything went bad on us, my job was to call it. If, for example, an autopilot failed, I would call it and give the new higher decision height we would then have to work with – all standard procedure. The Captain would only reply, 'Checked.' He would have to say this so that I knew he was aware of the new circumstances – a team is a team.

Everything went fine and, as the aircraft reached the flare height and started to ease the nose up for the landing, I made the obligatory call of, 'Flare Green,' taking my cue from the indicator light, labelled *FLARE*, turning green. I'm really clever this way. Even after the landing, I still had to stay looking inside because, even after touchdown, the autopilots still keep the aircraft tracking down the middle of the runway by using the rudders. I had to monitor this tracking as well as the engines, first coming back to idle, then spooling up again as they powered up in reverse mode. I also had to make sure the speed brakes came up to dump the lift from the wings.

Once these duties were done and I heard the call, 'Disconnecting,' from the boss, which told me he had taken over the steering, I looked up and out down the runway. I got one hell of a shock. Every other time I'd looked out an aircraft's front windscreen at the runway, it was there. This dreary morning it wasn't there. This was disconcerting in a way that might have required a change of underwear. Instead of rolling down the runway, we were moving pretty fast through a snowfield. It was daylight and I could see this airport- sized white area very clearly. For a change I held back on the swearing and I'm glad I did. I suddenly realised that, of course they wouldn't have been able to sweep the runways. The snowfall had been big enough to stop any thought of this and the landing strip was still under shallow snow. I then noticed the runway side lights sticking up on either side of us. They didn't show up that brightly because it was full daylight by now and white lights against a white background is far from ideal visibility. They really should have had black lights. Sorry, that's just silly.

An airport Unimog (small 4WD truck), with a rotating brush sticking out in front, came out and swept the snow off the yellow taxiway centre-lines for us. We stuck our nose wheel on these lines and found our way to the huge grey terminal buildings with me hoping our main wheels stayed on the taxiways as well.

We went into the terminal and found the place full. No quiet little tropical airport this – it was big, noisy and crowded. We lined up with lots of other crew from other arriving flights and eventually got through immigration. Before picking up our bags, I failed to see any pretty young women with welcome flowers – not surprising since they weren't there.

What was there, moving through the terminal, was a group of human tanks.

These were German Special Forces soldiers – one serious bunch of dudes. For a start, they were all big men, way over six feet and built to go with it, which was just as well because they were wearing body armour, not padded vests but serious armour that looked like a big plate of steel in front of them. It was thick and heavy looking and obviously designed to stop real bullets. The armour was strapped on so they had their hands free to carry their weapons – mean-looking, medium-barrelled automatic rifles that had those straight magazines with about thirty rounds in them. What really got me though, was that these Special Forces soldiers had chosen to tape two of these magazines together for the quick reload. When the first magazine was empty, they could just turn it around, plug the full one in and continue the fight. These were people I would not want to tangle with. That was the idea of course. Germany has these walking tanks to stop any entanglement in its tracks. That particular morning, Margaret Thatcher was passing through the airport and Deutschland was not going to have any security problems.

We got into the big crew bus and went off to our hotel in Mainz, not really that far away, but a bus ride through peak hour is always a drag, especially after a gruelling night flight up from Asia. Finally, we made it into the warm hotel. The temperature outside hadn't got above zero and wasn't likely too for the few days we were there, so no pool parties on arrival just a look at the view from my double- or even triple-glazed hotel window, of the grey and misty Rhine River. After a daytime sleep, the go here in Mainz was to meet up and go off to the favourite 'pigs knuckle' joint – sorry, restaurant. Good German beer and a huge meal of pork and crackling would give you the energy you needed to make your way back to the hotel in the minus twelve degree darkness and almost enable you to ignore the freezing cold coming up through your thick socks and solid shoes – the cold seeping through the heavy pair of jeans could never be ignored, though. How did people live here through an entire winter? A three-day holiday in Germany at this time of year was not my first choice – give me French Polynesia anytime.

Frankfurt in summer, however, was my favourite stopover.

24

FLIGHTS WITH STRETCHERS

After too many years as a S/O without landing privileges, a mate and I were chosen to be checked out as *landing S/Os*. Pilot upgrade training had virtually stopped as one of the periodic downturns in the economic life of the airline hit. To keep the training department ticking over, management decided to 'pre-train' a couple of F/Os but not actually promote us. This meant we did the full training as well as the full landing qualification on the classic 747 and could be put up in rank instantly when required. I don't remember my mate and I complaining about this, we were just happy that something was at least happening in our careers.

The only problem was that once we were put onto the *landing list*, that is those qualified to land a Jumbo, we would have to take our place in line for what few landings were available to get any practice. After months of training, I found myself back flying as a S/O. This meant I sat behind the two more senior pilots and watched but every thirty-five days, I had to do a landing to remain *recent*. On most flights, the old skippers had no idea I was qualified to land and would just treat me as a junior paper pusher. I got to introducing myself by saying, 'I'm your F/O-type-S/O, Captain. I'm supposed to do landings too.'

All this got me were a lot of strange looks and more paper pushing treatment. So, every thirty-five days, I would be sent to do a landing on a day trip out of Sydney. These day trips were usually a flight down to Melbourne and back and I would just hope I could pull off a landing that we could walk away from without a limp. What little expertise I'd accumulated during my training was fading fast as the lack of practice set in.

On boarding the 747 for one such flight one morning, I saw quite a medical presence down the back of the aircraft. A certain number of seats had been converted into a hospital stretcher and an intensive care passenger was being looked after by a medical team. This passenger had come down from the United States like this and I was his pilot from Sydney to his hometown of Melbourne.

This bloke had been through the wars. On the US West Coast he had been knocked down by a car, I think, and ended up in hospital with bad head and neck injuries. Serious enough, but he had also lost all memory of who he was. His wallet and passport had been stolen at the accident scene – just not his day. The only luck he had was when, a long time later, his brother, while on a visit to New York, recognised his brother's photo in a US national newspaper. His backstory meant this guy was a big news story on his arrival in Australia, especially in Melbourne where it wasn't the footy season so they had plenty of room in the media.

Previously, I'd had mixed results from my sporadic attempts at alighting gently upon the earth during these landings I did to remain current. One such attempt in San Francisco wasn't very pretty. I knew it had gone on like a sack of potatoes and didn't need to be told by the American pilot waiting to use the runway, his one-word radio transmission said it all, 'Oomph!!' At least I hadn't had that much time to build up any real pilot's ego and, just as well, because this sort of stuff brings you down to earth with a thud, quite literally – all puns intended.

I was very aware that I'd better not crash it on this day with a celebrity down the back with a broken neck. The pressure was on. Luckily, the conditions weren't too nasty and the landing, while not the smoothest, was quite acceptable and wouldn't have snapped any vertebrae. It wasn't until I got home that evening in Sydney and watched several TV news videos of my landing in Melbourne that I realised just how badly this could have turned out.

Every TV crew in the country, it seemed, had positioned themselves high up on the Melbourne terminal building and I had obliged by landing very close to them so they could get the best close-up shots of my 'arrival'. The voice over had the story of the poor bloke finally arriving home. Missing, fortunately, was the bit about how this horrendously heavy landing had snapped his, and a few other passengers', necks – 'Now, let's watch that again in slow-motion replay.' I knew by just how much I, and the poor bloke down the back, had dodged that particular bullet. I don't think anybody else had a clue.

Normal flights sometimes had a poignancy that took away some of the usual shine. The regular three-hour 767 trip up to Noumea was a nice day out – daylight hours, relaxed, fun airport without the busy work of a mainland or Asian airport. The only downer was seeing the ambulance pull up at the back of the aircraft in Sydney. Usually it meant only one thing, a New Caledonian cancer patient was going home to die. They would come down to Australia for advanced treatment which we all know only works sometimes. These passengers were too sick to take a seat home – hence the stretchers down the back.

The saddest flight I think I ever did actually had no stretchers on it but did involve cancer patients going home. This particular day was a great day's work for me. To start with, it was a beautiful day for a Melbourne to Perth flight. The weather was great everywhere and the usual strong headwind had become a tailwind so we were going to make up a huge amount of time. Once I got to Perth, I would just jump on the first flight home as a passenger since I wasn't needed for the rest of the *pattern* up to Asia. So, for me, this day's work on the 767 was more like an easy day out.

It was, until the female flight attendants came up and asked whether they could bring a little eight-year-old girl up to the flight deck for a visit. Being before 9/11, we could do this and I said, of course they could. The head flight attendant then told me, just before this absolutely lovely little girl came in, that she had been in Melbourne for some advanced cancer treatment but it had failed and she was on her way home to die. I turned around to see a little girl almost exactly the same age as my daughter was then. But what really floored me was that she had exactly the same blonde hair and vivid blue eyes as my daughter, I was speechless until I recovered myself a bit.

I made a real fuss of her and said all the right things while I showed her stuff she would never see again. This was harrowing enough but it got way worse. Another female flight attendant came up and lent around the window side of me to have a quiet word so the young girl couldn't hear. The story was the mother, on arriving in Melbourne, presented with a few troubling symptoms herself and was checked over by the cancer specialists as well. It turned out she also had advanced cancer and was going home, with her dying daughter, to face a very uncertain future.

While the little girl was in the cabin with her, the mother had held herself together but as soon as she was alone with some very sympathetic and compassionate flight attendants she had actually collapsed onto the galley floor in distress. The flight attendants wanted me to look after the child while they desperately tried to get her mother back together. We completed the flight with the little girl and one flight attendant on the flight deck. I will never forget that delightful young girl or her eyes. As I have said there were no stretchers set up on that aircraft, maybe there should have been – for me.

The next time I saw a mini hospital set up was on a tsunami rescue flight up to South East Asia. It was Christmas 2004 and I had just got home from a London trip. Because I had taken a week's leave during this two-months roster period, I knew I would be one of the very few Captains who could be called on for extra duties that Christmas. I had days free but, more importantly, I had spare flying hours to offer. Pilots during busy periods, like Christmas, are always running up against these government restrictions on daily, weekly, monthly and yearly flying hours. I was *available* and I knew it.

The tsunami hit and did a huge amount of damage to the coastal areas of many countries with a death toll in the hundreds of thousands. This tragedy occurred in countries I knew well. Those affected were people I liked and respected. I rang and offered to crew any flight the Company might have going up to South East Asia. No doubt, with the unfolding tragedy, the Government would need not only the Air Force but probably Qantas as well to be involved in any humanitarian flights. When a quarter of a million people lose their lives and millions more are affected, stuff is going to have to be done.

Qantas has had a long history of helping during disasters – getting emergency responders to trouble spots and evacuating or repatriating victims. The greatest example of this was again just after Christmas back in 1974 when Qantas 747s flew numerous evacuation flights out of Darwin after Cyclone

Tracy trashed the city. Thousands of women and children were stacked onto Jumbos and flown to southern Australian cities. The greatest number of passengers (673) ever carried on an aircraft were squeezed in as arm rests were raised and rows of seats filled up with as many kids and mums as possible. This meant that the aircraft had to fly at low altitude all the way south as there were not enough oxygen masks if some pressurisation problem occurred.

Having rung and offered my services for any tsunami rescue, I hung up with that inner glow of having offered but not actually having to do anything. Silly me. I was called back within the hour. The Government wanted a Jumbo full of responders up into the region the next day. Saturday morning and I was on a mission to get the flight organised and up to Singapore so that a crew there could take it down to the Seychelles Islands and land while it was still daylight. It needed to arrive before dark because there was no guarantee that any lights would be working on the airport – the runway had been underwater for a bit as the tsunami did its thing.

From there, the aircraft was to go up to Sri Lanka, where medicos and supplies would be delivered. Rescue assessors, TV crews, reporters and medical crews including a group of Sri Lankan Australian doctors would be delivered to various places. This flight also had a serious security and immigration department presence. They were there to help any Aussies needing to get home. Last but not least, a small *evac* hospital was set up down the back with stretchers for any casualties deemed worthy of getting a ride home.

My job was clear but the Qantas Chief Pilot had turned up this Saturday morning to add his weight to any decisions I might have to make. He just gave me his mobile number and left me to it. By this stage, I was wondering what I'd got myself into. There were problems from the start. There were lots of cargo loading snags because of the unusual emergency supplies being loaded instead of normal baggage containers. This was a flight organised overnight, so people were coming from everywhere with minimum notice and a lot of them were running late. There were medical specialists arriving from interstate with minimum time to transfer to this international flight.

While I was sorting fuel and weight problems, I had my pilot crew work out the timings to ensure the aircraft could arrive in the Seychelles before dark. This was mission critical. It was no good doing a real good job of getting everyone and their gear on board if it was too late to actually get them to where they needed to be. I'd better not mess this up. I was beginning to see why the Chief Pilot had retreated to his office – he was no fool. By working backwards from the latest possible touchdown time at Seychelles airport, estimating as accurately as possible the flight time down from Singapore and the flight up to Singapore from Sydney, adding fuel-loading time in Singapore and a small 'fudge factor', a departure time was decided on. We had to wait until the last possible moment to give the latecomers every possible chance of making it on board.

As it turned out, not everybody nor every bit of cargo made it aboard for the now firmed-up deadline. A couple of aircraft were too late arriving at the domestic terminal and some medical supplies didn't turn up in time. As the deadline approached, I was down on the apron with the cargo loaders and their controllers. I was making time-pressure decisions before we took off. Usually pilots only get really pressed for time as the fuel is running out. I remember an old pilot saying once that a pilot was someone who made life-and-death decisions in an ever-diminishing time frame. Here was I making them before we even started burning the kerosene.

The load controllers were keeping me advised on the progress of a large pallet of medical supplies coming from the western suburbs. The biggest hospital out there had spent the night getting this essential gear ready. They would have spent time deciding what was needed, what they had available and then preparing it all for flying. The pallet, that would slide straight into our hold, would have been stacked carefully and weatherproofed with plastic wrapping. It was on its way through heavy traffic with a police escort with sirens blaring – these guys were really trying. The last update put the convoy just out of the comfort zone and I had to make one of those decisions that I was being paid for – in fact, I wasn't even sure I was being paid for this day since, like the rest of the crew, I was a volunteer and I had no idea what that meant in terms of pay. I had to send the word to stop trying – the flight was closed.

A special dispensation was arranged for this *Government Charter*, meaning we would be given all sorts of priority in terms of air traffic control. This would help with bypassing any queues of aircraft waiting to take off and in getting the shortest route away from Sydney. We took advantage of this as we departed and literally cut a few corners after take-off as we were given a track straight to Singapore. This was the great circle track, the shortest distance between us and Singapore.

We also stayed below the high-altitude jet stream winds which are nearly always against you if you are heading west across Australia. Staying low meant a higher fuel burn that had to be balanced against the saving in time. This is always a compromise. Pilots have all sorts of graphs and computers to make judgments of what speed and altitude is best. This flight was on a time limit and I had enough fuel to really go for it, low and fast, and let the taxpayer cop the fuel bill – I'll make an Air Force pilot yet.

There wasn't one paying passenger on board, so the public address I gave was different from normal. I congratulated our guests for being the people going up to Asia to do all this great work. I told them they had a volunteer crew on board but, while their time away was totally uncertain, what we Qantas people had signed up for was probably just spending New Year's Eve away from Sydney. We knew who the real heroes were. In response to this PA, I got a letter from downstairs. It was from my oldest mate from school and all it said was, 'So, you do fucking work sometimes.' This unexpected semi-abusive note, that was also a bit unfair, was a mystery to me until I remembered that this mate, a prominent orthopaedic surgeon, had operated on all sorts of sportsmen and women, including a few Sri Lankan cricketers. He had contacts up in Sri Lanka and would no doubt be going there to help. What I didn't know was that he had many contacts with Sri Lankan doctors working in Melbourne, which was really why he was on board. Qantas had rung him and offered him, and as many fellow doctors as he could organise, a trip up to Colombo if they could get themselves ready and out to Melbourne airport by early Saturday morning.

This formidable team of doctors was on board now and my mate was letting me know that, after thirty years of flying overseas, he was finally flying with me. Such was his expertise that, for years, he had done more than his fair share of flying in order to give lectures overseas. I've never forgiven him for reconstructing the shoulder of Sri Lanka's best spin bowler – being a doctor is one thing but that was almost treasonous.

I went into the cabin and did the rounds of all the groups on board. They might have had requests for messages to be sent or any number of requirements. This was a special flight and things were being done on the fly. (Did I actually just say that?) I met the Sri Lankan doctors and caught up with my mate. Meanwhile, we were getting requests from the film crews and journalists on board for information updates and flight-deck access.

This was post-9/11 so, usually, the flight deck was off limits, but this was not a Regular Public Transport (RPT) flight, it was a charter and could therefore have slightly different rules applied. I asked the Chief Pilot back in Sydney and he came up with permission from the authority for journalists to be allowed on the flight deck once we had left Australia – two at a time, two plain-clothes SAS type killers with them and no cameras. I hadn't seen anybody on a flight deck, except crew, since 9/11 and now there were new rules.

As we flew over Indonesia, we were able to point out the string of volcanoes that is, in fact, the Indonesian islands. We couldn't see all the way to where the tsunami-causing earthquake had occurred, but the journos were happy. They were getting some good visual briefings and all for free. For the landing into Singapore, my mate was suddenly upgraded to journalist/surgeon so that a guy I'd known since primary school was able to sit behind me for the landing. Just to make sure he behaved himself, a security killer sat behind him. You can never trust these old schoolmates – sometimes they whip out their scalpels and fix up a Sri Lankan cricketer or two.

As a young flying instructor, I had one flight that really didn't achieve its aim. I had been given the job of supplying the prize in a children's competition. A ten-year-old boy had won an hour's flight over Melbourne and I was the pilot. The sickly-looking little boy and his father turned up for the flight and off we went in a little four-seater Cessna. I don't remember it being any more bumpy than usual, but that didn't mean much. In these small bug-smashers, airsickness was always a possibility. I used to carry a supply of sick bags in my back pocket and had, by this stage, developed a fairly quick draw. First sign of heaving and I had a bag in front of him, or her, already opened for business. The motive wasn't entirely altruistic of course. I would have been the one to clean out the aircraft if vomit went everywhere.

Shortly into the flight, this kid needed a bag and, while I persisted for a while, he wasn't getting any better and certainly wasn't enjoying himself. About halfway through I offered the father the opportunity to go back and give his son some relief. He vehemently resisted any idea of not getting the full hour's worth of prize. While I was concerned for the kid, he wasn't in any real danger of dehydration or anything, he was just getting more miserable as the flight went on. The dad was having a ball. I used every trick in the book to make sure I got the aircraft back on *blocks* and shut down just as the hour ticked over– this bastard father wasn't getting a second he wasn't entitled too.

Fast forward about forty years and I was given the opportunity of upsetting about two hundred sickly young kids and I had, again, exactly one hour in which to do it. Once a year, Qantas donates a flight to a charity that is sponsored by the company and Qantas staff. The Pathfinders Charity has been around for years and looks after sick children, some of them blind, but others with all sorts of conditions. I had donated money over the years to this charity but never time – still I was certainly a supporter. This particular year's flight was coming up and a good mate, Toby, was due to fly it. Unfortunately, he was off flying duties, due to a medical problem and needed a replacement. He rang, explained the situation and had me committed on the spot.

The aim was to take about two hundred deserving kids, their carers and medical teams as well as a double load of volunteer cabin crew, up for a spin. Who was I to refuse to help when asked? There are good people who you must always help. Qantas had given the aircraft up for the hour and there was a time set to hand over to the ground staff so that the Jumbo could be prepped for a regular service.

The flight would be up and down the coast with great views of Sydney and its beaches on both sides as we went to and fro at as low an altitude as we could. Sounds simple, but I knew differently. This was going to be hard work and I had prepared carefully. For a start, the Captain of this flight could pick his pilot team. No shortage of volunteers, I'm glad to say, and I did it on merit. While any junior Qantas pilots would have been right on top of the requirements, I chose blokes I had seen fly who I knew would be nothing but professional and who wouldn't be distracted by the occasion. To prevent myself being distracted, I was very happy for 'Captain Toby' to be the voice from the flight deck and to do all the PR involved. I was the designated driver and was determined to be on task.

The flight would go up and down the coast but would also have to go up and down the *steps*, those invisible circular rings around a major airport that define the *controlled* area. Big jets had to be in this area, or more correctly volume, as this was where Air Traffic Control could keep an eye on you and keep you away from any other traffic. Near the airport, the controlled area extended all the way to the ground, further away and there were lower limits that progressively got higher. For instance, if you were twenty miles away from the airport you would have to be at least five thousand feet high, thirty miles ten thousand and so on. If the aim was to keep as low as possible for the great views, I would have to skip up and down depending how close to the airport I was. All this had to be done at about two hundred and fifty knots. Mess it up and you could find yourself face to face with a non-ATC-controlled Cessna, which would be very bad for everyone. Even if there was no conflicting traffic, the Captain would be up the proverbial creek when ATC noticed, and they had us on radar all the time.

I had been watching the weather all day and was hoping for light winds and a smooth atmosphere to minimise airsickness. Any climbing, descending and turns were to be as gentle as possible as well. This fun flight was a workout but I knew what I was getting into –it was a worthwhile thing to do. The flight went as planned. Junior pilots were briefed to keep an eye on the old Captain to make sure he wasn't missing any steps (of any sort) and total attention focussed on the operation, please. This was meant to be fun – but not for us.

The scenery was great, kids were made a fuss of and there was a brief respite in many a troubled life. Carers were able to let the cabin crew entertain their charges for a bit. Fun and games all round, hard work for me, but I'll always thank Toby for making me do it.

When we got back to the terminal, right on the hour, by the way – I'd had forty years of practice by then – we had an open house on the flight deck. I had to stand at the flight deck door and send the ground engineers away. It was still the kids' time and the engineers could take over when planned but not a second before. Captains are always time Nazis but usually for a reason. These kids were going to get their allotted, and some more, if I could scare enough ground engineers away.

During this time, the flight crew and I were having our chance to interact and enjoy time with the kids and their grateful carers. The kids beamed with open delight at seeing all the whiz-bang TV screens and dials. One girl came in and put her hand on the back of one of the seats in the rear of the flight deck. Her comment, 'Ah, lamb's wool,' was right on the money but I thought it was a strange thing to focus on among all the razzle dazzle – we had all sorts of lights flashing by this stage. I was confused until I suddenly realised that this little girl was blind – she was seeing things through her fingers.

I was hoping I had kept the airsickness rate down and asked some of the medical people. They were happy as, wait for it, the number of seizures was down this year. I wasn't the only one working on this 'joy flight'. As we got off, the rather large crew had their photo taken in the passenger terminal. I made sure to thank the cabin crew on behalf of the Company – they were indeed great ambassadors. I recognised one passenger at this stage. He was in civilian clothes but was a Captain mate who I knew had been the pilot of this special flight in previous years. This year, he had been one of the helpers down the back. I fronted him and asked why he wasn't doing it anymore. His answer was telling – it was too much work and the pilot was always in danger of getting an incident report against him.

Having said this, he just smiled – he knew.

25

LIGHTNING

All pilots get hit by lightning, most while protected by a metal cage. Pilots who do enough flying in the tropics will most likely get zapped at some stage. Lightning strikes are surprisingly common anywhere there are Cbs. 'Cb' is short for Cumulonimbus, those big clouds we know as thunderstorm cells. These monsters are formed when there is a lot of energy about in the form of tropical heat, mix in some tropical moisture and up goes the warm, moist air, literally, and a Cb is formed. Away from the tropics, you get masses of cold air moving around forcing up the warmer, moist air and the same thing happens – a Cb is formed. In both cases, you have to have some 'instability' in the air as well but, once you start getting technical in all this, I suspect you end up with a butterfly flapping its wings in Africa.

So, a storm is brewing. Hot moist air goes up and clouds form when the water vapour condenses into small water droplets. These are usually too small to drop down as rain and are kept up by the rising air that got the moisture up there in the first place. Up the warm air goes until, eventually, it is no longer warmer than the air already there and it stops going up. Simple science says that, because it is now the same temperature, it won't be any less dense so why should it expect to get a hand up from its equals?

Up there, the cloud droplets can move around, bump into each other and form raindrops. Then down they go with a lot of, now cooler, air – remember it's all relative. If the updrafts are strong enough they can be pushed back up to the freezing level and form ice particles. Send these little troublemakers up and down a few times while they collect more water and you have hailstones – not at all the pilot's friends, or anybody else's really.

If this emerging Cb is getting enough 'convectional' heat energy to do some good upping, and therefore downing, of air masses, there will be some rubbing together of bits of water and ice and electrons will start to charge around (sorry!). Electrical differences in various parts of the cloud will emerge and eventually when the Cb enters its 'mature stage', discharges happen. This is called lightning and it occurs because, even in its mature stage, the components of the cloud have never really developed a way of resolving their differences and have resorted to violence. Mind you, the concept of a democratic cloud is up there with mandated support for air molecules – probably never going to happen.

By the way, I am not the first dingbat to talk about weather and politics in the same sentence. Years ago, I found some old notes from a meteorology lecture from cadet days. In discussing the Coriolis force that makes washbasin water spin as it goes down the gurgler and weather patterns spin, I found I had copied down what the lecturer had said, 'Wind is like Government, it only moves as a result of pressure and even then it tends to go in circles.'

I'll refrain from regulating the rain and just go with what is. The internal discharges inside the Cb mean that three out of four lightning bolts occur within the cloud. That still leaves room for the ones we see coming out of the cloud, of course. If there is enough opposite charge on the ground to that in the cloud, down comes a bolt, and sometimes back up the same path and down again. It's all pretty violent and unregulated – sorry, I backslid there, just like the lightning. What happens? Does it get over enthusiastic and send too many electrons down and then calls some back up? All pretty messy, really.

Luckily, what comes down is really high in volts (a billion) but surprisingly low in amperage – relatively anyway. It's like a super high-pressure hose with a very small hole for the water to come out of. The water will spray a long way but the very thin stream won't knock you over like a water cannon will when it hits you. Combine this with the fact that the lightning flash is a series of very short duration pulses that tend to scoot around the outside surface of objects that they hit and you can see why my dad, and a good mate on a separate occasion, survived being hit by lightning. The relatively small amount of current was mostly able to zap around their wet clothes to the ground. Incidentally, the mate who was hit, is named Bolton – I kid you not.

When lightning hits a modern aircraft, it's no big deal. The current is confined to the outside skin and then dissipated to the air – please note, I didn't say 'grounded', to the air. If you look closely at the trailing edges of aircraft wings and tails you will see thin little conductive rods sticking out. These *static wicks* are there to get rid of any build-up of static charge due to the airflow but they also help in getting rid of lightning in the skin.

The metal skin, and this includes the copper mesh imbedded in the new carbon fibre skins of modern aircraft, acts as a 'Faraday Cage' and stops any zappy stuff getting inside to hurt us watery, carbon-based life forms. Delicate electronics are also protected. This is a good thing but sometimes, luckily very rarely, a bit of disruptive voltage sneaks in and a bit of damage is done to radar, radios and the like. If there are vulnerable aerials sticking out then the 'Faraday' is not perfect.

Flying a 767 from Sydney to Melbourne on my first flight after a five-week break, I had my biggest strike, but not my biggest high voltage event, in an aircraft. This particular lightning strike also put me into a pretty exclusive club. The bolt came up and out of the developing Cb and I was hit from BELOW. I'm not sure how many pilots have mismanaged enough to have this happen to them but I thought we were high enough above the clouds and in the daylight there had been no flashes visible within the sucker. With my luck, it may well have been the opening salvo from this brand-new thunder cell.

We had been watching the *build-up* with our radar, of course, and the heavy returns from the water drops inside certainly indicated a volume of our atmosphere that was worth avoiding. Water drops are nothing. Their mates, the hailstones, are something else, but the updrafts and downdrafts are the real danger. We could easily *exceed the G tolerances of the airframe*. That is just 'engineer' speak for we could snap something vital. So we kept well away, or so I thought, from what was not even a mature build up. Nevertheless, there was the characteristic BANG, a little jump, maybe it was just us pilots jumping, and a lot of swearing. The idea of going back on leave was suddenly looking good and I'd only been back at work about an hour. Why the swearing you ask? Well, pilots don't like surprises.

On the ground in Melbourne and the aircraft had to be checked. I went around underneath the aircraft with the engineers and they pointed out the *Morse code* effect on the path the discharge had followed. Little burnt ticks along the fuselage, dit dit dit—dit dit dit—dit—dar. Not enough damage to let air out but they stuck some tape over the worst bits and repaired them later.

I mentioned above the biggest electrical 'event' I saw. A bit of explanation is required because this stuff is not common knowledge since, usually, only pilots get to see St Elmo's Fire. If there is electrical build-up in the atmosphere around the moving aircraft, then static discharges can quite often be seen snaking across the pilots' windscreens. It is like little baby lightning bolts with multiple arms zipping all over the window. Very pretty really, but every pilot now knows that, when this happens, they are in the right place not only for a lightshow but also the right place for a possible lightning strike. Because all things are relative, if the electrified air moves past a stationary object, the same effects can be seen.

Old-time sailors saw these static discharges when thunderstorms caused electrified wind to blow through their rigging. Sparks and little trails of light would splutter and stream above them.

Pretty scary for someone who used a candle to read by – no wonder they called it Saint Elmo's Fire after the patron saint of sailors. Blaming gods for unknown phenomena is not new. Thor was the man when it came to hammering out thunder and lightning on his heavenly anvil. Thunderclouds do quite often form an anvil shape, maybe that's why the ancient Norse went with the Thor hammering idea. All I'm saying is that the scientists who insist the anvil shape is the result of the cloud levelling off and spreading out due to the upper level winds just haven't read enough Viking mythology. Flying in the tropics after sunset when the build-ups are still around is where I saw most of my share of St Elmo's.

Quite often, the cabin crew would fill up the back of the flight deck to enjoy the show.

Another form of static build-up would occur in these conditions especially with the first generation of jets. On a dark and stormy night – sorry – every now and then a glow would form in front of the nose. With the flight deck lights way down low, this white glow could be seen as a dimly lit area moving with the aircraft just in front of the nose – spooky.

It was probably some form of what they call 'ball lightning'. This phenomenon happened rarely, if ever, on the more modern, better 'earthed' aircraft. The old 707s was where I saw it a lot. It happened so often that the old skippers, back in the day, devised a fix. They would just crack the speed brakes a bit, the metal panels on top of the wing would rise a smidgen and a better discharge path was formed. The glow would disappear.

By the time I was flying the 767, seeing this glow was pretty rare indeed. By the way, the glow looks just like the white auroras you see at high latitudes at night. I remember flying underneath a huge array of this moving glow near Antarctica one night – looked like a glowing pulsating cloud. The sun's particles and the Earth's magnetic field can give any thunderstorm a run for its money when it comes to lightshows. The minuscule glow that forms in front of an aircraft is still impressive. One, because it is right there in front of you and, two, because it doesn't feel real and just shouldn't be there.

One night, just south of Singapore in a 767, the St Elmo's Fire had a reasonable audience with pilots and cabin crew watching away. We were in cloud and, while the show was on, both us pilots were actually focusing on the radar screens. The returns were pretty much filling the screen with red, not the preferred colour – actually, no colour is what you want. A blank screen is a good screen and the returns on this cloud had gone from blank to green to yellow to red indicating more or bigger water drops ahead. With probable turbulence ahead, I called an end to the fun and the cabin crew departed as the seatbelt signs went on.

The F/O and I now noticed a glow forming in front of us. Very rare indeed but not yet concerning. What got us more interested, and concerned, were the arms of static electricity that started to branch out from the nose of the aircraft. These stationary lightning bolts seemed about as thick as an arm and just splayed out in front of us as if the aircraft had suddenly sprouted a dozen or so really thick undulating whiskers about ten metres long.

Neither of us twenty-five-year veterans had seen anything like it before. They weren't very bright, like real lightning, but we knew we were looking at one mean display of natural power. It was both awe-inspiring and frightening at the same time and we were mesmerised by the display.

In less than a minute, the arms seemed to start to flare a bit. The natural reaction of both of us was to stop watching and to throw our arms across our eyes and duck down forward under the glare shield. We were expecting one mother of a discharge and, a split second later, we got it. KABOOM and a FLASH which came through our tightly shut eyelids. I don't need to experience a police flash-bang grenade, thanks, I had just seen one. Two somewhat shaken pilots then checked every electrical circuit we could think of but found no problems – the aluminium skin had shielded us from this unusual 'lightning strike'.

Thunderstorms have immense energy. Over their short lives of a few hours, they can generate and dissipate a couple of nuclear bombs worth. These things have to be respected by any pilot and, while their noisy lightshows and hail stones are dangerous, the real danger to aircraft they present is actually silent and invisible. Aircraft flying near, or especially under, Cbs can get caught in the deadly downdrafts which spill out from them. These winds are now called *microbursts*, but if that's what they call them, I'd hate to meet a normal or a big burst. 'Micro' implies small and manageable like a little yappy dog that you just say boo to make it run away. The air masses spilling out from the bottom of thunderstorms are massive and dangerous, not micro.

Imagine flying under a big cloud and suddenly there is a big dump of air straight down – not good. To avoid becoming part of the ground-based scenery, you have to climb very quickly relative to the downward flowing air just to maintain altitude – it's all relative remember. This climbing will only save you if the down rush is not more than the 'up' ability of your aircraft.

You would think this is the worst-case scenario but *microbursts* have another deadly trick up their sleeves that can be even worse. As the air spills down, it gets to the ground and spreads out in all directions. The wind is now coming from the centre of the cloud wherever a distant observer is. When an aircraft starts to fly under a Cb that is *bursting*, it first encounters a headwind as it starts to go below the cloud, then a downdraft, and then, as it starts to exit from underneath, it will encounter a tailwind.

What this all means is that the aircraft is going to struggle to fulfil its function and therefore scare the you know what out of its pilot. The aircraft, as it starts flying under the cloud, initially is flying into a headwind of, say, forty knots. It needs to fly with, say, one hundred and forty knots over the wing to stay up. So it's actually doing one hundred knots relative to the ground.

A short time later the headwind suddenly changes to a vertical downdraft as the aircraft comes under the spilling air. Here's the thing. The aircraft, which was doing one hundred knots over the ground is still doing that, but the wind component over the wings is now zero. Remember, the aircraft needs a one hundred and forty knot relative airflow to keep flying, but all of a sudden this *shear* has produced a forty-knot deficit. Extra power must be applied to accelerate the aircraft to one hundred and forty knots relative to the ground to achieve this.

Hold on, there is also a downdraft and the aircraft must climb relative to this to maintain altitude which takes more power. Let's hope that all the available power is not used up doing this because the final straw is about to be slammed onto the camel's back.

As the aircraft starts to exit from under the cloud, the wind is now becoming a tailwind. This means that, even if the aircraft has accelerated up to its necessary one hundred and forty knots relative to the ground, all of a sudden the relative wind over the wings drops as the tailwind takes effect. If the wind blowing out from the cloud is still forty knots then, suddenly, the poor little aircraft has to provide power to accelerate itself back up another forty knots of airspeed to negate this *shear* as well. By the way, if it achieves this, it's now doing one hundred and eighty knots relative to the ground. Poor little engines providing two lots of acceleration and one climb in a given time frame. Let's hope that the wind shears and the downdrafts don't exceed the acceleration ability of the aircraft.

Fly under a nasty enough microburst and you're cactus. You can give yourself a better chance by having an aircraft with a good power-to-weight ratio. Power to weight determines your acceleration and that is the key to survival. But even the best P/W ratio won't save you if you encounter a big, active enough Cb.

A discussion on lightning has moved onto the real killer, wind shear, and rightly so. Wind shear has killed a lot of people and is the danger pilots have trained for in simulators ever since this very real danger was first recognised. The parameters of the accidents that have occurred are fed into the simulators and pilots get to fight against the elements. This is all to train pilots to do the correct things as soon as possible when shear happens. Aircraft computers now interpret rapid speed and height losses and give warnings. Escape manoeuvres are displayed and actions are practised so that they become instinctive.

Possible areas of wind shear are avoided wherever possible and aviation continues to improve its safety record.

Out in the real world, risks are weighed and approaches made in weather conditions that could turn nasty on you. I flew a 767 two-engine aircraft into the old Kuala Lumpur airport one day under a huge tropical cloud. The air was absolutely still but I was ready for any rapid change and I was glad to be flying a twin jet at its landing weight. The best airline scenario for the power-to-weight ratio is a twin at its landing weight. I explain in another section of this book (P132) why two engines is the way to go. Because of the engine-failure rules, twin-engine aircraft have way more power to weight than their four-engine cousins. This day, flying into Malaysia, I was ready but no downdrafts or shear happened. Yes, there were lightning bolts jabbing out of the sky and blasting into the ground on either side of us but lightning wasn't what we were worried about.

You still have to keep your wits about you flying anywhere near cloud build-ups even if wind shear seems unlikely. Flying a Jumbo into Melbourne years later the weather was relatively clear. I was tracking to a point where I would turn onto *final* approach and I was watching a funny little build-up quite close to the point where I would have to turn onto the runway heading.

No thunderstorms had been reported by the tower and all I was watching was some rain coming out of this cloud. I was making sure we wouldn't enter the rain and lose visibility with the runway since I was doing a *visual* approach and not relying totally on instruments – Orville Wright would have been proud of me.

My concern changed from worrying about the rain when, suddenly, out of the blue, well grey actually, came a vicious lightning bolt which exploded onto an electrical substation underneath. Sparks and fury everywhere and one old, not bold, Captain immediately turned away. Why go there if you don't have to?

My turn away was quick and I keyed my radio and told the air traffic controllers I was turning away and would do a circuit around the airport and approach from the clear side. I didn't have time to get the F/O to make this call for me. The tower cleared me instantly and began telling other approaching aircraft what the Qantas Jumbo was doing and that it might be a good idea if they followed suit. All I did was what any pilot would do, err on the side of caution.

26

NOT ALL THE FUN WAS IN THE AIR

Most training a pilot does is not fun. Challenging, stressful, time-pressured are better ways of describing it. A pilot's training starts with learning to fly and doesn't stop until they retire. The customers expect a totally capable pilot and that's what they get. I had my last simulator session very close to my retirement. As you would expect, I still had to prove my competency.

Every pilot is trained to a high standard but some airlines have a higher standard than others. This is a result of the safety culture of the particular airline or the safety and operational standards set by the airline's regulator. The regulator, not the airline, issues licenses to pilots. The airline does the training and testing but is overseen by the appropriate government department.

A pilot is very aware who issues their license as well as the all-important medical certificate. Doctors who issue certificates to pilots, in turn, have their own sub-branch of the regulator to make sure that they are qualified in the appropriate specialised area of Aviation Medicine (AVMED). The manual issued to these Designated Aviation Medical Examiners, DAMEs, as they are known in Australia, sets out a list of stressors that can arise from a pilot's lifestyle. Pilots *'must be capable of performing all the activities and of exercising all the privileges that are permitted under the class of licence held. Such activities may include flight (either as a private or professional pilot):*

For prolonged duration, often as part of a shift roster Subject to disrupted sleep and time zone changes.

In a variety of weather conditions.

Subject to extremes of temperature, humidity, atmospheric pressure, noise, vibration and acceleration.

Reliant on support services (including provision of food and water) of varying quality and reliability.

With little or no medical/health support.

With the potential for an emergency/mass casualty/survival situation to occur with little or no warning.'

Why did I want to become a pilot again? Oh, that's right – the fun. The last point though, explains the need for a fit, well-trained pilot.

Among all the stressors listed above the heaviest one is not actually mentioned – training, in all its forms, is that mega-stressor. Passing the exams, having check flights, doing regular simulator checks and getting through the frequent emergency days with their competency standards are the things that give pilots nightmares – along with the curries in India consumed just before bedtime.

If a pilot is well trained, both when they first learn to fly and when qualifying in an airline, that is the best defence against a disaster scenario occurring. Pretty obvious. If there is no crash, there is no mass casualty or survival situation to deal with in the first place. It cannot be assumed, however, that you will never come unstuck so you must plan for the worst and airlines must train for it.

Training for the worst involves training for the best. Airlines train their pilots to the highest standard of flying they can but to achieve world's best standard is hard. While ultimately satisfying for the pilot, it is not really fun – it's bloody serious – but, if you work at it, there is occasionally room for fun to be had.

My first experience of emergency ground training was way back as a cadet pilot. The Company had to demonstrate to the regulator that a new configuration of seats was capable of being evacuated in the required time. That meant a whole mob of fit young people, mostly young men, being organised to sit in the cabin of a 707 at Sydney airport one evening. When the starter's pistol went off everyone had to jump out instantly.

If you did this for the Company, you got a voucher for a free meal. We cadets were addicted to two things at the time, beer and food, so this was an opportunity worth jumping at. Not that we really had much choice in the matter. The company wanted a mob of fit young people and we were mistakenly identified as being in that category. Too much beer and food may well have been the problem. My recall of that night was that, when the signal was given, everybody just tumbled out of the nearest exit. Nothing like a real evacuation with older people, incapacitated people, small screaming children and whatever else you would have to deal with in reality. But a box was ticked, and cadets got fed. It wasn't training as such but it was fun.

Once I was on the 707 as a junior pilot, it was actual training and things were serious. We had to demonstrate proficiency in how to handle evacuations on land and sea, put out fires, use oxygen on ourselves and passengers and, if need be, subdue and restrain unruly passengers – over the years, I can assure you, the handcuff–bondage link was done to death. We learnt how to open passenger-cabin doors, deploy slides, prevent access to the doors until the slides were safe and then get the passengers off ASAP.

If doors or over-wing exits were blocked by fire, we were taught to redirect passengers to usable ones. I still remember being taught how to run down the armrests on the aisle seats to get past passenger-blocked aisles. Great fun, not sure what it would have been like for real. All this stuff was physical and practical and, as such, was carried out in cabin simulators or rafts in big indoor pools. We would wear swimming gear under a lightweight pair of overalls. Shoes if it was ground training, bare feet for the wet drills.

Once a year we were checked for proficiency and went back into the ground school, with its pool, for more of this fun. It all happened during an *Emergency Procedures Day* that included the normal refreshers for the emergency equipment and the procedures to be used in any mishap. We were then quizzed on life rafts plus their equipment, door slides, over-wing slides and how to operate doors and windows. By windows, I mean over-wing exits which are small plugs with a window in them. They are pulled in from the wall of the aircraft and people can get out onto the wing. We had to demonstrate our ability to alert the passengers and to get them ready to evacuate while we opened the door or window before directing them to usable exits, remembering that some may be blocked by fire or structural damage.

This stuff and more took up most of the day before a written exam requiring knowledge of all sorts of emergency procedures, location of equipment, first aid, esoteric knowledge – like how long you could stay conscious in an unpressurised aircraft – and a thousand other things I'm glad to be able to let go of now to make room for new stuff. Oh, it may not surprise anyone, but you go unconscious quicker the higher the altitude, although I have seen crew members out cold at sea level but alcohol was usually involved in those cases.

This losing consciousness, when there is not much oxygen around, was demonstrated to me and my fellow cadets long before we got anywhere near flying jets. They took us out to an Australian Air Force base near Sydney and put us into one of those pressure chambers or, in this case, a low-pressure chamber, curiously the same cylindrical shape as high pressure chambers – there is strength in the circle it would seem. Once we were in the chamber, they stuck really cool oxygen masks on us, ones we hadn't seen before, with the nose and mouth covering hanging loose so we were breathing the ambient air.

The Air Force blokes then sucked the air out while we tried to do cognitive things like writing numbers backwards from a hundred on a sheet of paper. I remember starting off alright, no problems, and then coming to with an instructor holding the mask over my nose and mouth as I breathed normally. No slowly losing it, just zonk and you're gone – but there were some peculiar scribbles and numbers on the paper. All a bit scary but that, of course, was the aim of the exercise – scare the young blokes so they might actually remember in the future. Not many, if any, airline pilots have to do this exercise anymore. It does have its dangers, as you might imagine, but we were young and we were having a ball.

Even the medical lecture given in class back at our college was a scream. The nurse was teaching us about artificial respiration but made the mistake of asking the class why we breathed. She was probably looking for an intelligent answer – her first mistake – that involved something about getting oxygen into our bodies. Then she made her second mistake. She asked a couple of my fellow cadets individually.

The first bloke just replied that he breathed because it was a habit he had got into at a very early age. She tried to ignore this and quickly pointed to the bloke beside him and asked him. Unfortunately, this was not her day, because this cadet had been a medical student and he proceeded to give a full anatomical, autonomic nervous system run-down on how one might ingest oxygen, how it got into the blood and what happened next.

In defence, we were bored and it was a long day of lectures. We knew that when the nurse stormed out in disgust, we might not see her again. The medical section got us back though. A day or so later, a senior doctor turned up and gave us a lecture that included some graphic slides. The slides were not of breathing-related stuff but of venereal diseases, and were indeed graphic. This bloke had gone through the medical books and got the stuff you never show patients and zapped us with it.

So, years later, as a junior S/O on the 707, I knew enough to pass the written exams, that was the easy part. Demonstrating my proficiency in the practical exercises had its moments, and I was about to be put back in my place. A few pilots, and a much larger number of cabin crew, both male and female, were lined up in our overalls in the 707 cabin simulator.

This cabin mock-up was a fuselage section ten to fifteen metres long inside a training building. It was set up with normal passenger seats with an aisle down the middle. There were proper aircraft doors at the ends, one opening onto a flat area and the other onto a drop simulating the fall to the ground in a real aircraft. The cabin crew were mostly men a bit older than me and a couple of 'hosties', as female flight attendants were called then. One of these women was pretty short with red hair. I'd married my redhead about this time and I should have known to expect what happened next.

The first exercise involved all but two of us being the passengers and when the pretend emergency happened these 'passengers' were expected to act like passengers, that meant the two unfortunates selected as crew would have to get a basically uncooperative and pretend-panicking group of people out the *usable* exits without letting them open the wrong exits in their panic. Once this was done, the area had to be checked for passengers or children stuck in seats. The two crew had to do all this within a time limit in much reduced lighting with a whole lot of stage smoke just to make it more fun.

Of course, I was selected with the small redhead to be the crew. This sort of selection followed me for the next thirty-five years. On one of my last unarmed combat classes I was paired with a small female flight attendant to demonstrate how a small person could take on a big bloke in a small galley and do some real damage without getting hurt too much. I got a bit physically hurt in the fight but the exercise with the redhead hurt my pride.

The pretend 707 raced down the runway and then boom, we were stopped after coming off the runway, or whatever scenario the instructor/sadists had come up with on the day. They weren't really sadists. They were just trying to make it as real as they could so the training would be worthwhile. Anyway the sadists then poured the smoke in, set off the red lights in the exits where there was fire to make them unusable and dimmed the lights.

This was the signal for the 'passengers' to go apeshit. This was their moment of fun and they were going to make the most of it. They jumped up, yelling as they ran in circles, fell over, got back up, tried to open the exits with fire lapping at them and generally made a real nuisance of themselves. They were actually being paid to carry on like this.

I thought, well okay, I'm the big bloke here. I'm going to have to sort this out. In the split second I was thinking this, a pair of white overalls, topped with red streaming hair, shot out in front of me and proceeded to fix things pretty bloody rapidly. Exits were opened, passengers were dragged away from blocked exits, instructions were shouted, big blokes were being pushed and pulled in all the right directions and I was just admiring all this from a distance. I thought I better get in and help. However, every time I saw a problem to fix the white and red flash was already onto it. Everybody off, areas checked, big dolls simulating unconscious children searched for and found then we both evacuated – significantly, with the red flash holding the doll. I never again underestimated just how well cabin crew were trained and have always been that little bit more wary of my wife.

Fast forward nearly thirty years and there were new aspects to training. Pilots had been getting trained in CRM – Cockpit Resource Management – for some time. This was really a logical way of saying teamwork is important. In the flight deck it meant that, while there was a hierarchy, things got done a lot more efficiently and safely if everyone had the appropriate input into any problem solving. Junior pilots were encouraged to speak up if necessary and senior pilots encouraged to listen and take on board all information.

All of this, you would think, is how it would have always worked. Well, not so much. When the first ground courses in CRM were starting, the main presenter commented to me that there were two types of pilots attending the courses. The first type – the majority – already practised good CRM and didn't actually need to do the course but would enthusiastically enter into the spirit and nitty-gritty of what was being taught. The second group was way smaller. They were the ones still running 'one-man bands' and had little concept of this 'teamwork' thing. They were the ones who needed the training and, of course, said my mate, they were the ones just ignoring the instructors – in one famous case even reading a newspaper during class.

It was only a matter of time before cabin crews would be trained to become part of a bigger team that included the pilots. Again, the more confident flight attendants were already including the pilots in any concerns they had regarding the operation of the aircraft. The classic example of this passing on of a worry was on a flight from Brisbane to LAX towards the end of my flying.

There had been some grinding metallic noise on the climb-out of Brisbane and the CSM – Cabin Service Manager – had been alerted to this by the flight attendants in the forward galley who heard it. The cabin crew were highly encouraged to communicate concerns to the pilots as part of what was now CRM good practice. By this time the 'C' stood for Crew, not just Cockpit. We had moved on. This CSM called and alerted us to the noise. As the Captain on this 747-400, I wasn't about to ignore the information. I went through possible causes, noted the suspected location and reviewed in my mind what control I had over the electrical equipment nearby. This was good. I had time to prepare for a possible problem before it hit and all because CRM inspired teamwork was being used.

The chiller fan did, in fact, crap itself just after we levelled off in cruise. The F/O was just disappearing into the little crew rest at the rear of the flight deck, one S/O was just entering the toilet back there and the other S/O was just strapping himself in next to me.

The first indication was a strong acrid smell bursting into the flight deck. At the same time, the F/O looked forward and yelled, 'Smoke!' Houston, we have a problem.

My preparation now came in handy. I immediately switched off power to various fans and galleys that I knew would probably stop this impending fire from increasing. This was my third electrical fire on a Jumbo over the years and the other two had stopped as soon as the electrical short had been stopped by the removal of the flow of electrons. This third fire responded in the same way – the smoke and smell diminished rapidly. One S/O was sent downstairs to the suspected source and cabin crew were alerted. Meanwhile, the remaining S/O and I actioned the emergency checklist covering this contingency. The actions were exactly what I'd already done about a minute earlier. CRM had saved us a vital minute of burning before we stopped the ignition source – it had taken at least a minute to locate and action the emergency checklist.

Lots of back-up work and checks and we were able to confidently continue the flight. During the cruise, a compulsory wide-ranging enquiry was conducted using a satellite phone conference call. Operational, engineering, safety and medical departments were all involved, this was a modern airline, on top of its game, operating as it should.

The last question to me in this airborne enquiry was, 'When would you like to schedule the crew debriefing in Los Angeles?' Not, would I like too, just when – CRM protocols dictated this must happen. I chose to have the crew assemble in the first-class cabin after the passengers had got off in LAX. This was a *hats on* discussion, meaning it was a formal meeting, from the old navy term for a dressing down. Well, we weren't the old navy and the discussion involved me praising the good work of all involved, especially the cabin manager for his warning.

I also praised the expertise and skill of the S/Os who were instrumental in making sure things were safe in the cabin and how well they calmed the passengers – CRM all round.

This CRM training started for the cabin crews in the nineties, partly as a result of a lack of communication in an infamous crash in the UK where something the cabin crew knew could have helped salvage the situation. The pilots weren't sure which engine had gone pop. Some cabin crew had seen sparks coming from this engine but didn't tell anybody. So, pilots and cabin attendants had to learn to trust each other more and learn how to work together. To achieve this at Qantas, a program was trialled where a couple of Captains would be rostered to attend a two-day cabin crew emergency course and interact. A fellow Captain I had known since the cadet course and I were scheduled and we were going to have a ball. There is always pressure on a Captain when he or she goes to work, but these two days were great – no tests, no marking, no reaching standards, no pressure.

The cabin crew would be working pretty hard to pass their usual yearly checks, so they still had the pressure. The first day included a big exercise to teach CRM basics. It involved the classic 'build a bridge across an imaginary river using teamwork' exercise. This entailed getting information from each member of the 'team' and really asking the right questions. If one member knows where the rope is to hold the pieces of wood together but is briefed to only divulge the whereabouts if asked, then you better ask the right questions of the right people.

The facilitators made the mistake of forming two teams to build two bridges and further compounded the error by putting a Captain into each team. There had been no time limit set but, all of a sudden, the final of the world championship bridge-building competition had just been announced – in the minds of the two Captains anyway.

The chief facilitator was a retired Captain I knew well. He had delegated the two Captains on the course as 'helpers' who would assist if needed but generally just be part of the team. Bullshit. We were off and Captains can always turn on the command thing if needed. Why ask somebody where the rope is hidden in this big gymnasium if it can be found easily by sending out search parties? Why ask how the bridge should be built if it is obvious the stuff collected in the searches will only fit together one way? Why form a consultative construction group when one man can coordinate and build in a much quicker way? Whoops – did I just say one man.

Maybe the teamwork skills weren't being demonstrated as they might. My mate and I were both working flat out next to each other on the riverbank, depicted by a chalk line on the floor. Insults and small bits of equipment were being thrown but we were both making good progress – I mean both teams were making good progress.

We were kneeling beside each other tying knots in rope when the first sign of dissent appeared. Two of the older female flight attendants approached. They had obviously been observing this competition from afar and were totally unsatisfied with what they were seeing. They came up to us, not quite entering into the spirit of what was going on because they actually stood in the river to address us. They looked us straight in the eye and inquired, 'Is it a dick thing?' Neither of us bothered to answer. Of course, it was. Now get out the way.

My blind flight attendant, the person on my team with the blindfold, made it across the rickety bridge seconds before the other team's – a glorious victory. The retired Captain facilitator came up to us as we were shaking hands like the two

Australian open finalists, put his head between us and said two words, 'Fucking Captains!' My mate and I had no idea what he was on about. We had just had some great fun.

In fairness, we were putting in big time in other ways. The other Captain was a senior check Captain and had got his hands on a 767 simulator, one of those up on hydraulic stilts, with big TV screens for the visual effects. He took every flight attendant and gave them a bit of a fly and explained how pilots could get ultra-busy if things happened and that's why sometimes their calls went unanswered. This was all on his own time and he'd pulled in favours to get the simulator availability. The female flight attendants got their own back on me at the end of the second day but that was after the wet drill.

I hitched a ride home with three flight attendants at the end of the first day and was surprised by the concern one was expressing. She had been given the job of 'raft commander' in the wet drill the next day. Most of us would just be passengers but a few flight attendants would act as the crew members on the raft – she was to be the boss. I was beginning to realise that not everybody accepted responsibility easily or were as confident as pilots were expected to be. This course was teaching me stuff as well. My job on the raft the next day was to be a 'helpful passenger' – that is one who doesn't scream and run around falling over.

The wet drill days, with us leaping around in rafts in the dark, were always fun. The sadists were still around and had come up with some new tricks. If you hadn't got the roof and sidewalls up on your raft, you could expect a fire hose worth of water in your face at any time. Fun, if you like that sort of thing. We had, over the years, learnt to climb into these rafts using the strap ladders down the sides. Quite a bit of skill and strength was required and, with a slippery raft, teamwork was actually needed – strong arms always helped in these 'rescues'. Mind you, even if you were just minding your own business, walking around the pool you could suddenly find yourself flying through the air into the pool as a 'mate' accidently bumped you as hard as he could. It was a fun day after all.

This day we passengers were loaded into the raft first. It was actually a *slide-raft*, a combination of the slide attached to the doorway for evacuation and, if there was water instead of ground outside, then, magically, it was an instant raft. The air-filled sides of the slide were its buoyancy tubes. My Captain mate and I had been the first onto the slide-raft and were sent right down to the furthest end – coincidence or a reaction to the previous day or did they just want us out of the way? I asked the other Captain what his role was. He had been assigned the role of an interfering naval officer – this could be bad.

We were all wearing our white overalls and our yellow lifejackets – the designated crew members had orange ones. There were no orange lifejackets down our end of the raft. They were up at the door end unfastening the raft from the aircraft and retrieving equipment. The raft commander was doing alright, delegating collection duties, getting everybody's heads out of the way as the raft was set free from the pretend aircraft, so that nobody actually lost their heads as it dropped at a million miles an hour away from the doorstep. She was a good raft commander.

Up our end of the raft, a female passenger started screaming and yelling and moving around dangerously – she was rocking the boat. In answer to my mate's and my puzzled looks, she broke character for a second and said she was a 'panicking passenger' who had lost her family. When she started screaming again, action was called for. Two Captains just lifted her up and threw her overboard – problem fixed.

Now the Naval officer was getting ready to cause trouble – you could just sense it. The best solution to a problem is to not let it happen in the first place so I threw him overboard as well. It was pretty lonely now down my end of the raft and I was starting to feel a little responsible for what was happening. In an effort to cover my guilt over my part in these proceedings, I threw myself overboard.

The three of us wallowed around a bit – lifejackets can be quite conducive to wallowing rather than swimming – but eventually we decided we should get back aboard the raft and sit quietly this time. After negotiating the strap ladders with many hilarious attempts at 'helping' each other, we were eventually sitting back with all the others – three totally soaked miscreants among a whole lot of dry scowlers. They would inch away from us in an attempt, not only to stay dry, but also to avoid any chance of being associated with us troublemakers.

When the inside of a raft gets wet, a pool of water forms on the floor that moves all around the place with rocking and weight movement. This means that anyone sitting on the floor – which is all of us – gets a wet backside. Hey, if we got wet so should they. The debriefing by the instructor said it all. The exercise had gone well with the assigned crew members doing a good job. That meant the nervous young female flight attendant had impressed as raft commander. He then looked at his notes and at three wet people and said, 'Not sure what was happening down the other end of the raft. Won't bother talking about it.' Just as well, because I was starting to get the hang of throwing people into pools and a sadist hitting the water wouldn't have bothered me in the least.

The medical training was the last activity of the day. This was done in a big room with three rows of three economy seats set up for demonstrating how to help patients in seats. This is where the cabin crew got their own back on a Captain – in this case, me. The medical instructor picked me as the biggest person in the room. No flight attendant is actually allowed to be as tall as me. I was also older than the rest and well into the nineties kilogram wise. I was sent to sit in the middle seat of the middle row and told to collapse and not to move or help in any way. Do absolutely nothing and get paid – a bit like what people actually think pilots do. I was up for it.

The four smallest female flight attendants were told to go for it. They knew what to do and attacked the task with relish. They grabbed a nearby passenger blanket and surrounded me. There was much pushing and shoving of the blanket to get it under me – we won't go into too many details here, but there wasn't much hesitation about how they accomplished this. Eventually, they each had a corner of the blanket weighed down with way over twenty kilograms each. They just had to lift this dead weight out of the seats and get me flat on the floor ready to stick the defibrillator on to me. The defibrillator was the great machine you hooked a patient up to if he or she needed zapping. They managed very well – no spilling anybody onto the floor or anything.

Once on the floor, I was still under instructions to stay still. The cabin crew, realising this, had a great time while one of them was busy preparing the zapper. They had noticed a whole mob of plastic dummies lying around me which would be used for things like chest pumping – something you can't practise on real people. The dummies have movable arms and legs so the flight attendants had great fun placing these all over me in very compromising ways while ensuring I understood I couldn't move. They were having a ball at my expense. What a great bit of fun to be involved in – two days of fun, in fact. Australians can find amusement almost anywhere.

27

FLYING SKILLS

The two Qantas jumbos were approaching for their early morning arrival into LAX (Los Angeles). One was the service from Melbourne and the other from Sydney. They had flown across the Pacific almost in formation in that they were within eyesight of each other from the point where the Sydney service came up and joined its stablemate from Melbourne as that aircraft passed by Sydney. This was, and is, the way it goes. All the company aircraft from the east coast would convoy up to LA and then any passengers going on to New York would join up on one of these Jumbos and off to the Big Apple they would go. This system mostly worked.

Of the two aircraft from Melbourne and Sydney, I was flying the second in line – the one from Sydney. The memorable bit of this flight, however, was the approaches and landings of these two aircraft. Usually on arrival, the approach was done via a very circuitous routing over Santa Catalina Island then across to the California coast and up across Newport Beach to join the final approach. Low and slow and fully controlled by Air Traffic Control – lots of aircraft, lots of sorting to fit them all into the approach sequence. It rankled with pilots that, for twelve hours in cruise, they would finesse their altitude and speed to save every kilo of fuel just to find themselves approaching LAX down in the fuel- sucking lower altitudes flying all over the place following ATC (Air Traffic Control) directions. Thousands of kilos of fuel could be burnt flying away from the airport before being turned back in for the approach.

On the subject of fuel, the lifeblood of any flight; the pilot needs to know how much fuel is on board for two reasons. The first is to know how much weight is being carried around. The second is to know how much fuel is available to burn to do this carrying. Now since both these things are dependent on how many hydro-carbon molecules, in the form of kerosene, are on board then pilots only want to know what weight they are dealing with.

Weight by the way is just the mass with gravity taken into account. Pilots therefore only talk about fuel as a weight, either pounds or kilograms depending on where you are. Whatever you do make sure you know what unit you are measuring in or you will either crash on take- off, because you are too heavy, or have silent engines way before they should be.

The ideal airport approach as far as the pilot is concerned is the one that is the most efficient in the use of fuel. A professional pilot wastes not a drop, to do so makes them something less than professional. On this magnificent Californian morning – definition: light winds with unlimited visibility under a clear sky –both Qantas aircraft were allowed by ATC to try for the pilot ideal for a change. We were so up for it. This morning there was a different approach in use. Instead of the big southern circle route, ATC tracked us straight onto the downwind leg. The downwind leg is a track parallel to the runway but about 4 miles to the side and significantly running in the opposite direction to the landing direction. This means that that at some point you have to do a 90-degree turn, fly 4 miles and then turn back towards the runway. Easy in two dimensions, not quite as easy in the three dimensions aircraft inhabit.

As you pass the runway on this downwind leg, you are going away from the runway at speed and at a specific altitude. The trick is to be able to turn back at just the right distance to give yourself the exact amount of *air miles* to be able to dissipate this speed/altitude energy so that you arrive over the touchdown end of the runway with between 60 and 100 feet of altitude and at the exact landing speed. Air miles can be tricky. They like to maintain their independence from *ground miles* and to do this they like a good strong wind. If, for instance, you fly between two points 100 miles apart and it takes you 1 hour, then you have gone 100 ground miles. If there is a headwind of 50 mph then, in that hour, you have actually flown 150 air miles. As I said, tricky, and then there is the tailwind situation to think of as well. Remember, for an aircraft going in the opposite direction to you, its tail wind is your headwind, (one aircraft's freedom fighter is another aircraft's terrorist.) When you change direction on your approach by 180 degrees, you end up experiencing both cases – even more tricky.

Energy and air miles are the factors in the pilot's calculations – remember, a heavier aircraft will have more energy as well – and he or she better get it right or the dreaded waste of fuel will occur. Allow too many air miles and you end up pouring on the power to push the extra air out of the way to get to the runway; don't use enough and you are too fast or high to land and you have to *go around* and have another go at the cost of at least 5 tonnes of fuel (lots of litres.)

Two Jumbos, two Captains flying them and the friendly Yank on the radio was being very obliging. He knew that pilots hate flying even one air mile more than necessary. He said to my mate in front as he was flying on this downwind leg, 'Qantas 93 cleared own turn in, cleared final 24 left.' This meant the Captain could use his judgement and turn in when he reckoned he could do his perfect approach. He did exactly that. Me? I was ready when a few minutes later I got the same clearance. Never let a chance go by.

The ATC controller was watching his radar like a hawk, of course, keeping an eye on how our approaches were going – he wouldn't pass either of us over to the tower until he was sure that we had nailed our approaches and didn't need to *go around* into the crowded skies above. The Captain from Melbourne did a good job. I know this because the controller complimented him with, 'Good job Qantas, call tower 133.9.' When I came around the corner onto final right on the numbers (correct speed, distance appropriate altitude) I got the, 'Excellent job Qantas, call tower 133.9.' Excellent! The competition with a workmate was always on – boys will be boys.

As I came over the fence, I noticed the Melbourne Jumbo taxiing back on the parallel taxiway very close to my intended touchdown point. I'd better not stuff up the landing, the boys in that aircraft would have the best view on the airport. The conditions were, as I said, perfect and it went on as smooth as it can get. In the customs hall, we met the other crew and their F/O asked who did our landing – they were impressed. I couldn't help it, I gave a little nod and then said, probably unnecessarily, 'I got an "Excellent job Qantas" as well.' These blokes were ready for this sort of stuff of course, I was told exactly where I could put it – I miss the mateship of customs halls.

Keeping skill levels up for the bragging rights over some mates is one thing, having them there for when peoples' lives depend on them is another thing altogether.

Peoples' lives depending on pilot skills is a given. I'm talking about those, thankfully rare, occasions when the brown stuff hits the fan and the pilot has to get his or her act together to try and fix it or at least help. Again, one hour from Los Angeles on another beautiful morning and I was on the radio declaring a *Pan* emergency. *Pan* is one level below *Mayday* and I was declaring to ATC that something was wrong and I would really like some help.

About an hour earlier, a woman passenger had collapsed into her seat. Luckily this was noticed and the cabin crew had got right onto it. A doctor was nearby and, with his help, first aid and diagnosis was started and the passenger, now patient, was stabilised a bit using the oxygen mask. I was informed, of course, and asked to receive continuous updates, this was not just 'nice to know' information, it was vital for me to organise the appropriate level of medical help on the ground and time was important. As we got closer, the doctor helping downstairs asked to see me as he was obviously concerned and wanted to get his message across directly. Once he told me it was vital to get the woman on the ground and into proper emergency care ASAP, I had no choice, the operational aspects of the flight entered the semi-emergency *Pan* phase and a medical emergency was declared to ATC.

ATC have their protocols and an ambulance with a specialist crew was called to meet the aircraft at the gate. ATC then cleared me for a high-speed, short as possible approach. I was allowed to go where I wanted to get to the runway and to go as fast as I could. Those piloting skills that we loved practising were to be used in earnest this time. The mission was to get on the ground as quickly as possible but that meant achieving that without getting too fast and having to do a missed approach which would require another attempt at landing. It would take a lot of extra time if I fucked it up and that was not the aim at all. So down I went, fast as I could, cutting corners where possible and watching my *descent profile* like a hawk. I was ensuring I would make it down to the touchdown point at the right speed.

All went well, no mistakes, and I reckon I did one of the quickest approaches ever seen from a Jumbo into LAX. Not boasting here – I just happened to be the bloke tasked on this particular day, any proper pilot would have done the same. A reasonably quick taxi to the gate and I noted with satisfaction, as the parking brake went on, that the ambulance was pulling up at the stairs going up to the aerobridge that was now attaching itself to the aircraft. A few seconds later, the paramedics were sprinting up the stairs with all their equipment. The timing was perfect – yes, very satisfying.

This wasn't the only time an ambulance pulled up at the gate at the same time as I did. The other time had been a few years earlier in Perth, Western Australia. I was the Captain of a 767 coming over from the eastern states when we had a very similar incident. The woman this time collapsed onto the passenger beside her and fate decreed that he just happened to be a senior diagnostic physician attached to Perth's largest hospital. If you're going to collapse, try to arrange this if you can, it really makes a difference. He got the woman out onto the floor and started to resuscitate her instantly – there were no signs of life apparent at the start.

The 767 was nearing the top of descent point when I got the urgent message from the back. Get us to an ambulance now! Perth isn't LAX and the chances of fifty or sixty aircraft being in the way really wasn't there so I really didn't have to declare an emergency. An ambulance was ordered, with an emphasis on speed conveyed. No good getting the woman to the airport terminal just to wait fifteen minutes for an ambulance to drive up without its siren blaring. ATC then gave me 'medical' status and I was cleared to do the fast straight-in approach this time as well. Again, high speed all the way down and an eagle eye on the descent path. There was a decision to be made as to which runway to use. This depended, of course, on the wind. The runway assigned was the duty runway and did have a headwind on it. Since the terminal was midway along the runway, there would be a taxi of about an equal length with either landing direction, I just went with the flow, literally.

After the steep, fast and short approach, I touched down and jumped on the brakes less roll out meant less taxi distance back. Once on the taxiway, I broke the norm again as I got the little 767 moving way above the usual speed. Taxi speeds are kept down for a variety of reasons: other aircraft, corners, and brake temperatures being the main ones. Other traffic is obvious, going around corners in a vehicle totally not suited for cornering is also obvious but hot brakes is not so obvious.

Aircraft brakes get hot whenever you have to apply them. That's what the multiple disc brakes do; they take the energy of motion and convert it to heat. Since the energy of motion goes up by the square of the speed, then doubling your speed gives you four times the energy; four times your usual speed and you have sixteen times the energy. When you put the brakes on, up go the brake temperatures. This is no biggie for the brakes and wheels which are made out of hard strong metals. The tyres, however, are just rubber filled with nitrogen – not as tough as they think they are – get them too hot and the pressure from the hot nitrogen will make them burst. This is dangerous. Bits of exploded rubber shooting around like shrapnel can kill ground engineers or pilots walking past the hot wheels. To prevent this, there are plugs that melt and let the pressurised nitrogen out before bursting temperature is reached.

It is embarrassing for a pilot to mismanage the brake energy and melt the plugs. An aircraft with flat tyres stuck out on a taxiway is hard to hide and hard to hide from. I was now going to have to strike a compromise; taxi fast with already hot brakes from the landing but do it without melting any thermo plugs. The temperature indicators for each wheel were rising and I knew it. There is always a big time lag with the indication and really, just after landing, all you can do is try to access the rate of rise to give you a clue as how bad it will end up.

I did taxi at way above normal speed but kept my big feet off the brake pedals as much as I could. By the way, a heavy aircraft bouncing up and down on a bumpy taxiway also increases tyre temperature – you have to be careful of that as well. After taxiing at the taxiway record speed – it probably still stands – I eased on the brakes and came to a stop at the gate. Same thing as in LA, the ambulance arrived at our nose as I came to the stop. I'm betting the ambulance driver is still claiming credit for timing his arrival to exactly when the aircraft pulled up. I don't care who gets the credit, a woman's life was in the balance and the driver and I had done our best.

Thinking about all the incidents I had with passenger illness over the years, it's sad to realise that only on one occasion did I find out about the outcome for the passenger. The system wasn't set up to provide feedback to anybody who didn't need to know. I always took the 'glass half full' approach and assumed things worked out well.

The arrival of Covid 19 has brought back a virus memory from the early 2000s. A memory of one of the hardest situations I ever had to deal with during my career. At the height of the SARS (severe acute respiratory syndrome) epidemic in the early 2000s, we had a passenger come down with the classic symptoms. We were returning to Australia from a very infected area and the passenger had been in that region for some time.

He was immediately isolated, as much as possible, by placing him in one corner of an economy section. All the other passengers were moved away and, indeed, he ended up being the only passenger in the whole section. Now it came down to making the decision as to who should look after him.

I remember being in the cabin with the cabin manager, who was very eager to pass the buck to the captain when it came to deciding who the carer should be. It was logical that the female flight attendant who had already dealt with him should continue doing so. I took her and the manager aside and explained my decision. It was a decision based on logic and practicality but it also put a young woman's life at risk. The captain's role is demanding at times and this was one such time. Of course, the demand placed on me was nothing compared to the demand I placed on the young woman.

Once we were on the ground in Sydney, medical staff came on board, covered from head to toe in full protective suits – clothing the young flight attendant did not have during her time with the patient.

I sent in a report praising her work and recommended the highest recognition for her dedication to duty. Again, I never heard anything back from the company about either the suspected SARS patient or the flight attendant.

28

LONG-DISTANCE FLYING

Long-haul flying has its peculiar properties and they all have to be taken into account before you blast off merrily towards the other side of the planet. Take off with enough fuel to carry the aircraft and its payload to your destination and you would end up landing, or ditching, somewhat short of where you wanted to be. You would have failed to take into account the amount of fuel it takes to carry the fuel. Any advanced pilot has to do courses in flight-planning and pass the exams – so many things have to be taken into account to get from A to B. Fuel to get somewhere good to land is the key. By this I mean, it's no good arriving somewhere with plenty of fuel just to find the airport unusable. That can lead to landing, by definition, somewhere unsuitable – see earlier references to land and ocean.

So, now we are getting somewhere. Isn't that the aim in all this? Anyway, we are getting there. If we have a suitable airport to land at – you ready for this? –they are called *suitable airports*, and enough fuel to achieve this flight – you guessed it – is *flight fuel*. The rest of the stuff is all add-on. Suitable airports must, of course, have suitable weather at your arrival time otherwise they aren't suitable. We are now getting down to definitions of what a suitable airport is. I won't bore you with what levels of weather are allowed and for how long such suitable weather must be forecast either side of your ETA. Suffice to say, it all gets complicated even without *acceptable* and *usable* airports around just to confuse things.

When you take off on a long-haul flight, these airports are so far away in time that the weather forecasts have use-by dates that expire before you get to them. Weirdly defined airports without valid weather forecasts are the domain of long-haul flying. When you take off on a long-haul flight, you do so on the proverbial wing and a prayer and you'd better have all sorts of *contingency* plans for all sorts of possible scenarios. What happens if a donk shits itself here? What happens if a window blows there and you end up flying unpressurised in the thick air at low level? Is there enough fuel to get to an *emergency* airport? After all, three engines burn way more fuel than four – if you don't want to fall out of the sky, that is. What if you are over the back of the Himalayas on the *Silk Road* route and you have a mask-dropping event or an engine fail and you can't actually descend very far?

Those mountains are high. There are a lot of add-ons but they are just add-ons. Food, water, crew hours, airport hours, fire truck availability, airspace restrictions, electronic airport aids serviceability, aircraft serviceability, pilot fitness – on and on goes the list of add-ons. Believe it or not, empty toilets are a big factor. The preparation for these long flights and, to a lesser extent the shorter ones, is important and lengthy. Pre-flight duties of the pilots include the *paperwork* where all of the above, plus factors like flight-planning, fuel-ordering, weather analysis, aircraft weight and balance and routing problems are all taken on board – well, into account. Actually, a huge amount of paperwork does end up going on board. Captains sign for a lot of stuff in the briefing office and on the aircraft. Check out a

Captain and see just how fast they can do the signature – takes years to get it so quick.

One add-on you see in long-haul is passenger issues. In other parts of this book I have described a couple of pre-flight passenger interactions. There were many more, as you might expect, in my nearly forty years of globetrotting. While some passengers were too drunk or sick to travel, others were really desperate to get onto the aircraft and get home.

One evening I was the F/O on a flight out of Bombay. The crew were squeezing through the crowded Bombay Airport terminal when the Captain I was with was grabbed by a distraught mother with a baby in her arms. She made sure she got the Captain's attention by grabbing him by his tie. Long ago pilots' ties became breakaway ties for just this reason. No good fighting someone and providing your opponent with a choking device free of charge. The crying mother knew, as we did, that our aircraft was full but she was desperate to get her sick child back to Australia. The Captain eyeballed me and shouted, 'Paperwork!' It was so crowded and noisy he had to shout this order twice. He went with the mum and the S/O and I departed to briefing. The Captain took about forty-five minutes to heavy the ground staff into getting this desperate couple on board. Just on this point, why people think it's cool to travel the Third World with babies and young kids I'll never know. I've seen too many really sick youngsters a long way from any decent medical care.

Later, as a Captain, I had to be *route checked* from Singapore to London as part of the changeover checks for the 747-400s. The check pilot and I were walking through the Singapore terminal on our way to briefing. Cue distraught woman confrontation. On this occasion, she was a European flight attendant desperate to get home after being stuck in Singapore with all flights full. She stopped us and the *checkie*, a good mate by the way, sized up the situation and instantly handed the problem over to me – way easier to do the paperwork. As he told me later, he also thought that I should get back into the swing of long-haul with all its problems. I had been hiding from really long-haul prior to this check flight having just spent fifteen years flying closer to home on the 767. Anyway, the flight attendant made it to Europe and I was given a refresher in all those long-haul add-on differences that I hadn't really missed.

Long-haul in the Southern Hemisphere quite often involves going near, or over, Antarctica. After I retired, for instance, my wife and I took a cruise down to Antarctica from South America and promptly ventured even further south than the ship had gone on our flight home. Such is the result of great circle flying. Great circles are no mysteries. The equator is a great circle, the Greenwich Meridian is a half great circle from the North Pole to the South Pole. Any two points on the Earth's surface can be joined by a segment of a great circle. Just get a globe and join the points up but you have to do it on a globe not a flat map. The Earth is not flat – sorry, *Flat Earthers*, it's not. If you use a bit of string and pull it tight the great circle segment will be formed. All great circles have the centre of the circle at the centre of the Earth. These great circle segments are the shortest distance between two points on the Earth's surface, that's why we use them and that's what makes them 'great'.

What this means is that if you want to fly from Buenos Aires to Sydney, which is a very long way, then you fly the great circle that takes you down over the ice. This was what I was about to do one really hot South American night but not before I and my tech crew had some fun and games we would rather have done without. All the pre-flight planning had been done. The weather on the East Coast of Australia and in New Zealand checked out.

These places were a long time away but we would update weather forecasts in flight and land where we could – hopefully in Sydney. I wanted to go home but only if Sydney was suitable – that was the law.

We were also watching the crazy weather at the Buenos Aires airport from where we were about to take off. Wind changes were starting to happen as a cool change, that is a weather front, passed over the airport. This made it hard to choose which runway to use.

The two factors that would help with our maximum weight take-off would be a strong headwind and a cooler temperature. Headwind meant free airspeed over the wings and a cooler temperature meant more dense air over your wings, the equivalent to more free airspeed. Cooler temperatures also meant better performance from the four jet engines ready to convert chemical energy into kinetic and potential energy to get us to Sydney.

That's what they do, these monsters, and they have to be able burn the fuel at a prodigious rate to achieve this – we weighed over four hundred tonnes. They would get bloody hot inside and, at take-off, I knew there would be four very hot fires sitting under wings filled up with 185 tonnes of kerosene. (Over 230,000 litres or 61,000 US gallons). A lot of stored energy and four ignition sources nearby ready to release said energy, almost instantaneously, if things went pear-shaped.

Thirty-five degrees Celsius at midnight with a vicious wind and temperature change expected when the front hits. The hotter the temperature before the change, the stronger the winds when it arrives with big quick swings in wind direction. On more than one occasion, I have sat on the ground and watched a front pass over an airport. Wait until things calm down and you get closer to the *Old* pilot status all pilots eventually choose over the *Bold*. This night we were fooled. The wind changed so that it blew straight down a long runway and, although the temperature hadn't dropped much, things looked suitable for take-off.

We took off, watching the engines like hawks. They were being asked for everything they safely had to give and we were certainly not being blasé about anything.

A diversion here to explain what pilots train for: the worst possible case is what they train for and simulator sessions are full of engines misbehaving at lift-off. The aircraft is at minimum flying speed and you have minimum altitude at the beginning of a flight.

Remember all my earlier ravings about energy? This stage of the flight is when the aircraft has the minimum energy for flying – minimum kinetic and zero potential. If you then go and reduce the input of this sorely needed commodity by having an engine failure – not good.

On this occasion we didn't have a failure but one of these energy converters misbehaved at this crucial stage by getting a little over enthusiastic. We became aware when one of the temperature bars on the engine screens turned red exactly on lift-off – not a good colour anywhere on any screen. One of the four fires had got too hot and we had to sort it, and soon. This is what I'd trained for.

I was flying the aircraft. The F/O was monitoring both the flying and the engines and the S/O sitting between but slightly behind us was doing the same. These blokes knew the score. It wasn't good, and they called it, 'Over temp number three!' The aircraft computers knew the score. They not only turned things red but actually wrote on the screens for us,

'Over temp No. 3.' I just muttered the compulsory expletive under my breath.

This is where our old friend Murphy decided to enforce his law. Aircraft don't like windshear – see my earlier explanations (P219) concerning its impact while flying low near thunderstorms or near windy airports. Murphy decided to bring some strong wind changes into this evening's entertainment. Being Murphy, he introduced these at the worst possible time – exactly the same time the *over temp* hit.

Wait a second. There is no Murphy, or deity, responsible for any of this. It's just physics and applied science. We know what causes wind fronts. We know what we're doing with big powerful engines and we just needed to take ownership of the consequences of fooling around with these things.

I did take ownership. That was my role and the reason I got paid. I would have to *manage* the situation which is where training and experience kicks in. Hoping and praying just wasn't on the agenda. The gusty turbulence that hit us was the hidden wind changes just above the ground of which the benign wind on the ground had given no indication.

Turbulence is one thing – we were experiencing enough to drop the wings twenty to thirty degrees off the horizontal in both directions and the airspeed was starting to waver – but windshear is another thing altogether. Having seen vicious windshear, I was acutely aware that, if I suddenly went into a bit of sky with less relative headwind, it would mean a loss of airspeed and, with no more power available to get it back up, I would have to trade altitude for speed, that is, trade potential for kinetic energy. We didn't have much altitude – we were still bloody low.

Back to the *over temp*. A bad and prolonged *over temp* can result in a failure of turbine blades, complete loss of thrust and the possibility of engine disintegration. This is called a *catastrophic* engine failure. No one wants to be near a catastrophe. This night I glanced, for the very short time I could look away from the flight instruments, especially the speed and altitude readouts, and noted that the temperature was in the red but not by much. The engine wasn't going to go bang. The fix for an *overtemperature* is pretty simple, reduce the amount of fuel so there is less fire. Basic science stuff again but science will also tell you that less fire means less energy and I might need every bit I had available if the *shear* went pear-shaped.

The F/O put his hand up on the thrust lever of the hot engine. They were my thrust levers. I was the pilot flying and I had control of them even though my hand wasn't on them at this stage because I had both hands on the control wheel. He wouldn't have pulled the engine back to get the temperature down out of the red until I ordered it and checked he had the correct lever in his fingers. He was just getting ready and maybe doing that quiet managing up thing by gently reminding me there was an action needed – subtle bastard.

My mind had gone into emergency mode. I was in that total concentration mindset you must be in when flying aircraft at various critical times. I saw this thrust-lever-grabbing and said, loudly enough to be heard I can assure you, 'Leave it. I need it.' I was applying a compromise. Maybe damage an engine but maintain maximum power. Risk a slight chance of escalating the overheat against keeping a safety margin with the power. I was being paid but not enough.

About twenty seconds into all this, the wind variations and turbulence settled down at last – not much *shear* at all as it turned out. Now the climb was starting to resemble all the rest I'd done on these magnificent 747-400s, so it was the time to call for the thrust reduction. Carefully monitored thrust reduction and the red went away and all engine indications came back to normal.

Management didn't end there, of course. We had a long, great circle extravaganza ahead of us and we'd just had a donk go red. This was where modern technology came into play. Satellites, computers and satellite phones all proved very handy. Qantas engineers had been watching everything from a little control centre somewhere in Sydney, where they were linked with our aircraft. By the way, jet-engine manufacturers have their own monitoring rooms – all very 'big brother'. They watch most jet engines operating at any given moment – literally tens of thousands of engines that will trigger an alert on a screen if any go a bit silly.

The option of returning to Buenos Aires was, of course, the default. This would have meant dumping a hundred and forty-odd thousand litres of hydrocarbons into the atmosphere to lighten the Jumbo to its maximum landing weight. Yes, aircraft can be light enough to fly but too heavy to put on the ground – all to do with the forces the airframe experienced if you banged it on when landing.

I could land these aircraft like the proverbial 'cat pissing on glass' but, unless you had a dire emergency, you had to comply and not land overweight. Is a cat doing anything to glass relevant? I don't know. This was a saying about smooth landings and I went along with it. Oh, don't get me wrong here. I, and probably every 747 pilot, could land these aircraft smoothly but I could also bang it on – very occasionally.

The engineers in Sydney came good. As we rang them on our climb, they were watching the incident that had occurred with our engine on their screens. They actually had way more relayed data than we could access and could see exactly how hot things had got and how long the exceedance had gone on for. I was very pleased when given the all clear – very slightly over the limit as far as the temperature went and the engineer on the phone almost scoffed at the small amount of time I'd let it run high for.

The engineers went into their safety protocols and deemed the engine completely safe to use over the ice. We flew home with no problems. The engine stayed in Sydney for an hour or so and then went on to London. My decisions had been vindicated. When you have signed, with one of your very fast signatures, for a *serviceable* aircraft and then bring it back broken, the first bloke they look for is the owner of the signature – as Captain you're responsible.

29

THE THREE-CARD TRICK

If there is one thing that unites the world we live in, it's the three-card trick. I've seen it all over the world for decades. It's an enlightening insight into the society around it. I will give you three different examples from three different cultures First the trick. It involves the trickster, and maybe a team to help him, plus a cardboard carton or a wooden crate to put the cards on. Two small-value cards and a court card, usually a queen, are flipped over then tossed around the board. You win by picking where the queen ends up. You cannot win unless the card sharp lets you and even then you've probably lost your wallet to the pickpocket who uses your joy at winning as the distraction they needed. That is not the only reason for a team. They are there to pretend to be fellow tourists and to get you take your money out. Hey, the nice-looking lady with the big camera just made a few dollars surely I can. Big teams even have multiple lookouts since this scam is illegal in most places.

I first saw the trick in London in the early seventies. I enjoyed walking around central London doing a bit of touristy stuff but I also liked to get off the beaten track and the sleazier the area the more interesting I found it. Soho was just the right mix – interesting bookshops and cafes plus a bit of street life. So, there they were. A group of people milling around a card sharp obviously having a good time and, what's this, someone just won a fiver. A fiver back then was a lot of dosh to a bloke who had only been given ten or fifteen pounds to buy beer and food for the three-day London stopover. So little mister greedy pants now became part of the audience – winners all no doubt because the card sharp was obviously inept. I was really smart though. I didn't jump straight in, I watched for a while to pick up on any scams. So this crowd of about eight or ten people were all blokes, mostly young and a bit scruffy. I fitted right in.

I watched as other guys picked the same card I did and won the money that I didn't because I was still sussing out this new source of income. This happened enough times that I thought I'd better get on board the gravy train before the hopeless card sharp gave up and went home. Did I twig to the fact that the people winning were the card sharp's brothers and cousins? Of course not. I was a hick from the suburbs. In fact, one of the few places I haven't encountered this trick is in my hometown, Melbourne. By now I'd built up enough courage to get some money out and about six pickpockets had noted where I kept my wallet, the farce was about to unfold.

Suddenly, before any money was lost, mayhem broke out. The scruffiest young bloke in the crowd, with at least a four-day growth on his face and a cheap leather jacket, suddenly swooped around to the back of the cardboard box. To me this was like someone jumping up on the stage during a performance – absolutely the wrong thing to do. It would never have happened in Melbourne. He not only broke theatrical etiquette, he broke all rules of good manners by applying a vicious headlock on the card sharp. Total surprise followed as this scruffy thug said, with a very upmarket English accent, 'Come along with me please, sir. You're under arrest.' All this was disconcerting enough but what happened next in the little crowd really flummoxed me. At least three gang members were grabbed, flattened or headlocked as other plain-clothes coppers did their thing.

Well, fight or flight? I certainly wasn't going to fight anybody, so I hoofed it. A much surprised young man decided to wise up a bit. At some point I could well have been the only non-actor in what was quite a large theatrical production – 'street smart' was not a term that applied to me. Fitting, I suppose, that all this went down in the shadow of some of the oldest working theatres on the planet.

A few years later and after a some more encounters with this trick in different places around the world, I came across a game in operation in Athens. This time I was determined to get close to it for the first time since London. I was in Athens on a longish five-day layover and my wife was with me. I was going to show my wife the scam and then we would run away. I had learnt that this was what you did, you certainly didn't partake and you went early before the mayhem.

We were in the centre of Athens in the park near the parliament, close to where the Greek army guards in their tutus goosestep around with the pom poms on their feet – by the way, recruiting for the Greek army must be the hardest job in the world. The game had been set up in a corner of the park on this lovely warm evening and money would be made. I pointed the game out to my lovely and we started to walk over for a closer look. As we started to move, I noticed an elderly Greek gentleman on a park bench watching us. He seemed concerned and was looking towards our destination. This bloke had been around and had obviously developed some street smarts. He knew what was about to happen and he was going to do something about it. He was between us and the game but a little to one side.

This elderly Greek was a man on a mission. He struggled to get up off the bench and, once up, nearly fell back down, his walking stick just preventing this. Once up, and semi-mobile, he moved on an intercept course with us. By now I was beginning to suspect what he was up to. This bloke was going to look after the innocent tourists. He stopped us. No English, of course, so it was all Greek to me (sorry). The walking stick was thrust out to emphasise his point that no amount of me thanking him in Greek was actually going to get us past him. My wife and I beat a retreat and the moment was over. Greeks are like this, mostly, and I just filed this experience away in the ever-building memory of how great people can be all over the world.

How great people can be, indeed. So how would you classify this little experience? In the nineties, I spent a bit of time in Nagoya, a Japanese city with not a lot going for it except that it was a Japanese city. They are always interesting and full of surprises and if you don't enjoy the strangeness and differences, you just aren't trying. I was trying on one Nagoya stopover. I'd found out how to get to visit a huge Toyota assembly plant in nearby Toyota City – I kid you not. This huge complex of Toyota factories and houses was a short train ride out of Nagoya and I was determined to see the marvel that was Japanese manufacturing first hand. Globalisation hadn't yet shifted a lot of car production out of Japan and I was going to see what made Japan great. I learned a huge lesson in Japanese politeness and manners.

I had got myself to the correct rail station and then onto the appropriate local bus. The entrance to the factory was at two hundred yen. The Japanese had developed a method of measuring distance in money – very clever. As I got into the bus, I told the driver my destination – Toyota and the number of fingers for the number of the factory seemed to work. I paid my money and all I had to do then was wait for the money counter above the driver's head to reach two hundred yen and I was at the right stop. It was drizzling this day but I knew there was only a short walk to the entrance from the stop so I wouldn't get too wet.

As the counter hit the destination price, I was ready to go. The driver made a special effort to alert me and a young woman on the bus said, 'Toyota,' and something in Japanese and pointed up the hill to the gates. She got off the bus at the same stop and offered to share her umbrella with me for the short walk. Very nice of her. We walked in silence for a minute or so – two people, two languages, two cultures. I managed to thank her in Japanese at the gate. I used the more formal version as she had been very helpful. I even said goodbye properly. I ran the last bit to the covered door and it was there, while waiting for the tour guide, that I suddenly twigged. After we parted, the young angel turned back the way we had come. I did a quick run out to the gate and looked. There she was at the bus stop, standing under her umbrella, waiting for the next bus.

Back in those days, India had to be seen to be believed. I spent quite a few layovers in Bombay (Mumbai) and had a real eye-opener on my first visit. I had arrived at dawn after a trip where I, as the S/O, had done most of the HF radio work, scratchy hash-filled frequencies with multiple calls *stepping* on each other was the norm on these radios.

Bombay control seemed to have weak transmitters and receivers and was just a real pain to try to communicate with. When I got there and was driven through the early morning streets, I could see that this country had way different priorities as to where it spent its money, HF radios were down the list and you could understand why. People sleeping and living on the streets everywhere and, when I say living, that involves all aspects of toilet use as well. The poverty, the filth, the stench and the squeeze of people was just overwhelming. India was an acquired taste but I did eventually develop an appreciation of the people and how they coped.

Fast forward a few years and I was with a new pilot on his first visit to India. I took him on a walking tour of Bombay and showed him the streets. He was overwhelmed, as expected – people lying down on the side of the road ready to die who would only accept donations to pay the body collectors. There was a special place they would be taken after death to be dealt with by the vultures.

The young bloke from Adelaide was taken aback and was ready to intervene when a beggar got too close to a corporate building and the stick-wielding security blokes had him screaming in pain. I had to hold him back to prevent this rough justice spreading to us – we walked on. When we came to the 'thieves market' we stopped and watched in awe. This was a huge area with tens of thousands of people, mostly young men, selling everything, and then some, to anybody who'd buy. One row of small shops sold clock parts, another used watches, others clothes – on and on it went.

Ten thousand poor Indians and two rich white blokes – it's all relative. We were the only non-Indians around and had been for hours. My mate expressed a derisive view of all this – it was not First World stuff. So, I decided to pass on what I'd learnt. I asked him how many young Indian blokes with no money he could see and how many coppers. The answer was correct – ten thousand and none. I asked him how many white guys with a month or two average Indian income in their pockets he could see. Two was correct – just us. Last question – are there any small groups eying us off, any pickpockets sidling up behind us, any sign at all really that we're in any danger? He was surprised when he realised that no, there was no threat. Now reverse the situation and put two incredibly wealthy Indians in a poor, unpoliced Australian marketplace and ask them how they feel.

Indians had learnt to live together and nonviolence was a help. Don't get me wrong, bad stuff still goes down, just not as much as you would expect. I told my mate that I had seen Indians trick money out of people but not with using violence.

I still show people how they should always have money counted out into a pile of notes and not count a fanned-out bunch of notes. During the Middle East Yom Kippur war in the early seventies, I was stuck with a crew in New Delhi for a week or so as the airways closed up. We had to change money on the black market and I recall having watched a steward get fleeced on the street one day. With one or two notes folded over and then cleverly placed to hide the fact that that the folded notes were being counted twice in the fan is how it was done. The steward, and I swear it wasn't me, did the deal. He carefully counted the fanned-out money and, as the street dealer departed, did a quick recount and discovered the shortfall. We looked back at a football crowd of street vendors and no money changer anywhere. No coppers anywhere, a million poorer people (financially only) and two isolated white blokes with obvious money. Tricks, yes, but no robbery with menace or violence.

Walking back along the waterfront in Bombay, after a few hours with the new pilot, I spied a street cricket game in progress. A mob of ten young blokes were having some real fun under a bridge. These Bombay street cricket matches are not to be taken lightly. One time, I saw one develop from a mere dozen kids to about a hundred in only a few minutes when I and the flight steward I was walking with, joined the original game. The word had got around that there were two Aussie blokes playing and for a few moments in a street kid's life, the chance of playing internationally against the great foes, the Aussies, was there in real life. Never let a chance go by. The steward, who actually played for the cabin crew team, and I couldn't get away for hours, every kid had to bowl and then bat against us, exhausting in a backstreet lined with rubbish bins.

Back to the game on the waterfront. It was being played on a nice walkway under a bridge – no street kids here. As we approached, but still probably a hundred metres away, the cricket game stopped. Our alert radars flickered to life – something was up. What replaced it was a fully functioning three-card set-up – wooden crate, cards – and suddenly all these strangers were trying to win money off a card sharp they had never seen before. The card sharp, who looked exactly like the last batsman, was a totally different guy. I told my mate what was going down, or what was up, make your own choice, as we ambled up to the game. There was no way past. They had chosen a choke point on the path and used the bridge tactically as well.

We had no wallets and only a certain amount of cash, necessary precautions on these streets, but we had a plan for dealing with any unforeseen eventuality. These guys could have stopped us, waved their cricket bats around a bit and asked for a 'donation' had they wanted to. They chose instead the three-card trick. Then it was on – hilarious attempts to show us how easy it was to win money off the dipstick with the cards. As these attempts got more frantic, the more we laughed with them, not at them – there were ten of them, after all, and they did have bats, so we kept it friendly.

After quite a while of frustration for the scammers and much laughter on both sides, they began to realise that we were streetwise – more than I had been in London – they weren't stupid. Finally, a truce was declared and honour satisfied as the plan my mate and I had decided on was put into action. We reached into our pockets and produced a ten rupee note for each cricketer – I mean stranger. They were happy, we had had a great friendly time and India continued on its merry way.

I was pleased to note on my last trip before retiring, during a nostalgic wander around the Fisherman's Wharf tourist area of San Francisco, a cardboard carton being set up in a quiet little nook and a black guy getting his cards out. This was thirty-eight years after I had seen that first carton appear on a London street. It's good to know that some traditions just refuse to die – after all, this trick has been around since the turn of the fifteenth century.

ANTARCTIC FLYOVERS

As an international pilot based in the Southern Hemisphere, I did my share of flying down over the southern ice. Not too much, I'm glad to say. The poles are where the ice is but also where the radiation is. Those spectacular northern and southern lights at the poles are just the visual manifestation of a whole lot of nasty sun-produced radiation being let into our atmosphere by the earth's magnetic field. The magnetic field lines dip into the earth at the poles and in comes the radiation. Luckily, the strong field around the rest of the Earth deflects the nasties away – most of them anyway – there are still elevated levels at jet cruising altitudes, just not as much as at the poles. Too much polar flying and your exposure starts to approach cancer-causing level. A Qantas pilot mate, an ex-fighter pilot, started studying inflight radiation and ended up with a PhD in the field, (magnetic that is, sorry). He, and many others, have made radiation management the usual for aircrew now.

I did nearly all my polar flying en route to South Africa and South America but there was one special trip I did straight to the ice. Back in the late seventies, Qantas conducted sightseeing Jumbo-jet charters down to Antarctica and one day I was lucky to be rostered. The flight was to be eleven-and-a-half hours long and would take the passengers down and back with a high level of cabin service. Once over the Antarctic coast, the aircraft would descend and give the best possible views of the ground features – both man-made and natural. I was to be the S/O on this *Classic* Jumbo – that just meant it was one of the older models without the *glass cockpit*. It had computers, but only for navigation, and even those had severe limitations – GPS was decades away. It was state-of-the-art but the art was primitive.

We had a *heavy* crew to compensate for the lack of technology. Apart from the three pilots, with me being the junior, there was the flight engineer and a special navigator for this near-polar flight. As well as all of these, a specialist radio operator was sent because communications would be tricky. Last but not least, we had a glaciologist on board to help with the low-level navigation and to provide commentary. He was not specifically part of the Qantas crew, but was the only person on board who had been down there on the ground. Of the six *flight crew*, three would not be needed in later years when Qantas started up these trips again using more modern aircraft. The flight engineer's job was taken over by technology. Monitoring computers did the job this crew member used to do. The radio operator's job disappeared as satellite communication became the norm and the navigator lost his job to GPS and other advances in aviation electronics.

Having done the special day of 'arctic survival training', this big crew was ready. The next day we, and the excited passengers, set off with good weather forecast for our flight and destination – for what that was worth. State-of-the-art weather forecasting was about as advanced as it was in aviation – in other words, not nearly as good as it is today. We would know the weather when we got there. The forecast for the flight down was good but, remember, the poles are where the world's strongest winds are and, along with them, incredibly fast-changing weather conditions. We were just hoping the cloud base and visibility would allow the passengers to get their money's worth. Luck was with us. The day proved magnificent and we got low enough to see the glaciers and the early explorers' huts.

Glaciers are great things to see from ships or from the land but the only way to really see what they are like is from the air – light aircraft if you can, or from a low-flying airliner they are extraordinary. The big ones in Antarctica are something else and I for one had a ball on this trip. It was now time for me to earn my pay. The return trip was where the other technical crew used the junior members to their advantage. If I'd been one of them, I'd have done the same.

Once established on the return cruise, the Captain, F/O, navigator, radio operator and the glaciologist went downstairs and joined the party of excited, happy passengers. These passengers had just seen one of the best shows available on Earth and were having a ball. The Qantas S/O is an F/O, or for that matter a Captain only with less stripes – well almost. The level of skill the S/O had to achieve was comparable to the other two ranks. S/Os were just not given the final, costly in those days, landing training. Okay, this is probably a bit simplistic since the roles of the more senior pilots do entail more sophisticated duties. However, my level of training did mean that when the Captain and F/O went downstairs and left me in control of this 747 five hours from anywhere, they knew I was sufficiently qualified to not fuck it up.

The Flight Engineer was sitting behind me. He was there not only to monitor the engines and aircraft systems, but also to make sure I didn't have a medical problem. I wasn't planning on any medical problems but I did plan to do my job. This meant flying the aircraft, navigating the aircraft and communicating with the air traffic controllers. I was happy to be left to *manage* the operation.

This meant, if anything went *non-normal*, I would handle it. I knew the emergency procedures as well as anyone and had been tested to ensure this. Nothing special about me, that was just how it was, and is, in a real airline. Even if this Jumbo decided to tip upside down, I was trained in *jet upset* recovery techniques and, no, it doesn't mean offering a shoulder to cry on to the big blubbering diddums, it meant I could recover the aircraft safely from *unusual attitudes*. There are airlines around the world that don't do this sort of training, even now. Occasionally, I'm asked, since all airlines are the same, why wouldn't you just go with the cheapest? I simply point out that there are some airlines Qantas pilots will not allow their families to fly on and I haven't found a Qantas pilot yet that wouldn't jump at the chance to save some money. (Please note, I resisted the obvious double meaning joke about an aircraft's unusual attitude.)

The other *tech* crew stayed downstairs and the F/E and I were left upstairs alone to do our thing. The engineer did the fuel balancing and management and sorted out the pressurisation and thrust changes needed when we climbed as the aircraft got lighter. He just got on with his job and so did I. Flight management on this cruise also meant trying to make the flight take the agreed eleven and a half hours, to achieve this involved me in some tricky little navigation calculations.

The clock had been started as we pushed back from the terminal in Sydney and would be switched off as the brakes came on back at the terminal. So how was it going and what was the info I was getting to work this out with? The rudimentary navigation computers were giving me a time of arrival at a certain point on the approach to Sydney. GIGO – Garbage In Garbage Out – is what I was contending with. The computers were calculating using the current wind and using the distance to run to get to this point. With any wind component change, or airspeed change, the ground speed would vary and the calculation was therefore garbage. I did a fairly detailed plan from this point to the airport terminal – speeds and distances to touchdown, taking into account the likely approach. I then calculated the taxi time as best I could. This gave me a time to aim for at this approach point.

With an ETA to aim for, I then applied likely wind changes over the route to the point and applied the revised average speed to the distance to go. It's not rocket science, but a bit of educated guesswork with winds is needed. I then used my slide rule, still no worthwhile electronic calculators, and came up with a speed to aim at. The pilot slide rules were actually circular ones so you could stick them in your shirt pocket. I carried one there for donkey's years and only stopped when I noticed I'd gone digital.

The speed I was now aiming for was a TAS, a True Air Speed, this would equate when the wind component – headwind or tailwind – is added to the desired ground speed. All this sounds easy but factors like flying into strong headwinds or with strong tailwinds mess with your calculations if you're not careful. If you get slowed by a strong headwind, you are going slower for a longer time and the headwind has more time to slow you – tailwinds do the opposite. You have to take these things into account and I'd had my little computer spinning, believe me. Just on this windy point, as a 400-metre runner as a youth, I was very aware that any wind slowed your time over the one-lap run. You pushed into the wind for more time than you had the tailwind helping you. Sitting in a 747 over the Southern Ocean didn't alter this rule.

I'd got my best guesstimate for the speed I should hold, worked out what *Indicated Air Speed* that would equate to and slowed to that speed. If I had, in fact, slowed right down to this speed, the aircraft would have gone into slow-speed buffet and the engineer would have probably, rightfully, belted me across the head with the crash axe. Mind you, if I'd needed to speed up too much to achieve the desired IAS, I would have got the aircraft flying up into the high-speed buffet with similar consequences for the back of my head.

The 747 was flying like all high-flying jets in that range of speed with an upper limit imposed by the speed of sound and a lower limit imposed by the stall speed of the aircraft. *Stall* by the way is when the wing stops working, not the engine – it's not a car. The higher you fly an aircraft into its weight and temperature limits, the closer you get to *Coffin Corner* where there is a diminishing speed range you can safely fly in. I've flown with the Jumbo unable to fly more than a few knots faster or slower. No young, well-trained S/O was going anywhere near these limits so I could only slow so much.

I slowed to this acceptable speed. It wasn't what I wanted but, hey, it would stretch the charter time closer to the desired and save some fuel – win-win. By the way, the option of going faster, if I needed to, would entail more calculations if I didn't want to use too much fuel and compromise our reserves. The crash axe could possibly get a workout if I started to use too much – the Engineer wanted to get home in one piece. Drag increases in proportion to the square of the speed and therefore the fuel usage does too. Then you go into compressibility drag as you approach the speed of sound – I knew all this, as I should have.

The other pilots eventually returned, happy as farts in a bottle by the way, and took over from me. They followed my speed plan but they weren't personally involved like I was and you could tell they didn't really care – no skin in the game, as it were. The approach pretty much followed my assumptions of four or five hours earlier and we made our approach into the Sydney night-time rush hour.

Things always get busy at this stage and the next thing I knew we were parking our brakes and the pilots were switching off their clocks. I remembered and checked the time – eleven hours thirty minutes to the minute. I'd got a little satisfaction out of the day even though I hadn't got to party with the passengers – S/Os learn to get their kicks where they can. Naturally, the other pilots didn't recognise my feat – that would have broken the rule of not acknowledging any achievement by the S/O. This was, after all, the good old days.

Fast forward nearly thirty years and I was again down over the ice, this time flying between Australia and South Africa – different time, different aircraft. It was still a Jumbo but it was a 747-400 model, the latest glass cockpit edition. This *Electric Jumbo*, as it was called when it first came out, was a different state-of-the-art. Electronics had advanced to the point where, as I said earlier, the Flight Engineer and the Navigator were no longer needed. Dedicated Radio Operators had really disappeared decades before.

All you needed in these aircraft, anywhere over the Earth's surface, was two pilots, and that was the F/O and me on this day. Sitting in the wispy clouds, communicating with Australia and Africa via satellites, navigating via the GPS satellites and letting the computers monitor our aircraft systems, we were living out the old-time aviators' dreams – well, almost. I was hoping to get some great views of the Antarctic continent as well as the sea ice and icebergs I knew to be below us.

The GPS map was showing us coming up over a tip of land and it was frustrating being in cloud. We couldn't see a thing. Luckily, the visibility gods beamed on us a moment later and the view just opened up – incredible sea ice with imbedded icebergs, flat snow- covered coastal ground underneath us, all lit by that spectacular slanting light you get at these latitudes. The first officer got out of her seat and started snapping great photos from both sides of the flight deck.

Such scenery had to be shared. I knew I would be interrupting videos and some passenger's sleep but this was a chance you couldn't let go by. I got onto the PA and did the 'tour bus' commentary. In the baggage collection area in Joh-burg many passengers came up and thanked me. 'Glad we didn't let that chance go by,' they said.

All these years after my first trip to Antarctica, there was an added feature. Some cabin crew members came up and had a go at me. Apparently some passengers had been woken, seen the view, and then requested cups of tea or drinks. These disgruntled cabin crew had had to do some work. The F/O and I lamented the stunted lives some people live. This vibrant, female F/O certainly lived life to the full. Sadly, she was killed a few years later in a parachute accident in the US. I cherish the photos of that day over the ice that she copied onto a CD for me.

31

SAN FRANCISCO

San Francisco was a favourite destination. The stopovers were great with interesting things to do and fascinating bars and restaurants. The flying to get onto the airport could be challenging – a real workout at times. The airport was an old one with parallel runways but the spacing between the runways was suitable for a previous era. Air Traffic Control seemed hard-pressed to handle the number of aircraft coming and going and, especially at the peak time of our arrival up from Honolulu, things were usually hectic. This was the early nineties and I was a fairly new skipper but I just loved flying the relatively smaller 767s, particularly into tricky airports.

We would fly onto the extended centre-line of the main parallel runways at about eight miles. The nautical mile is still the standard in most of the world and pilots can't actually think in kilometres until they get into a car – I can't, anyway. It's as if I live in two different worlds with two different measuring systems. I don't just use metric or imperial, I live them, depending on what I'm doing. No converting goes on – just use. It must be like that for people who can think in a different language – no translation in your head, just think and talk.

We would come into San Fran at a right angle to a lot of air traffic that had joined the extended runway centre-lines way out as they approached the airport from the eastern states. We were the rarity coming from the ocean side. Imagine two lines of aircraft approaching the parallel westerly runways and the occasional interloper, like us, joining this parade from the south.

On one clear busy night, the controller literally slotted us in where he could. We were assigned the far runway, which meant crossing through the path of other aircraft coming in the from the east. There was no fancy radar positioning with minimum separation standards this night. We were just headed in the right direction and then the responsibility for separation was handed over to us. *Own separation* this was called – it meant you looked out the window and separated yourself from other aircraft. On this occasion, there was an American Airlines Jumbo coming down the final approach of the near runway and we were on a collision course with it. The controller gave us our instructions and moved on to other aircraft: 'Qantas, your traffic is two o'clock, seven forty-seven final for two eight left cleared own separation final two eight right, call tower one twenty point five established.' (Say this as quickly as you can in a broad American accent – that's how he did it.)

We had been watching this Jumbo getting bigger and bigger in our windscreens and had been waiting for some command from ATC, either a directional change or an altitude instruction. Instead, we got the do-it-yourself option and don't fuck it up. I'll try and get you up to speed with the situation. Two big jets would've hit unless someone did something.

The yanks in the Jumbo were no doubt watching us like hawks but they would've heard the instruction to me to do something. They continued flying down the glideslope of their runway and didn't deviate to the side at all. The yank skipper knew I was relying on this – he'd been a pro for probably much longer than I had been at this stage.

I had to do something to avoid this aircraft flying right-to-left in front of me. If I turned left in front of him I would lose sight of him and he was too close to ensure separation – gotta love that word – so I didn't do that. I could've turned right and tried to pass behind him, but again, by rolling to turn, I would've put him under my belly – aircraft's that is – and lost sight of him. I didn't do that either but, luckily, I had the third dimension to play with. If I had gone over the top of him, again I would've presented the underside of my 767 to him and again lost visual contact with him. He would've freaked at me doing this because he would've known that I would lose visuals, and you just don't do that. You guessed it, I had to go under him to get to my approach path on the other side.

You can use the autopilot at this stage to do all the manoeuvring necessary but the quick actions needed doing stuff like this means most pilots will hand fly. Actions can be taken very rapidly manually and the autopilot can be a bit too gentle. Off went the power and down went the nose. We were already descending at about five hundred feet per minute – remember I have no idea how much that is in metres or cubits. What I do know is that the Jumbo was maintaining a similar descent rate. He was on the glideslope and would not deviate. I had to increase my descent rate to ensure altitude separation and that meant getting as far below our friend as we could without getting too low. In a car going downhill, if you want to increase your rate of altitude loss, you can speed up – this works for aircraft too. Pilots call it trading altitude for speed. You can reverse that equation if you want – just not at the moment, thank you.

You can't speed up too much, there are speed limits, actual maximums and minimums you must observe at various stages of your approach and various flap setting maximums and minimums. The undercarriage has its own maximum. So, I dived, but I had limits to how vicious I could make my dive. It was best to start as early as possible. The instruction to go visual separation had come over the radio and within a second or so I was descending. Concentration, anticipation, experience and situational awareness is what it is all about – this was just another day, or night, at the office.

If you push the nose down too hard on a *dive* like this you can induce a negative G- force that equals the positive 1 G that gravity provides. You would be weightless and so would your passengers and crew down the back. If a passenger's laptop started for the roof you could expect some surprise, which would turn to anger as it crashed back down when gravity returned. I had to get the aircraft descending but I couldn't go all fighter pilot. I had paying passengers aboard and they had a right not to be scared. All flying is a compromise and there are limits on everything. Flying a *flight sim* on a computer is one thing – flying a real aircraft is something else.

We got a magnificent view of the underside of the Jumbo. It was dark, but a surprising amount of light was coming up from the ground and our eyes were well and truly night adapted – we'd had the flight deck lights way down for hours to ensure this. Very rarely have I seen a brightly lit flight deck at night. We scooted over to our approach *localiser* – the thin radio beam that would take us down the centre-line of our runway, 28R and also joined the glideslope on that runway – another beam coming up the approach. By following these two beams we would arrive at the approach end of the runway. The Jumbo had got a bit of a head start but, remember, we had sped up a bit and, by the time we had slowed, we had caught up and were now flying alongside our big brother. We had, in fact, traded our extra speed back into altitude. We had a magnificent, but scary, view of this accompanying Jumbo. At 750 feet (436 cubits) apart this is one of the closest parallel approach paths in the world and you don't usually fly down them alongside another big jet.

I chose to fly to San Francisco for my last flight ever. I was now flying a 747-400, the arrival was in the morning instead of the evening and, on this day, the weather was beautiful. No traffic to worry about, calm conditions with cool morning temperature ensuring there were no heat bumps around. The approach and landing was an easy visual approach and the only pressure was to make an appropriately smooth landing in such conditions. The F/O, assigned to this flight at the last minute, was on his first flight after checkout on this type of aircraft and the old skipper was being observed very carefully. The conditions allowed me to put on a 'greaser' and I have a fond mental audio recording of the young bloke announcing, as we trundled down the runway, 'You've got to be happy with that!' I know he might have only seen a handful of landings on the 747-400 but I was receptive. This newbie had been put on the flight to do a landing but that may well not have happened. It was my last trip, after all, and it was expected that I would just hog both landings – the one I had just done and the one back in Sydney. As we pulled off the runway in SFO, I glanced over to him and told him I was indeed satisfied and it was his aircraft on the way home. This meant he'd fly the sector and do the landing back in Sydney.

This was seen as an incredibly generous move on my part but I knew the truth. A few trips earlier I had run into a pilot mate in Los Angeles, and he'd given me some advice. He told me to start doing all the landings a couple of months before retiring and as soon as I jagged a good one to just give the rest away to the F/Os. That way my enduring memory would be that I could always do great landings. I remembered this as we turned off the runway – generous my arse, I was just following good advice.

The young – it's all relative – F/O flew a flawless sector home with a very acceptable landing at the end. So good, in fact, that I willingly accepted the congratulations on a 'Magnificent last landing, Captain,' from Sydney control tower. Hey, I'm generous, not nice. A few years into retirement, I was amazed to see on the news that a large Boeing had crashed onto the same runway in SFO. The conditions were again morning perfect and there was no excuse except incompetence. There are indeed differences in airline standards.

In the earlier days, arriving in San Francisco from Honolulu meant you could unwind a bit by going out on the town. We would get to the hotel in good time to change and set off for favourite bars and eateries. They weren't always the most salubrious establishments but the beer and hot pastrami sandwiches were second to none. This town has always been a late-night town and they really know how to party. I can remember coming out of a trad jazz club at three o'clock in the morning once to see two of the toughest looking coppers I'd ever seen with their guns hanging off their belts like old western gunslingers. These cops were joking around with a guy who was up on a soapbox selling something to anybody interested. This was the very early seventies and a lot was happening. My lady friend, a local, pointed out that the bloke on the soapbox was selling 'pot', as they called it back then. This was an interesting town.

A lot of the bars were piano bars that were always good for some local flavour. One young woman was amazed at how good my English was after hearing me sing along with the bar.

I pointed out that I came from a progressive country where every child was taught English in school. If Americans thought we were Austrians, I wasn't going to disappoint them. The entertainers were always great and the beer was still cheap.

Every now and then you had to go and find a different bar. My favourite would sometimes go pear-shaped. One night, a huge white Texan, complete with Stetson, leant over and offered the piano man a five dollar note. 'Here's five bucks to play *The Yellow Rose of Texas*.' About a second later a huge local black man leant over the piano. 'Here's ten bucks NOT to play *The Yellow Rose of Texas*.' Two seconds later, my mate and I exited onto the street. Two seconds after that we heard the first glass being broken.

Same bar a few years later and I was nearly knocked out of my seat from behind as a fight broke out – nearly spilt my beer. This time we watched as the bartender leapt the counter and threw the instigator out the door but, once the drunk stuck his head back in and told everybody he was coming back with something, my mates and I did the two-second departure once again. It may be San Francisco, but it's still the USA, and it's not just the cops that have cowboy pistols.

You didn't have to wait for the sun to go down to see the cultural rainbow that is San Fran. Coming into town from the airport late one morning, I noticed that our crew bus had more than the usual number of gay guys on board. I discovered the reason once we hit the downtown area. It was the day of the big gay street party and it would all blast off very shortly.

Also on the bus was a brand-new female S/O on her first trip out of Australia. Her eyes were everywhere and, when we pulled up at a red light outside a nightclub that had a line of people all wanting to get in, she was right onto it. The nightclubbers were dressed to kill and the little black party dresses in San Fran are just that little bit smaller I assure you – especially at eleven in the morning.

Our new traveller turned to the other junior pilot, who'd been around a while, 'Why isn't the big black security dude letting those two girls in?' she asked. The girls in question were two of the most lusciously dressed creatures I'd ever seen. His answer was a classic, 'Ah, they're not exactly girls, Wendy. You're not in Kansas anymore.' San Francisco has never been Kansas but we all knew what he meant.

Little black party dresses were nothing to what I and the F/O saw or, more accurately, didn't see, later that afternoon. Following the rule that no chance should be passed by, we had ventured out to a Costco store. My mate needed to stock up on vanilla coffee and I was up for a walk. The store was in the blocked-off party area – quite a few city blocks, as it turned out. When we fronted up to the security gates, all naive and Australian, they greeted us as gentlemen and grinned as they let us in.

I soon found out the reason for the grinning. They knew what we would find on the streets. Every form of gay subculture was on display – lifestyles I had heard about but never seen. There were also things I'd never dreamed of on display, and that is what it was, of course, one gigantic proud display – good on them. A lot of risqué stuff everywhere but anywhere I looked an even more risqué scene would present itself.

There was one subgroup proudly walking around with their absolutely gorgeous 'ladies' who were dressed almost identically. These ladies had magnificently coiffured hair (wigs, probably) and all wore magnificent tight-fitting gowns that came down to their stilettos. These gowns sometimes had little trains at the back and were, without exception, all vivid white and, again without exception, completely body-hugging and see-through.

Every one of the 'ladies' was also completely naked under these lacy masterpieces – they were a sight to behold. This was classy stuff and the mixture of black-leather-clad bikies, completely naked blokes being led around by chains attached to their privates and a hundred other mind-snapping visions was just what you would expect to see on a trip to Costco to pick up some coffee. Well, it was in San Francisco anyway.

I made the mistake of emailing a bit of this story back to a mob of new pilots I was mentoring at the time. I was making a point about knowledge levels needed at this stage of their training and using Wendy's experiences on the aircraft on the way to San Fran as a guide. For colour and interest, I talked a little about the street party. To their credit, my little ducklings just went for it – never let a chance go by. They congratulated me on getting to the party and gave me the dates I should be in other cities around the world to enjoy similar events. They were learning fast.

32

TRAVELLING THE WORLD

Travelling the world, I got to see and do lots. The main thing I miss in retirement is the mateship of fellow pilots and cabin crews but there are many aspects of flying that makes retirement day for pilots the saddest day of their career. I realised that I would no longer see and do the things I took for granted.

To see a circular rainbow is a privilege rarely granted. To experience two sunrises or two sunsets a few minutes apart was always fun – I used to work at achieving them if I could. To see the back of the Himalayas with the huge expanse of mountain range reaching down towards Nepal was always magnificent. To fly at night over the fishing fleet in the Gulf of Siam and imagine you are looking down into a starry night sky is weird – those fish- attracting lights are bright. To lose count of how many shooting stars I saw in one night was easy – there was always another night to start the count again. To look vertically up to the pulsating Aurora Australis is mesmerising, I assure you.

To watch tropical sunsets or desert sunrises with their vivid and subtle colours was something I never tired of. The fact that I was awake during so many dawns had its compensations, and flying with a magnificent sunset or sunrise off to the side meant that I experienced not just one view but, because of the speed, I had an ever-changing vista that meant I got dozens of magnificent mental photos for the price of one. To look out over the snow-covered steppes of Russia and wonder how people survive and get around down there is what I did in the quiet cruise periods on the way to a bustling tropical Asian city full of light and people. I would always look out on the approach from the south into Manila because on a good day you could see a big island in the sea that had a lake in it and the lake had an island in it. In turn, this island had a lake in it and, you guessed it, this lake had a small island in it. I'd love to know if this is true anywhere else on the planet. Uh oh ... early 2020 and kaboom! Taal volcano, the island in the middle of the lake, has just erupted. I wonder if, in a few months when the smoke and ash clear, whether that view will still exist.

The contrast between leaving snowy London and landing in Karachi in forty-five degree heat or of flying through severe smog but then climbing and popping out of the *inversion* into the crystal-clear, unlimited visibility above it are just some of the things I had taken for granted. To fly a jet just above some flat cloud is to *cloud surf* and must be done when you can – never let that chance go by. The sense of speed and flight is only enhanced when you get to play with your shadow. To have the sun behind you so that when you approach a wall of cloud you see a haloed shadow of a four-engine jet getting bigger and bigger and then you hit it – unforgettable.

To see the wingtip vortices from a preceding jet cause a swirling hole in some low cloud above London is a sight. To hit the swirling air a short time later and to have to take over from the Jumbo's autopilot because the turbulence is too violent for it to handle – pilot heaven. I flew over Melbourne one night and watched a portion of the city come down with a power fault that caused a ripple of light failures that then repeated. I was alone above this part of Melbourne and the only person to have this view of wave after wave of lights. I haven't seen St Elmo's fire for years now and I regret that. I just took these things for granted but knew I would miss them when I stopped flying – and I do.

I miss the fun on the ground with that extended group of mates that was every Qantas crew I flew with. To be part of the crew applauded off the Paris Metro by a peak hour crowd of Parisians after we had tipsily entertained them with a risqué version of charades was par for the course. (Okay, we were drunk, not tipsy, and risqué is not a strong enough word either.) To be ordered to tap dance across the Heathrow Airport apron with the rest of the Jumbo technical crew to our crew bus was what happened because the Captain ordered it knowing there was a captive audience of four hundred passengers waiting for their buses. Playing tennis at the Mauritius hotel was great but you did have to run the gauntlet of the huge black spiders hanging from the trees on the path to the courts. If an Australian says a spider is huge, it's probably bigger than anything he has seen at home and that makes it BIG.

To leap, after dinner, fully clothed into the lagoon surrounding the balcony restaurant in Tahiti was a tradition. (You had to watch your feet as there were two huge Moray eels to contend with.) To skinny dip at midnight in a lot of places was also just what we did. Coming last in the Shanghai go-cart races due to my bad power-to-weight ratio was to be expected. The win in the computer racing car competition in Tokyo was totally unexpected. To crawl around in Viet Cong tunnels after the war was scary. To shoot a few rounds with their old AK47s was even scarier. Okay every now and then I would visit some incredible art or science museum just to have a break from all this. The 3D movie recreation of a moon landing in the British Science Museum was incredible but the Van Gogh paintings in Amsterdam were three dimensional as well.

There was not only the natural scenery but also the flying-generated scenery, by which I mean things that could only happen while flying. An example of this is what happened one late afternoon approaching Sydney from New Zealand. It was rush hour and we were told to do a holding pattern to lose some time. We were able to do this at a reasonably high altitude and after one go-around the *racetrack* pattern, we were allowed to descend and turn in for our approach. I looked back out of the side flight-deck window and saw the 'mind photo' that is still in my storage. There above us in the deepening blue sky was a perfect racetrack-shaped *con trail*. This condensation trail formed from the water vapour in our jet exhaust was a beautiful white, sharply defined pattern. There was no entry trail or exit trail, the atmospheric conditions were obviously just right at that level only and we had a glorious view of the track we had followed.

What made this view something out of the box, however, was that at the precise moment I looked, the rising full moon was seen exactly in the middle of the racetrack. Of course, there was no mobile phone camera or any other cameras for that matter and I didn't get the cover of Flight International. I now knew, however, why a lot of pilots carry cameras at all times. There are great websites with pilot photos, check them out and you'll see why I miss all this scenery. Luckily, there are very few photos of the fun we got up to, as crews, on the ground.

The best by far airborne scenery is the circular rainbow. To see this rare but stunning vision you have to be up in the air with the sun behind you shining onto, or more correctly into, water droplets. With the light waves being internally reflected and bounced back by the droplets, the observer sees a circle of colour as the reflections form a cone back to his or her eyes. The angle of the cone is at the magic rainbow angle of about 40 degrees. Since there is a slight difference in the angle of reflection with each wavelength of light, the cone of light is seen as a rainbow, in this case a complete circular rainbow. No good going up a mountain to try to see this. The mountain would block the bottom half of the sunlight from getting to the water drops and you would only see the normal half circle of rainbow. By the way, if conditions are right with really strong sunlight, you can see double rainbows. I saw a really bright double once in country Australia. The outer rainbow is caused by the sunlight being internally reflected twice inside the droplets. This means the second rainbow is seen as a weaker mirror image of the main one. This sort of stuff has always blown my mind.

I mentioned a haloed shadow before. From an aircraft you can see another great little sunlight effect – the aircraft's shadow has a halo of bright light around it. The Americans call it the 'glory', as you would expect, while others call it a Brocken spectre. If the sunlight is bright enough this 'halo' will break up into wavelengths and the halo becomes a small rainbow. Get the sun right behind you as you fly into a wall of cloud and the effect is spooky – a dark 'ghost' plane, surrounded by light, comes out of the cloud and hits you just as you lose all visibility. This effect is stuck in my brain as a video rather than a photo.

More passengers than aircrew actually see the clouds that form over the top of wings as the pressure and temperature becomes ideal to turn water vapour into water droplets. I have, over the years, been a passenger and have always enjoyed the view of this 'ectoplasm' forming and revealing the airflow over and around the wings and wing tips. It's actually just condensation but 'ectoplasm' sounds so cool. Air Force dudes, because they are cooler than most, refer to the condensation forming near speed of sound shock waves or on top of their wings as they pull on the 'Gs' as ectoplasm. They're allowed to. I was asked only the other day why aircraft dump fuel as they approach Sydney airport. My answer didn't mention fuel but did include moisture, temperature and low pressure, especially at the wingtips and at the sides of lowered flaps. The resultant streaming white stuff looks like fuel being dumped and I congratulated the observer for noticing. I also silently thanked him for not mentioning 'chemical trails', I like to answer intelligent questions.

One other phenomenon I have seen also required me being in the passenger cabin to observe. On my first-ever trip to London in a 707, the Captain was training me in everything he could think of. At one point, when he reckoned the sun angle was right, he increased the aircraft's speed to closer to the speed of sound and sent me down into the cabin to look at the airflow over the wings. The airflow over the top of the wing is sped up a bit by the wing curvature and was therefore just going supersonic. The shimmering line I could just make out was a shock wave forming. I didn't point this out to the passengers watching me look out of the window.

I have flown over, around and beside volcanoes, banked to look down into smouldering semi-active craters, watched erupting monsters spewing dark bulbous clouds up to almost our altitude. I've flown close beside Mount Everest and over the remains of Mount St Helens. I've wondered at the serenity of Mt Fuji at dawn. I've looked down into the watery grave of Krakatoa. I miss volcanoes. I miss the Hawaiian Islands

– volcanic in origin, fantastic in character. Mount Everest isn't a volcano but it is big, okay?

It was fun seeing volcanoes as you flew over them but they are actually bloody dangerous where aircraft are concerned. When an Icelandic volcano erupted a couple of years ago, it shut down half the world's air traffic. Volcanic dust and jet turbines do not mix. A British Airways Jumbo flew into a volcanic cloud over Indonesia one night about thirty years ago, all the engines literally ground to a halt. They were very lucky to get the engines started again to make it to an airport. After this incident, Qantas pilots, who flew over more volcanoes going up into Asia than most international pilots did, were trained in volcanic cloud recognition – they stink and are electrified – and how to get out of them ASAP. I was up on the rim of an Indonesian smoking volcano once. The sulphurous fumes were almost overwhelming and this one was sleeping. Whatever you do, don't have an avocado milkshake straight after a smelly volcano visit. On reflection don't ever have an avocado milkshake.

One day in 1998, flying up to Fukuoka in Japan, we passed by an erupting Mount Unzen. That was its last major eruption and just as well – this volcano is a killer. The horrible scenes of the billowing pyroclastic clouds rushing down its sides are all over the internet. I saw it get really aggressive that day. The huge ash clouds were dark and angry and had climbed pretty high but not as high as we were cruising, luckily. We descended shortly after passing this event and spent the next couple of days in another interesting Japanese city.

The hotel room had a television, of course, but no English channels, so watching the news coverage of the eruption was pretty frustrating – great visuals but the voice over and wording on the screen were in Klingon or Japanese, one of the two.

That reminds me of watching TV in Japan one rainy night. I was waiting for the movie *Road Warrior* (*Mad Max*) with Mel Gibson to come on. This must have been a big event for the TV channel because it was interviewing the star live before the movie started. I was so impressed with Mel. The host would ask him a question in Japanese and he would answer in English. This went on until the third question was asked, in Japanese, and Mel lent forward and said, 'Sorry, mate. I've forgotten the third question.' After a quick prompt in English, Mel gave an excellent answer about the movie's director. This was only one example of how TV fooled me around the world. Once, channel surfing in London at 3.00 am, I came upon the Australian show, *Police Rescue*. The scene was of the hero abseiling down a cliff to a crashed light aircraft. After much adventure, the rescuer reached the aircraft, leant in and spoke to the injured pilot in perfect Italian.

You would think I would have wised up to all this over the years. I mean, on my very first stay outside of Australia, I was exploring my hotel room in Hong Kong. It had a big bed and its own bathroom and a television – luxury. I stuck the TV on and found myself watching my favourite American show *FBI*. Again, there was the hero going down the mountain but, in this case, he was leaning out of his car's window, shooting at the baddie in the car in front. Many screeching turns later, the G man managed to run the fugitive off the side of the road. He jumped out and stuck his gun in the side window and spoke in perfect Cantonese. I just fell off the bed in surprise.

Two days of watching incomprehensible news coverage in Fukuoka and I was none the wiser when it came to just how bad the eruption was. How high the clouds had got – I had no idea. When we got to the briefing room at the airport to collect our flight plan and to review the weather and *notams* (notices to airmen), we would get some good information, or so I hoped. Unfortunately, the information was sketchy and there were what could only be guesses as to how high the nasty stuff had reached. The flight plan sent up from Sydney had us flying very near the volcano. We would still be on our climb as we passed.

This is where pilots have to actually use their knowledge, experience and expertise to do something. Bullshit. They just have to do what anybody would do and employ a bit of caution in relation to what could, if you let it, become a dangerous event. Yes, as an experienced pilot with knowledge about the upper level jet streams, I would now apply what I knew to manage the situation but all I was doing was being airline pilot cautious.

The forecast wind at the top of our climb, at Mount Unzen's position, was a strong westerly. No surprises there, this was jet stream altitude and latitude and they are predominately from the west. They can also be much stronger than any surface winds – it's all hurricane strength up there. We have known about these winds for a while. During the Second World War, the Japanese actually used them to carry balloon bombs over to the US west coast. A few unfortunates were incredibly unlucky to be killed. A lot more Americans were killed by that other divine wind, the Kamikaze – the Japanese know about wind. A little-known fact is that the British also used balloons, carried on the prevailing winds, to attack Germany during the war. (No need for bombs, they dragged cables over electricity wires to cause blackouts.)

The unfortunate thing about this night's wind was that it would blow the volcanic clouds straight through our planned track. Someone in Sydney had run the flight plan without taking this into account. That's why you have a pilot with, literally, his or her skin in the game to decide what route and altitude might actually be flown. We changed the route to much further west, upwind of the eruption, we then let air traffic control know our new track and left for home. All this didn't stop us peering and sniffing our way past the volcano as we went by in the dark. Volcanos were great scenery during the day, not so much fun at night.

As for the two sunset, two sunrise, thing, zooming up or down just after sunrise or sunset is the way you get them. I have been known to delay a take-off until the sun just dips below the horizon or dive into a descent just as the sun pops up at dawn. To make the sun reverse direction either way is to become a god. You have to work at these time-travel pastimes but, if someone gives you a couple of hundred million dollars' worth of machinery to do it with, you may as well go for it. Just don't tell the Flat Earth Society – it will only upset them.

No, wrong. Always have a go at the flat Earthers, in every field, and never let a chance go by.

33
GREAT TIMES ON THE GROUND

I'm no travel writer as I have said before. I have travelled of course and I've had some great times – interesting times and some funny times. Most came about because I was a pilot back in those days and just happened to be in the right place at the right time. I would work at not letting any chances go by and, quite often, interesting things happened.

On one flight into Mexico City when I was the young S/O, the young Flight Engineer and I wanted to go to the bullfights but time was short. I remember the Captain coming back onto the Flight Deck after his break and questioning why we had the poor little 707 going flat out. When we told him, he didn't order any slowdown, in fact, he was now on board with the bullfight idea – and fuel was free back then, I think.

This Captain had been a Squadron Leader flying fighters for the RAF and was prone to organise all his crew members onto mopeds for around-the-island bike races in Bermuda. He was always calling himself 'red leader' and forming us into 'squadrons' – he was obviously missing his old job. I have a vivid memory of one such race. Having helped a hostie to start her moped, I and the rest of the 'squadron' had to chase her across a golf course before she stacked it. She had never ridden a bike before, let alone a motorbike. Only severe illness got you out of these adventures – being unable to ride was no excuse. We did get to the bull fights, only to see them rained out for the first time in years. Today, as a more mature person, I'm kind of glad.

On one three-day stopover in Tahiti, I had a great chance. The Pacific Games were due to start and the opening ceremony was happening on one of the three days. The beachside hotel we were staying in was a great place to kill time but an opening ceremony had to be seen. I couldn't get any other crew to come with me, which still puzzles me because, as I said, crews did a lot together back then. There were Islanders from all over the Pacific at the makeshift stadium and I was determined to go.

I caught a 'Le Truck', which was the main form of transport on the island, basically a truck or a ute (a pickup) with wooden benches on the back covered by a wooden roof. I had a magic day absorbing the tremendous atmosphere of fun and happiness these people generated. I've done island dancing where you try and keep up with the young women in the grass skirts a few times in Tahiti and this was one such occasion. I went to a rehearsal for the opening ceremony of the Sydney Olympics but I remember more from this fabulous day in Papeete.

Karachi was the stopover port on the way from Europe to Australia for the migrant charters of the early seventies. We would pick up migrants in various European and Mediterranean destinations and fly them down to Karachi where another crew would take them on to Australia. These migrant charters were great. I got to see Malta, Stuttgart, Vienna and Istanbul as well as this port city in Pakistan. Karachi provided a lot of fun and adventure and the crews really did stick together there.

On the flight from London with one mob of 'ten-pound poms' (the amount these English migrants paid to come to Australia), we had a couple of wags in the cabin crew who were up for some fun. The chief steward came up and asked the Captain if it was okay for a steward and a hostie to swap uniforms and serve the breakfast into Karachi cross-dressed. The Captain gave his permission but said they would have to stay in drag all the way to the airport hostel where we stayed. It was on. Clothes were ferried between two toilets and a magnificent creature emerged from one and Charlie Chaplin from the other.

Brunhilde, the hostie from hell, complete with masses of makeup, huge red lips and a massive beauty spot plastered on her cheek, proceeded to take charge over the PA system. 'Ze meal is about to be served and you vill put ze little tray tables down, NOT NOW, NOT NOW, VAIT UNTIL I TELZ YOU.' On and on she went. Mind you, when she tried to walk with her high heels flopping over to the side and the gusset of her pantyhose just above her knees, she did lose some of her authority.

Meanwhile, the small hostie had been transformed, with the baggy trousers and a borrowed walking stick, into Charlie Chaplin. She would do the characteristic walk up and down the aisle with the walking stick rotating as only Charlie, and this very funny woman, could manage. The passengers loved it and the Pakistani airport officials and workers came from everywhere to stare at these crazy Australians.

The hostel we stayed at was called Speedbird House. It belonged to BOAC, the airline that became British Airways. Only crew stayed there and with a communal dining room, a swimming pool and little cells to sleep in it was a pretty unique stopover for us. Usually, only three 707 crews at a time – two Qantas and one Birdseed. No prizes for guessing what Speedbird, the BOAC call sign, had morphed into. There would be pre-dinner drinks followed by a dinner where crews were expected to occupy their own dedicated table – all very pukka. It was, after all, just after the colonial era and you could easily imagine yourself back in the Raj. Two tables of Australians in a formal setting after a few drinks cannot, of course, be trusted to behave. Quite often insults would fly between the tables and that would end in hilarious food fights – as you would expect.

On one such evening, there were the three tables, one lot of Birdseeds and two Aussies. We were all being very polite and the F/O on our table was determined that us Australians would behave ourselves for once. He was English and didn't want us to degrade ourselves in front of his old countrymen and women. The initial volleys of bread rolls had just started and he was desperate to keep us from retaliating. 'No, don't lower yourself, gentlemen,' he said while holding his pipe in his mouth. This guy was old school and decorum mattered.

We held back but, a few seconds later, a banana skin sailed over on a perfect trajectory'. It hit him on the top of his head and then flopped and balanced itself over his pipe stem with equal amounts of skin on both sides – brilliant shot. We all looked aghast at this vision and waited for his reaction. He slowly stood up, took the pipe out of his mouth, looked at the skin still draped over the stem and announced, 'There are limits of course,' and then he just started hurling whatever he could find. He was now an Australian.

In the hotter months on this stopover, you had to virtually live in the pool. With the aid of a floppy hat and some sunglasses, I read *The Godfather* in this pool. Getting into the pool wouldn't wait and the tradition was that when you arrived from the airport you went straight over to the pool, fully dressed in your uniform, and just jumped in. Points were awarded for best entry. You would stay there too – drinks, food and entertainment, in the form of playing cards, were duly delivered. As long as the cards were waterproof, you could use the water surface for the table, just don't jump around.

On one of these lazy mornings, the British arrived, looked down into the pool at a mob of fully uniformed Australian pilots and stewards and made some derogatory remarks about colonials. The Captain just looked up from his cards and said, 'It's okay, it's okay they're plastic coated.' By the way, some of the Birdseeds were known to follow this uniform/pool tradition as well. A Qantas pilot mate witnessed one BOAC crew line up next to the pool. They all skulled a beer then marched in a line around to the diving board where they launched themselves into the water. I'm betting their Captain had been a fighter pilot in the RAF and was probably known as blue leader.

Again, in trying to stay aircrew oriented, I will now talk about *crew rooms*, those dedicated rooms, some actually conference rooms, set aside by the hotels we stayed at for crew to meet and party in. I've seen as many as two hundred crew at Christmas parties and such and quite often a good mix of airlines are represented. I can remember holding a practical session in one crew room on how to win at eBay. This was fairly new at the time and I was bidding on a pair of pilot sunglasses. It was in the LA hotel and I had an audience behind me as I used one of the computers supplied for our use. Again, a different time. Very little, and expensive, wi-fi and unsmart phones meant you couldn't hide in your room and do this stuff on your personal device. I got the glasses at a good price and didn't have to just keep bidding. This was lucky, as I couldn't lose the race with all the build-up and advice I had been throwing around. These crew rooms were used for all sorts of things, not only parties, although I seem to remember that alcohol was always a participant.

There was one crew room party that we pilots got invited to in Singapore that kept the great tradition of cross-dressing going. We went down to the cabin crew hotel, at this time we had separate pubs for some reason, and walked in on a big one. Mostly Qantas people, a few European female flight attendants and some American pilots from somewhere and, unusually, quite a few gays. A good mix and it was on. The Qantas cabin crew had rung around and insisted on everyone cross-dressing. We pilots weren't told because we had very few women to swap duds with and I now suspect that this whole cross-dressing idea was just a great way of getting into a female flight attendant's room and having an excuse for everybody to get their gear off. How many couples didn't make it to the party, I'll never know.

The party descended into the rude phase with quite a few of the 'ladies' becoming mysteriously pregnant. You could tell that this was the case because there were suddenly huge dress-covered bellies appearing all over the place. I noticed there was a corresponding number of party balloons disappearing. This was milked for all the crudity the alcohol could conjure up and then the birthing activity began. For some reason I was given a camera and designated 'birth photographer'. It just got cruder and everybody had a great time. Some of the more straitlaced Europeans seemed to think we had gone too far but I knew we hadn't really got started. The American pilots were having a ball and one Captain turned to me and said, 'Just love you Aussies, great fun. I mean the way your gay guys got dressed up in drag, great.' He was dumbfounded, of course, when I pointed out that the gay blokes were off to a special party soon and none of them had actually cross-dressed.

Fun times, but every now and then, the unusual would take precedent. One night, while I was standing just outside the aircraft door, supervising the loading of migrants in Istanbul, I watched two coppers dragging a bloke up the stairs. I stopped them at the top and gently reminded the police that Australia didn't actually take convicts anymore. The interpreter told me that the police had just stopped this guy from bringing his donkey onto the aircraft. How else was he supposed to get around in Australia when he got there was how he saw it? So he was resisting pretty hard. The rifle crack from behind the hangar was loud enough to grab everyone's attention and when the police pointed out to our mate that that was it, the donkey was no more, he calmed instantly and wandered, very sadly, onto the aircraft. The world was made up of more than Melbourne suburbs it would appear.

On that trip, after getting to Karachi, I and the F/E were wandering along a street near the airport when jeep-loads of troops suddenly cleared the footpaths. We were pushed into an alley and a young soldier with an old British Sten gun held us at gunpoint. When there is no English being spoken and there are nervous young blokes with machine guns, the adrenalin flows – I can tell you. A couple of minutes later, a Presidential motorcade zoomed past and we realised what was happening. The soldiers instantly ignored us and ran to their jeep. We, somewhat shakily, went back to the hostel for a few hundred beers. I had heard enough guns going off near airports for one trip.

One stopover in Manila went pear-shaped on us after we got to the hotel. President Marcos was deposed in a coup – I promise we had nothing to do with it – and chaos ruled for a few days. The airport was closed and there was a changing of the guard. We knew this because guards all over the place just disappeared. In fact, all sorts of uniformed people were trying to sell us their guns or anything else they had – times had changed.

I still have a couple of police badges I did buy to keep these now unemployed people with guns happy. The Philippines, with its close ties to the US, had obviously modelled their police badges on the yanks so these badges look like every badge ever worn by American TV cops – big, golden and flashy. Why wouldn't you buy one, especially if it meant that you and a few mates could then sneak into a newly vacated Presidential Palace and take a squiz?

This we did and it was a surreal experience. Filipinos are wonderfully friendly people but we were as cautious as we could be. We purposefully didn't carry cameras because cameras can make people nervous. This means that I have no hard proof of just how many shoes I saw in rack after rack in Imelda Marcos' dressing-rooms but I still have that 'mind photo' I can tell you.

Tokyo is a big city. I started going up there in the early seventies when the highlight of the night flight would be to spy the Japan Airlines aircraft flying down to Sydney. Two aircraft passing in the night. Fly up into that part of Asia now and if you can't see dozens of aircraft zipping around you just aren't trying. The world has changed as aviation has grown. I often think that the world is connected by aircraft to such an extent now as to make national differences familiar rather than scary. This can only mean that it is harder for the nationalists to formulate distrust and hate to the level of starting big wars. There are plenty of other 'isms' to worry about but blind nationalism is on the decline and that's been a biggie when it comes to war.

This optimism doesn't take away the fact that, over forty years of travelling, I slowly formulated my definition of a nation: a nation is that group of people who considers themselves to be superior to every other group of people. Please name for me one nation that doesn't think of themselves as superior to all others. This superiority can be of a mild nature, like the gap between Australia and New Zealand as seen by both groups of people, or it can be extreme as in the vast gap between say the North Koreans and anybody else – again as perceived by either group. I'm just saying that, as we see more and more of each other around the world, the perceived superiority gap gets smaller. Eventually, instead of looking at inferior people, maybe we will all just see different people. I live in hope.

I'm not the first person to have idealistic aims for mass aviation. Juan Trippe, the legendary head of Pan Am, said in 1966 that he thought, 'Mass travel by air may prove to be more significant to world destiny than the Atom bomb.' He could see that with millions of people travelling and trading with each other and, eventually, learning to like each other, world tensions would ease. As I said, I live in hope.

I was talking about Tokyo being big, but there are really small buildings all over the place. You realise just how small some are when a young S/O who I was introducing to a favourite eating hole tried to steal a menu from this establishment. He wanted to take the menu home and show everyone how this place sold 'flied lice'. He had had his fair share of sake and took no account of the fact, as he tried to stuff this rather large menu up his shirt, that the restaurant was the size of an average Australian bathroom. Mama san, Papa san and fellow pilots just watched in awe as the dingbat tried to hide his activities from people inches away from him. Eventually, two of us had to carry him home.

Small buildings and the occasional monster like the hotel we stayed at – big, strong and built to withstand earthquakes. I was away from this hotel one day wandering the streets, looking at second-hand books in racks outside a row of little shops. These shops were only about two to three metres wide and only one or two storeys high but, surprisingly, free-standing – in that there was about a five-centimetre gap between them. While looking down at the books, I suddenly became aware that I was swaying a bit. There was no alcohol to blame for this so I looked up to see what was happening. As I looked along the street I saw a line of power poles which were swaying backwards and forwards in waves. At the same moment I heard a loud clacking sound from the top of the little shops.

I was going through my first earthquake. I watched everything very carefully but nothing seemed ready to fall. The little buildings were moving and tapping each other but the clever little gaps were preventing any breaking and collapsing. The Japanese had been dealing with earthquakes for thousands of years and I wasn't feeling at all superior to them.

The quake stopped fairly quickly and I skedaddled off back to the hotel. There the talk was all about how the concrete hotel had weathered this event. The building had wobbled and popped but there was no damage to speak of. One flight attendant getting out of the shower had run out into the corridor and promptly got stuck, naked, outside his room when the door locked behind him. A pilot on the other hand had displayed great presence of mind. He told me he had been lying on the bed, when things started moving and when a strip of wood twanged off his wardrobe and banged into the opposite wall he made a decision. He leant over to his bedside table, grabbed the beer can wobbling on top and opened it. He obviously followed the golden rule – never let a chance go by.

34

HISTORICAL HILARITY

This last little chapter is to pay tribute to my old man, a dad, a mentor and a fellow pilot. He died just before his ninety-ninth birthday while this book was being finished.

He was nothing but the consummate professional when it came to flying. He rose from humble depression-era beginnings to achieve respect within his profession from all who knew him and respect and love from those who knew him outside of work.

All this respectability didn't stop him having a great sense of humour. I think I got a bit of my warped one off him. He worked at making his flying days as much fun as possible and would delight in practical jokes whenever he could. The first one I witnessed Captain Austen perform was when I was a passenger on his flight from Melbourne up to Sydney back when I had a been a cadet for only a few months.

Before departure, we were standing just inside the doorway at the top of the stairs at the front door of his Boeing 727. He had been joshing with the *hosties* as the businessmen started up the steps – no aerobridges back then. I expected him to move into the flight deck but just as the first 'suit' came through the door, quick as a flash, he lifted the nearest hostie off her feet and deposited her in the overhead luggage rack. This forerunner of the overhead locker bins they use now was angled sharply upwards so bags wouldn't fall out in turbulence. This meant that if you found yourself up there with your stockinged legs dangling over the edge for all the passengers to see it was quite hard to get out and down. Up went the hostie and a chuckling Captain and his son retired quickly to the flight deck and closed the door. Never let a chance go by and run away if you can – I was learning.

In the later years of his flying, Dad wasn't so prone to manhandling cabin crew but he would quite often tell me of his latest little exploit. One example was when he was about to line up for take-off at Sydney airport one day. He watched another aircraft using the runway turn-off and knew that Sydney tower was about to call his aircraft and clear them for departure. The F/O would have to answer the radio call as Dad was the pilot flying.

He timed the conversation perfectly. He asked the F/O, just as the other aircraft started its turn off the strip, whether he had heard about the senior Captain who had just come out of the closet. 'Who?' the F/O asked. Just the reply Dad had been hoping for. He looked over at the F/O and said, in a very seductive voice, 'Give us a kiss and I'll tell you.' Shocked laughter and my father had to answer the tower's radio instruction himself, which was his plan all along. The F/Os loved flying with this Captain. This was all back in the sixties or seventies and the way women and the LGBT community were viewed was shameful. The things my old man got up to would, quite rightfully, be seen as unacceptable today, even though no malice was intended. He was one of the fairest blokes I know. Never once did I hear any sort of bigoted or sexist comment from him. He always took the underdog's side – a good role model for his kids.

My father may have calmed down a bit as he got older but the postwar years were when he worked at the 'fun' thing pretty bloody hard. New hosties were quite often the targets of these practical jokes but passengers weren't spared either. The long multi-stop flights through the outback in the DC3 were the main opportunities for some of the best scams these young pilots got up to.

If there was a new hostie on a flight, she was fair game for some 'fun' – I don't mean that sort either. These women were tough. The pilots were the least of their troubles. A male-dominated passenger list and the social attitudes of the times meant that no naive shrinking violets applied for this job – glamorous, it wasn't. So, cue newbie's first flight through the desert. She would give the cardboard box meals to the two pilots and then go back into the cabin. A short time later she would be called up to the cockpit – flight deck doesn't sound right for these old classics – to bring a sick bag up. The F/O's hangover was catching up with him apparently.

What the poor woman didn't know was that the small can of fruit salad in the F/Os lunchbox had been opened and was ready to be tipped into said vomit bag as she handed it over to him. A little distraction by the Captain and a lot of loud barfing from the F/O and the bag was full. Both Captain and hostie were absolutely disgusted by this and the F/O would be suitably embarrassed as he handed the bag back to the hostie. The Captain would then grab the bag and announce, 'Hey, there's good food in there and it's still warm.' He would grab his spoon and get stuck into the contents. Dad said there were all sorts of reactions to this scam.

The most innovative and athletic DC3 desert trick was the 'left behind co-pilot' ruse. This involved a short flight between two dirt strips only about five minutes flying apart. The DC3 would take off and cross a meandering river that was wide and usually dry, but still uncrossable by land vehicle. The short flight would mean that neither cattle station nor town was completely isolated. The hostie would close the main door down the back and the two pilots would get the aircraft airborne.

Straight after this the F/O would get out of his seat and hide amongst the mail bags at the back of the cockpit. The hostie would then be instructed over the phone to send the F/O up from the passenger cabin because it was time to get ready to land. She would run up and tell the Captain that he wasn't there and, of course, she didn't find him sitting in the right-hand pilot seat either. The Captain would feign being upset because now he would have to do all the work himself and pick up the left-behind F/O the next day on the way home.

Landing on the other side of the river the aircraft would come to a stop. The F/O had to quickly open a small door on the side of the cockpit, where the mail bags are accessed, and jump down out of the aircraft – he actually had to hang by his fingertips and then drop.

Once on the ground, he would run around to the main door and greet the hostie as she opened it. Puff, puff, 'Please don't lock me out again. Puff, puff. Do you know how hard it is to run that fast through a dry riverbed?'

As I said, passengers weren't spared. On the long boring sectors, Dad would go to the toilet right down the back of the aircraft. As he got out of his seat, he would attach two bits of thin cord to his control wheel and on emerging from the cockpit, would hand the ends to the passenger sitting in the front row on the right-hand side of the cabin. They could see the vacated seat and the ropes on the control wheel but, significantly, couldn't see the F/O actually flying the aircraft from the right-hand pilot's seat. Dad would hand over the cords and say, 'Keep it straight will you, mate. I'm busting for a pee.'

A toilet at the rear of a DC4 featured in another joke on the passengers. This was a much bigger four-engine aircraft with a cargo and baggage hold under the passengers. This underfloor cargo area was key to this scam and would be utilised on the longer boring sectors.

Having achieved the quiet cruise stage, one pilot may need to visit the toilet. He would march down past all the passengers and enter the toilet. When he was ready, he would take the rear panel off the toilet and enter the cargo space behind. He would refit the panel and go down under the floor and crawl through until he was under the cockpit where there was a trapdoor. Once back in his seat, the other pilot would then proceed to visit the cabin. The passengers would see this second pilot leave the cockpit without recalling the first returning. What was going on and who was flying this thing? If the pilots were really bored, the second bloke would visit the toilet and take the underground route home and then a third pilot would appear. This play acting could also work in reverse with multiple pilots magically appearing from the rear of the cabin and disappearing into what must be a very crowded cockpit. Messing with peoples' heads is of course essential in all this and subtlety has its own quality.

Hey, it wasn't always these old-timers or indeed only pilots that used the under floor for fun. On the original Jumbos, there was quite a large galley under the passenger cabin. Access was by a small one-man lift hidden inside the upstairs galley at one end of this underfloor wonder. Safety being safety there had to be an escape hatch at the far end of the space. If you pushed a big lever at the end of the subterranean galley, a section of the carpeted aisle above would tip up and you could run up the escape ladder. This escape hatch was between seats 44C and 44D – or thereabouts. I remember being down in the cabin when I was given the heads up.

The bloke in 44C had just ordered a gin and tonic. With a couple of flight attendants making sure there was nobody using the aisle the 'go' signal was given. One poor unsuspecting passenger was happily reading his magazine when an arm appeared from the floor beside him, a drink was clunked down on his tray table and a voice announced, 'Here's your G and T, mate!' The arm disappeared back into the floor as the cabin crew and a young S/O rolled around the galley in fits. Yep, I had a great laugh and I didn't have to crawl through all the bags and cargo to get it.

My brother and I, in keeping with our old man's sense of humour, plan to distribute small amounts of his ashes at various sporting ovals around Australia where his sporting career occurred in both cricket and Aussie rules footy. This is illegal for obvious reasons so we had to come up with a ruse Dad would have been proud of. We will do this distribution, of a responsibly token amount of ashes, as if we are POWs during WW2 and are the two blokes tasked with distributing the escape tunnel dirt under the watchful eyes of the German guards.

We will walk around innocently letting the little bit of ash escape from the holes in our trousers pockets. As we do this we'll be singing a couple of Dad's favourite wartime songs, just to distract the guards. The plans are evolving and my brother and I are having trouble keeping about six women, including our ninety-four-year-old mum, from gatecrashing this celebration. I'm just beginning to realise that these women aren't going to let this chance go by.

His grandson is currently doing some training in the very same flight training complex that the old training Captain started teaching at over sixty years ago. I just hope they don't have a course in overhead locker loading.

P.S. Since I wrote that last comment my son mentioned out of the blue that he had just watched a long boring company-produced video on how to lift luggage. I'm too scared to ask whether the overhead bins were mentioned. Aviation has given me so much over the years and it appears as if it isn't going to stop anytime soon.

RIP Captain V C Austen MAP (Master Air Pilot) 1918–2017

Thanks for the sense of humour and the chance to be your wicketkeeper when I was only fifteen. You were by far the best and fastest bowler I ever kept for.

See the GLOSSARY below.

Glossary of Terms

Explanations for those baffled by the Australian dialect.

I was in a tour bus in Scotland recently, the young woman guide told the bus that something had been around for **'donkey's years.'** I and the other Australian and British passengers knew what she meant but the Americans and Canadians had no idea. Well rhyming slang for 'years' is 'ears.' Donkeys ears are the longest around so 'donkey's years' (the ears morphed into years) is a bloody long time.

I'm Australian and have always used the word **'cactus'** for something that is broken. The word means more than broken really, totally f*#*d is more like it. Now I love this - its origins can be traced back to the Australian Air Force during the second world war. There are other possible derivations but being an old pilot, whose father was in the Australian Air Force during that war, I will have none of them mentioned here.

Another term I use in the book that comes from WW2, is the expression **'pear shaped.'** Again there are a few possible origins but the Oxford dictionary says it came from the British Air Force where a pilot trying to do perfect circular 'loops' would sometimes mess them up and fly a 'pear shape' instead. The term has come to mean something that has gone bad on you, something that wasn't a problem but now is. I did my share of pear shaped loops but I had no idea I was just perpetuating an expression and cementing it into the language.

The word that is used probably more than any other word in the book is '**bloke.**' Old English slang for 'man.' A bloke is one of the guys.

Just be careful you don't include a woman in your 'Come on you blokes, let's have a beer,' the woman, if she is Australian, may well '**deck**' you. Lying on your back on the floor with a swollen lip is when you know you've just been decked the Australian way.

Metric and imperial weights and measures are used throughout the book, hopefully readers in the USA will not get confused.

Main Measures:

A '**kilometre**' 1.6 kilometres equals a mile.

A '**kilogram**' 1 kilo equals 2.2 pounds.

A '**tonne**' 1 tonne equals 1.1 US ton.

A '**metre**' A metre is a yard and a bit. (a bit is always about 10%)

A '**klick**' is a kilometre in distance or as a speed, a kilometre per hour.

The physics course I did in high school was a beauty, it set you up for any higher education in that subject: it was in metric and was an American course. Go figure.

'**Donks**' as in donkeys as in engines. The cactus engine is a broken donk. (One 747 donk equals 60,000 horsepower: pretty big donkey.)

'**Mates/mateship**': a driving force in Australian males. Strong friendship but strictly hetro. Mostly.

'**Dipstick**' cleaned up version of 'dipshit' meaning someone exceptionally dim.

- **'Dropkick'** in Australian football a dropkick is the most erratic, useless type of kick. It has come to mean someone who is pretty useless.
- **'Cold enough to freeze the balls of a brass monkey'** means really cold. Apparently on an old sailing ship cannon balls would topple out of a brass triangular enclosure called a monkey if the brass shrank enough with the freezing cold. Yeah right.
- **'Dole-bludger,'** someone on the dole (unemployment benefits) who is too lazy to look for work.
- To take a **'squiz'** is to look closely. Squint and quiz; combine them and you get a close questioning look. I can't make this stuff up. P.S. I just heard Paul Hogan (Crocodile Dundee) on the radio, he reckons a great word he heard from a couple of fans was that they were having a 'gawk' at him. A similar thing to squiz and the price of fame for a film star I would think.
- To get the **'irrits'** is to get extremely annoyed or *irrit*ated.
- **'Herbing'** along is to travel fast.
- **'Cooee'** A loud drawn out call used to attract attention in the Australian bush. Not within 'cooee' is to be a long way away.
- **'Dingbat'** just what it sounds like, somebody more stupid than you.
- **'Deedoo Deedoo'** from the theme music to that great Sci-Fi TV show 'The Twilight Zone'
- It has come to mean something really bloody strange.
- **'Firies'** and **'Ambos'** Fire fighters and Ambulance crew.
- **'Billy Can'** small light-weight cooking pot. Usually used to boil water for tea or coffee.

Acknowledgments

In putting this book together I was aware that I would have to get two things right.

The first would be to get what I was saying accurate, the second would be to get the message across so that the non-aviator would enjoy the book. To do this I enlisted the help of fellow pilots to make sure I was getting it accurate and friends to make sure I was making it enjoyable.

Col Adams, Bronwyn Austen, Geoff Austen, Ernie Bolton, Bob Connolly, Tim Fitzpatrick, Bandula Gonsalkorale, Dilhara Gonsalkorale, Toby Gursanscky, Rene Herbert, Jon Hornibrook, Peter Hunter, John Joppich, Grant Keetley, Paul Limmer, Geoff Markwell, Naomi and Jeff Shaw, Stephen Wallace and Ray Vuilerman. The editors Russell Thomson and Peter Gray.

Thank you one and all. Thank you also to you the reader I hope you had a great flight.

Notes

A bit more information, explanation, photos and web locations of videos relevant to the stuff in the chapters. I've even put graphs and formulas in just to bore you to tears, feel free to ignore.

1 – CLOUD SURFING

I talk of a jet engine producing horsepower. They actually produce 'thrust', which is just another way of saying power. One pound of thrust equals one horsepower if the jet engine is moving at 325 knots. Strange, but jet engines came after the horse-drawn era and deserve their own definitions.

Jumbo on approach all 'dirtied up' with flaps and landing gear. This is actually a photo of Qantas' last 747 doing one of its last landings into Sydney.

2 – WHY BECOME A PILOT?

*Two retired airline pilots under an Auster.
Peter (left) flew us to Darwin.*

Inside the Auster – the Wright brothers wouldn't have been impressed.

3 – SECURITY ISSUES.

Video of hijacked aircraft being blown up in the desert. Qantas and I were lucky that day.
(https://www.youtube.com/watch?v=5de6fYWKDWU)

British, American and Swiss jets being blown up on Dawson's Field. The Qantas jet made it to London with no problems.

4 – CADET TRAINING.

Turning circles and angles of bank and apparent weight (G forces).

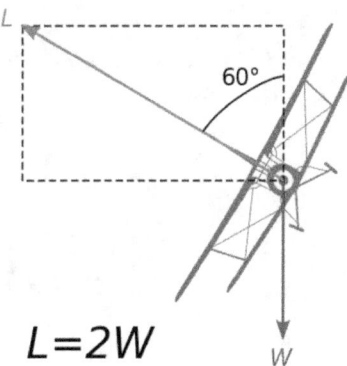

I've actually flown something that looks like this diagram aircraft. The maths are the same for a Tiger Moth and a Boeing 747.

It's all to do with the cosine and the tangent of the angle of bank. Roll the aircraft to its normal 15 to 20 degrees to go around a corner and passengers will notice a little increase in weight but not enough to be annoying. Increase the angle of bank to 60 degrees, what pilots call a steep turn, then the apparent gravity is suddenly doubled. It's a cosine thing.

The steeper the angle of bank, the smaller the turning circle. The tangent of the angle comes into play here; speed is the other factor. So, keeping the angle of bank at a passenger-friendly 15 degrees but maintaining your Concorde like two times the speed of sound speed makes the radius of turn ridiculous. Tipping your aircraft over enough to have a small turning circle would be even more ridiculous, your passengers would all black out as the blood left their brains with the extra G forces. It's like when Boeing loses engineers to Airbus – it's an aviation brain drain. (Sorry.)

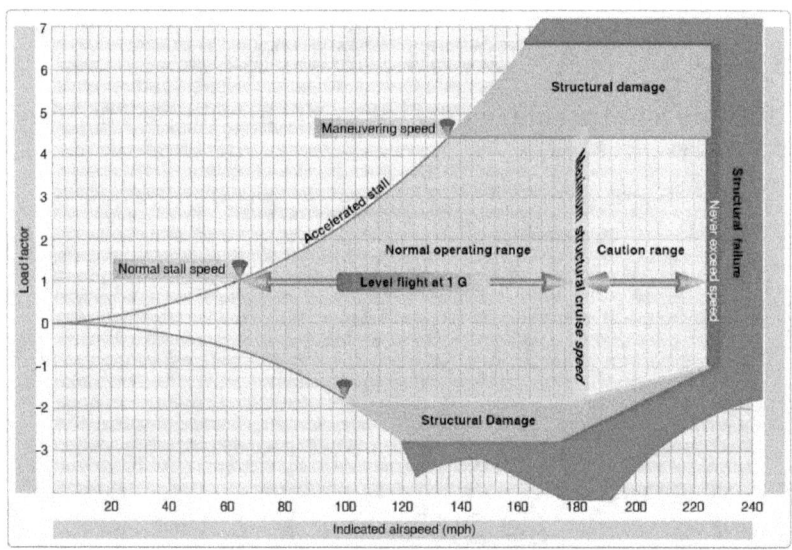

I have no idea what the above graph does or means but it looks fantastic.

I think it might have to with not stressing your aircraft to breaking point by applying too much G-force. Sounds like a thing that should be avoided.

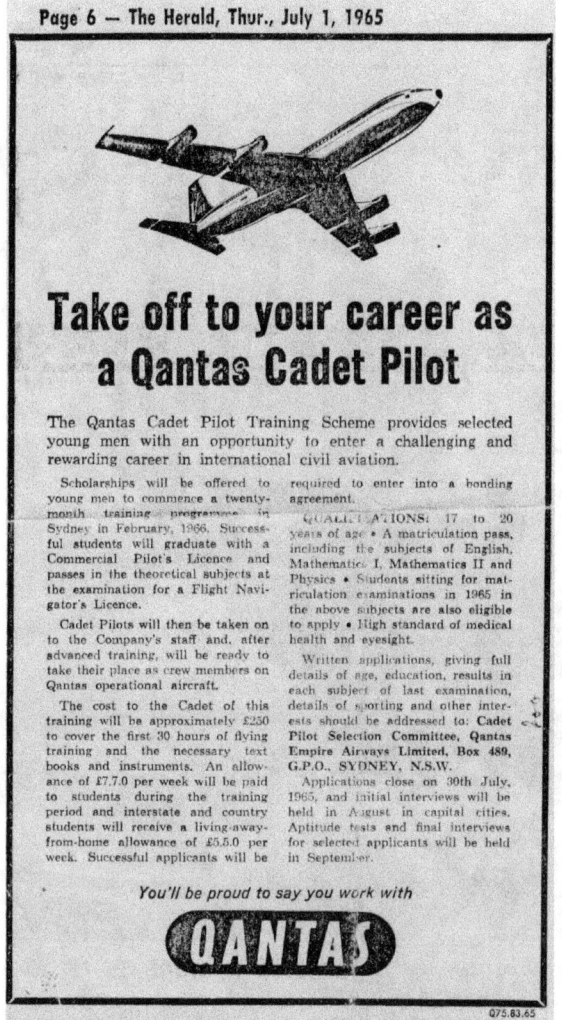

Qantas EMPIRE Airways will offer scholarships to young MEN and pay them in POUNDS, SHILLINGS and PENCE. Times had to change – and they did.

By the way, I didn't want a career as a Cadet Pilot; I wanted to progress further than that.

Ah, so young and innocent. Graduation of 4th course. Going up the back row I'm the 7th young 'space cadet'. That's what other Qantas people called us anyway.

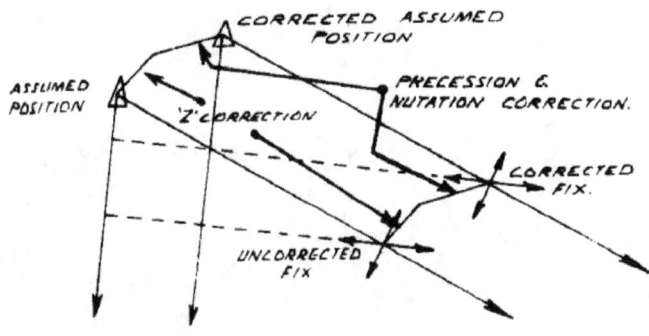

FIGURE 2 - CORRECTION OF THE ASSUMED POSITION
*From some old 'Astro Nav' notes- no wonder I had
no idea where I was most of the time.
Now I'm just not sure what I'm doing most of the time.*

5 — AILERONS.

With my aileron control problem back in the 90s in mind, I went looking in the Smithsonian Aerospace Museum recently. I found two little models depicting the two different flight control systems used in modern aircraft. There was the mechanical one with cables running through pulleys to the control surfaces like the ailerons and elevators. It was pretty flimsy and over the years the millions, and I do mean millions, of kids just hammering the joystick in all directions had taken its toll. The controls hardly moved and the control surfaces just flopped around a bit.

I moved on to the electronic fly-by-wire model – beautiful looking thing. The wires led from control handle through electronic circuit boards to little actuators on the ailerons and elevators. Now we were talking. This was how it should be; I took the control handle in my hand and moved it around. Nothing happened – nothing. Says it all, really. Somewhere the Swiss cheese had a hole in it and the electrons all fell out.

*Two photos through glass of the models in the Smithsonian.
I had to push little kids out of the way to get even these.*

*Wheel well shown with the doors open.
Usually they close up again after the wheel go up or down.
Lots of stuff inside it, cables and pulleys for a start.*

Animation of Undercarriage and the doors. (This one is an A380)
https://www.youtube.com/watch?v=P1Xarq1Yr1Y
On Takeoff—Doors open—Wheels up—Doors close.
On Landing—Doors open—Wheels down—Doors close.

Me doing the walk around inspection at the Avalon air show. This picture is in here not only to remind me of the rip in my uniform trouser leg but also to show what the wheel-well door looks like in comparison with the photo above it. The door closes back up after the gear comes down. The ground engineer had to open the door to see the great lump of ice covering the control line pulley. I've never seen the photos; I have enough nightmares without them thanks.

Dutch Roll video
(https://www.youtube.com/watch?v=Zmjam1evDD4)

Dutch Roll Damping Technique

AIRPLANE MOTION AND INDICATION

NOTE : DUTCH ROLL ½ CYCLE TIME - 2 TO 3 SECONDS

CORRECT WHEEL INPUTS

PILOT ACTION				
Roll motion to right stopped.	Rolling motion to left beginning.	Wing level.	Roll rate to left reducing.	Rolling motion to left stopped.
Wheel centered.	Wheel to right to counteract rolling motion to left.	Roll rate to left at maximum. Wheel to right approximately equal to max bank angle to left expected.	Wheel to right reduced.	Wheel centered.

It says use the ailerons; too bad if they don't work.

6 — UNUSUAL FLIGHTS.

Young flying instructor wearing warm flying jacket; it gets cold up there, down there in Melbourne.

The debate over how wings work goes on.

Increase the angle of attack of the wing and more air is forced down away from its initial relative path and in agreement with Newton's laws there is an equal upward push on the wing.

Increase the angle of attack of the wing and the curvature on the top of the wing forces the air that is travelling over the top to travel further in a given time and, because of this increase in speed, that air loses some of its pressure. (Bernoulli's principle.) The air underneath the wing has now gained relatively in pressure and therefore there is an upward push on the wing.

Both these statements are true. Flat-winged balsa wood gliders work without the classic curvature you see on an air foil shape. Curved upper surfaces really do reduce pressure on the upper surfaces of aircraft wings. I was called out of the flight deck to check out what was on the wing of a 767 one day over the Tasman Sea. Some type of rubber, non-skid surface had been laid on part of the wing before departure and unfortunately the glue hadn't dried properly. What I saw was this rubber being sucked up into a semi-sphere the size of half a basketball. I alleviated the passengers' fears by pointing out the most graphic example of reduced upper wing pressure anybody had ever seen. My exuberance and childlike glee at seeing this wasn't totally contrived, even though I was deliberately making light of the whole thing.

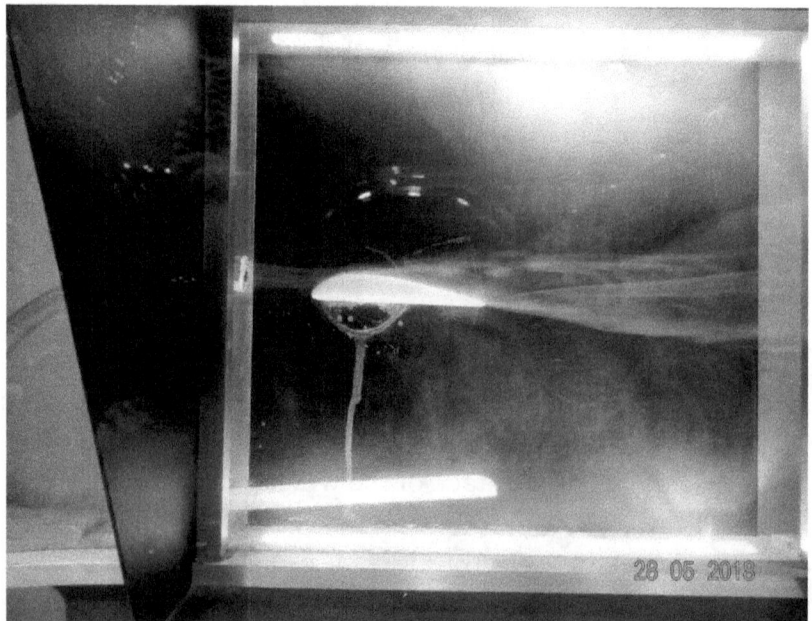

Here's another photo from the Smithsonian. I had to snap over the kids' heads. It was getting embarrassing elbowing them out of the way.

Here's a poem by another very young pilot killed in a mid-air collision. The author and Holly Smith were almost the same age when they died.

'High Flight'
Oh! I have slipped the surly bonds of Earth
And danced the skies on laughter-silvered wings;
Sunward I've climbed, and joined the tumbling mirth
of sun-split clouds – and done a hundred things
You have not dreamed of – wheeled and soared and swung
High in the sunlit silence. Hov'ring there,
I've chased the shouting wind along, and flung
My eager craft through footless halls of air ...
Up, up the long, delirious burning blue,
I've topped the wind-swept heights with easy grace
Where never lark, or even eagle flew –
And, while with silent, lifting mind I've trod
The high untrespassed sanctity of space,
Put out my hand, and touched the face of God.
                    John Gillespie Magee Jnr. RCAF.

7 – FLYING NEAR FIRES.

Aussie fires 2020

I mentioned 30,000 fire fighters on duty on one day. The Victorian CFA operates more than 4,000 vehicles, including 1,970 4WD tankers, 264 pumpers, 11 hydraulic platform (aerial) trucks, 28 rescue tenders, 16 hazmat vehicles plus numerous other vehicles including communications vans, lighting trucks, command and transport vehicles. This fleet is supplemented by more than 1,400 brigade-owned vehicles. There are 1,200 base radios, 5,800 vehicle radios, 3,000 handheld radios, 35,000 EAS pagers, 58 satellite terminals and 10,700 pre-conference telephone interceptors (whatever they are).

The CFA also leases a large fleet of firefighting aircraft to assist brigades throughout the busy Summer fire season. The fleet comprises rotary and fixed wing aircraft, from small single-engine planes up to Very Large Aerial Tankers, based on commercial passenger jets.

Those impressive numbers are for the small state of Victoria where I did my bushfire flying. The state where I live and where the Blue Mountains are, New South Wales, has the world's largest volunteer fire service. There are currently 75,000 volunteer bushfire firefighters. This does not include the 7,000 full-time firefighters and their 7,000 special volunteer helpers. This is for a state with the same population as Washington State USA or London. There are 6,000 firefighters in London. If you are an Englishman this means that a London firefighter is worth 15 New South Wales firefighters – either that, or fire is 15 times worse in NSW.

I heard a great Blue Mountains fire 'battle' story from an ex-Air Force Qantas mate. Well, what is it if not a battle when artillery is used and directed by forward observers? The battle was against a vicious little fire demon forcing its way up the side of a hill, determined to destroy a row of houses built on the downhill side of a road. The firefighters had managed to borrow a great water cannon from the nearby Air Force base and had it positioned on the road but, significantly, on the other side of the houses to the fire.

With the observers on the balconies of the threatened houses directing the water spurts from the big cannon with their radios, the pump operators put their shots over the houses to exactly where they were needed. No houses were lost on that street. The pump operators were totally dependent on directions over the radio and the landing shells had that great Kurt Vonnegut (*Slaughterhouse Five*) reverse war thing going and, instead of starting fires, these shells put them out.

For those in gentler climates, here are a couple of videos that may explain why Australians like me are wary of bushfires. They kill way more than all our spiders, snakes, crocodiles, jelly fish and sharks combined.
(https://youtu.be/lDTrqQM9NqM)
(https://www.youtube.com/watch?v=XMhUU1BBRdY)

8 – VERTIGO.

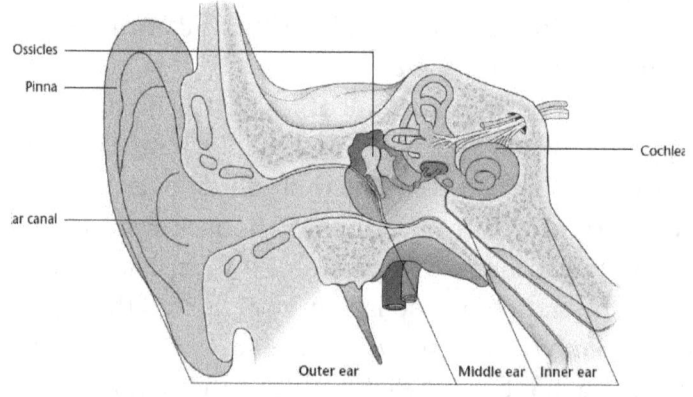

9 – EARTH SHADOW.

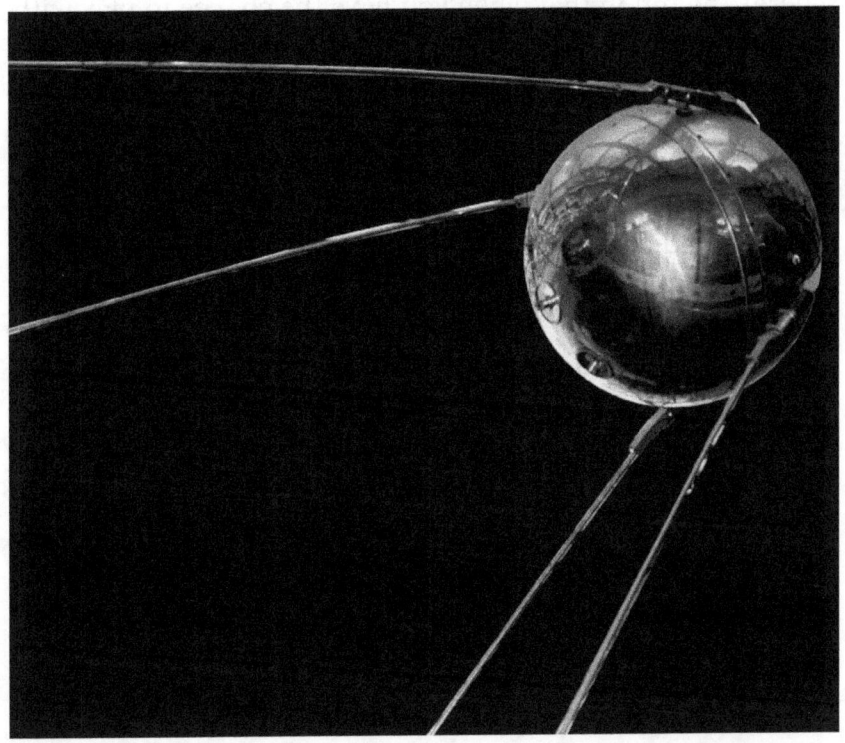

Sputnik started it all. Now there are nearly 5000 satellites.

Using formulas for volume of spheres, air density, hydrogen density (air is 15.5 times heavier than hydrogen) and the lead density of 11.4gm/cc you can, like I did, make a spreadsheet to find out how big your lead balloon needs to be to carry a small white mouse. So, 48 years after Frank and I started it on a tablecloth, I used a couple of modern-day tools to finish the calculation. The advantage of a spreadsheet is that you can fool around with the various parameters to your heart's content and you can try all the 'what ifs' you want.

My actuary coffee mate tells me to just use a formula. Where's the fun in that when you have the chance to play with a spreadsheet.

If you can get your lead down to a thickness of 2 mm you only need a balloon diameter of 1.2 m or 4 feet – theoretically, anyway. The impracticalities of thin lead and making a sphere out of it confines this project to paper only. Some academics used lead foil to build a balloon in the late 70s and the *MythBusters* did it again recently. Cheats, one and all – WTF is lead foil?

Captain Frank Brown or, as we young S/Os used to call him, Blank Frown, (pilots are just so witty) would have used spreadsheets all the time if he had access to them. When he was doing his stuff, unfortunately for him but good for the rest of us, they were just being invented by a couple of hippies who refused to take out a patent on them and instead gifted them to humankind – a great tool to be used forever more.

Sir Arthur C Clark, the famous science-fiction writer, like Frank Brown, worked in the RAF during the war as a boffin (scientist). I often wonder whether they met. Sir Arthur did all sorts of fancy stuff with radar but, right at the end of the war, he came up with the idea of putting communication satellites into geostationary orbits. Again, he didn't patent the idea, calling it an idea for humanity and not his or anybody else's to profit by. He had hippy ethics as well.

10 – EARLY DAYS.

The Mighty Boeing 707. This one has Flight Management Computers and a modern radar; a bit like putting cruise control onto a 1968 Volkswagen Beetle.

Early days all right! Check out the sideboards – you needed those if you wanted to talk to young women in mini-skirts. It was the 70s. The white-top caps disappeared from Qantas for 45 years and then made a comeback in 2017.

How to impress people who are seeing a white guy haggle for the first time in their lives ... One day in China, way off the beaten track, there was an interested audience to a street market purchase. About a half dozen blokes were watching how a creature from another universe would stand the hot blowtorch of street haggling. I had 8 yuan in my hand and I had spotted a small ceramic turtle, an ideal gift for the nine-year-old boy at home who was way into turtles.

A plan was hatched – 8 yuan in the hand, so that must be the price. I had no idea if that was a fair price but it was not a lot – so why not? The goods were displayed on a blanket on the ground and I asked the blanket holder, 'How much?' I was using hand language as these blokes only spoke Mandarin. The merchant pulled out a basic calculator and put a price of 12 for the turtle on the screen. Ridiculous – he was dreaming. I would only pay 4, significantly, the same amount below the fortune I held in my hand as the asking price was above. So, when his price came down by one, my offer would go up one, and eventually we would meet in the middle. Of course, the middle was 8. We met and I handed over my money.

Much satisfaction was gained by all the spectators. The white guy had haggled hard and a fair price was, by definition, achieved. But wait, one sharp-eyed spectator had noticed how easily I handed over the money, no counting out from a pile but instead I had just opened my hand. Well, he realised and told everybody very loudly of his discovery. The alien had known before the haggling started what the final price would be. There was stunned silence as these guys took this in. No, I didn't know the future but I can do quick mental arithmetic and I did know how much I had to play with.

11 – GUNS, DIAMONDS AND CASH.

Big diamond, downtown Jo-Burg.

Dehydrated animal carcasses, ready for the discerning buyer.

12 – ON THE CHANGING TIMES.

Captain Deborah Lawrie, first Aussie woman pilot in a major airline.

First Qantas women pilots. Sharelle Quinn and Ann Bennett. Note the one stripe of the Pilot Under Initial Training (PUIT.)

13 – ON SPACE AND STUFF.

On my recent pilot pilgrimage to the Smithsonian Air and Space Museum in Washington DC, I saw it all – sputniks hanging from the ceilings, Saturn V rocket engines, the insides of all the big Jumbo engines – you name it, it was there. I walked through the Skylab mock-up and I could see its fuel tank origins. I could also look up into the more empty spaces and see the running track. Lucky bastards, what I wouldn't give for just one vertical lap, or should that be one upside down lap, it's all relative to something.

Mock up of Skylab in the Smithsonian.

Lucky bastard
Video of astronauts having too much fun exercising.
(https://youtu.be/S_p7LiyOUx0)

Alan Shepard doing his thing.
Videos of Moon golf:
https://www.youtube.com/watch?v=BUwGe9zzxoE
https://www.youtube.com/watch?v=NTnoyaffOkQ

Apollo 14 landing video. I'm calling bullshit on this one, the last few minutes anyway, the real Alan Shepard didn't describe it like this.

(https://www.youtube.com/watch?v=W6rZvxhgxZg)

Space orbital formula

Space orbital formula

Vo (Orbital Velocity) Ve (Escape Velocity)

$Vo = \sqrt{gR}$

$Ve = \sqrt{2gR}$

Energy equates to the square of the velocity.
($\frac{1}{2}MV^2$) so energising above:

Energy (o) = ½ gRM and Energy (e) = gRM

Energy to escape = 2 times Energy to orbit.

(As I said – magic!)

15 – VIETNAM FLYING.

I just read some wartime history about the horrific casualties Royal Air Force light bomber crews suffered in the early months of WW2. The bombers, when and if they did return to base, would often drag their trailing radio aerials over houses near the airstrips and do quite a bit of damage.

B 52 bomber. Just what they looked like coming home from their missions.

In memory of those civilian aircrew and ground staff — who under control of the RAAF — operated unarmed aircraft in Papua New Guinea and over the Pacific and Indian Oceans during the Second World War. Their roles included evacuating civilians and soldiers from threatened areas, dropping supplies to troops, and keeping the air routes and lines of communication open.

Eighteen Australian civilian aircrew were killed during the war.

During the Vietnam War members of the Australian Task Force and other personnel of Australian Forces, Vietnam were transported to and from the country by chartered QANTAS aircraft flown by civilian aircrew.

Dedicated by "Skippy Squadron" (QANTAS civilian aircrew — Vietnam) on 30 January 2007, the 65th anniversary of the first QANTAS aircraft and crew lost to enemy action in the Second World War.

AUSTRALIAN WAR MEMORIAL   PL00126

Qantas 707 loading up with diggers

Squadron logo. The ribbons are for the medals awarded.

16 – REFUGEES.

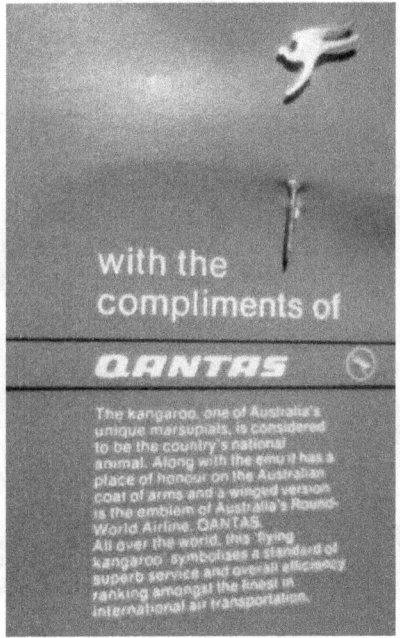

17 – LOS ANGELES RIOTS.

The video of Rodney King being beaten by the LAPD. Not for the squeamish. My daughter tells me she had to study this video in depth and the case that it sparked in law school.
https://www.youtube.com/watch?v=sb1WywIpUtY

Lots of fires like this all over LA.

18 – MELBOURNE BALLOON.

Melbourne balloon just recently. Gas, sparks and wicker don't go well together. Luckily, on this day, passengers and pilot weren't in the mix.

One of two balloons that crashed on the same day down there in Melbourne. Just what are they doing down there? I love that the Chinese tourists 'were whisked away' to a champagne breakfast.

Wheels spin up and the rubber gets deposited .
Here's a video.
https://youtu.be/fSodzuCwRYI

And no, you can't put little electric motors on the wheels to spin them up before landing. Lots of problems if you do that. Mismatch of wheel and landing speed, failed motor on one wheel, landing with the wheels not pointing straight down the runway are just the start. See this video for more and this bloke doesn't even go into gyroscopic forces messing with the aircraft.

https://youtu.be/AJRf1jDiaXw

19 – I ONLY FIGHT WOMEN PASSENGERS.

I found this post below on an aviation forum (not my spelling) By beerdrinker - Tue Dec 31, 2013 5:12 pm The middle of Australia is know as the Great Australian F**k All. Years ago a whit in the Oz CAA named a waypoint in the middle of this airspace GAFFA. Sadly no longer there.

And you wonder why the woman in Hong Kong wanted off the aircraft.

20 – MARS.

CONGRATULATIONS

You are now one in a million (or probably a lot more)

At 09:51 UTC (Universal Coordinated Time) 27/8/2003 when you were approximately 10 kilometres above the Earths surface, you were also directly under the planet Mars. At this precise moment Mars happened to be at its closest point to Earth in some 60,000 years. This combination of events brought you closer to our heavenly neighbour than almost all modern humans, making you "one in a million" or better.

This comes as a direct result of you being astute enough to arrange your travel itinerary so that you were aboard this Qantas flight 25 bound for Los Angeles out of Auckland New Zealand on the night of the red planet's closest point. Well done, especially as this was a close encounter at no extra expense.

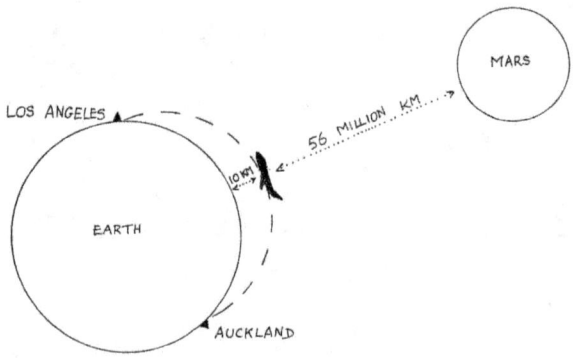

Feel free to tell your grandchildren about this achievement and be sure to point out that they will have to become deep space astronauts/cosmonauts to equal it.

Thank you, Captain W.V.Austen

There is one certificate holder for every 20 million people on Earth

Video of clever people doing clever things on Mars. As the closest human ever to Mars, I give them permission to keep doing so. (I'm pretty sure they couldn't care less what I say.)
https://www.youtube.com/watch?v=zeApJ2nuYmY

21 – TYPE WARS AND AIRSHOWS.

Windy Wellington approaches video – 36 seconds in, is a Qantas 767. I could easily be the bloke fighting the controls.
https://www.youtube.com/watch?v=IA7qkUeltNI

Flying a 767.

First glass cockpit aircraft I flew –the times were a-changin'. As a Captain, I saw my first female technical crew on this aircraft. A junior S/O was the first and she presented a problem. All the rest of these junior pilots were generically nicknamed 'Baldrick' after the smelly little Blackadder underling. This didn't fit this female S/O but, because she could easily have been the daughter of a couple of hippies, she was awarded the title 'Moonbeam' and it stuck for years. Checking the instruments in the photo above, you can see the climbing ability of a twin jet; 13,000 feet and climbing at an easy 3,500 feet a minute. 40 mph or 65 klicks vertical component; no wonder I went a quarter of the way to the moon.

Dad at the Avalon Air Show in a Dragon Rapide.

I'm behind him making sure he doesn't try to fly with this one pissed and broke; it doesn't look like it would fly with two healthy motors, let alone one. You just have to call those engines motors, don't you? By the way check out the motor that took me to Darwin in the Auster (photo above in the Chapter 2 notes.) Dad told a great story of carrying a dead body one day in one of these aircraft; got it in okay but then rigor mortis set in. It was a bugger to get out he said – we won't go into the details.

22 – SEX (X RATED)

*Qantas "Hosties" uniforms through the years,
I well remember the orange mini-skirts.*

Ah Tahiti!

23 – DIFFERENCES.

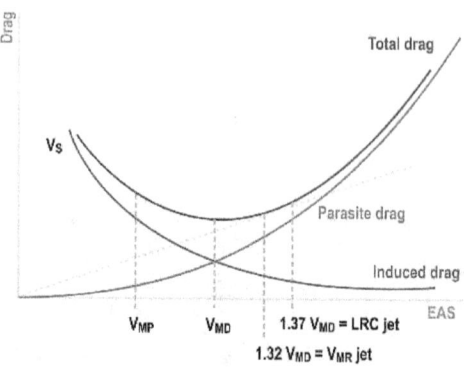

Vary the speed (EAS) and the drag varies; I used to understand graphs like this. EAS is short for Equivalent Air Speed; close enough to Indicated Air Speed.

EAS as a function of impact pressure and static pressure (valid for subsonic flow):

$$EAS = a_0 \sqrt{\frac{5P}{P_0}\left[\left(\frac{q_c}{P}+1\right)^{\frac{2}{7}}-1\right]}$$

And you wonder why I have kept the book as simple as I could.

Airport entrance

Bill Austen

Jumbo landing on snow-covered runway. Note how hard it is to see the runway lights in these conditions. You can pick out one just in front of No 3 engine but, even with a dark background, it's still hard to see; maybe black lights would have indeed been better. This is a later model Jumbo than the one I helped land in Frankfurt; you can tell by the winglets. I was once told by a Melbourne airport ground controller to, 'Follow the Virgin with the big tips.' His next comment was, 'I've always wanted to say that.'

Not as bad as the other ground controller up in Darwin who, when asked by the captain of a taxiing aircraft whether its rotating beacon was working replied, 'Yes it is, no it's not, yes it is, no it's not.' It gets hot up there in Darwin.

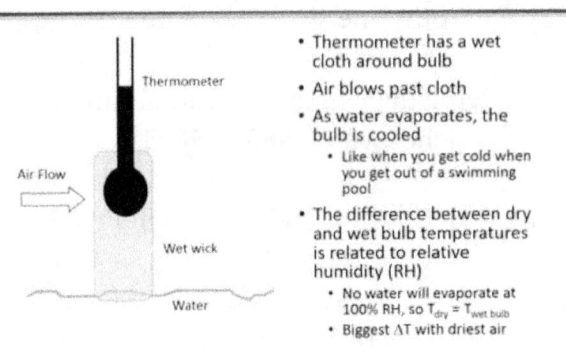

A wet bulb drawing.

The only wet bulb thermometer I'm interested in now is the one in my swimming pool.

I talk about losing nearly 99% of the aircraft's energy from cruise to touchdown.

Here's the proof but feel free to skip.

So a 1 kg aircraft at 500 knots cruising at 41000 feet has energy from its speed and altitude.

M = 1 kg   V = 500 kts = 257 mtrs/sec
H = 41000 ft = 12497 mtrs
G = 9.8 mtrs/sec^2

Energy from velocity (kinetic) = 1/2 MV^2 = 33024 joules
Energy from Height (potential) = MGH = 122470 joules
Total Energy = 155495 joules

Energy of the 1 kg aircraft touching down at 125 knots.
M = 1 kg   V = 125 kts = 61 m/s
H = 0 ft or mtrs
G = 9.8 mtrs/sec^2

Energy from velocity (kinetic) = 1/2 MV^2 = 1860 joules
Energy from Height (potential) = MGH = 0 joules
Total Energy = 1860 joules

Percentage of energy remaining
on touchdown = 1860/155495 = 1.2%

THE AIRCRAFT HAS LOST 98.8% OF ITS ENERGY BEFORE IT TOUCHES DOWN. THE REMAINING 1.2% IS ENOUGH TO SET FIRE TO THE BRAKES IF YOUR'E NOT CAREFUL.

24 – FLIGHTS WITH STRETCHERS.

'Classic' Boeing 747.

Note the Engineer's panel to the right. I became a First Officer on these.

The huge crew from the charity flight for the kids with disabilities. You can see the big bloke in the white shirt in the top centre; he's the very proud Captain who will always thank Captain Toby (seated bottom left) for getting him to do the flight.

747-400 'Electric Jumbo'

You can see the lamb's wool seat covers; the little blind girl got that right. I really hope this photo was taken inside a simulator.

The Sri Lankan tsunami damage was a catalyst for my surgeon mate. He and one other hero started to organise finance for a trauma centre on the east coast of Sri Lanka. It was opened in June 2018, one great effort by some dedicated people, one giant leap for humankind. I hereby officially forgive my mate for fixing up Sri Lanka's cricketers.

Video of the tsunami (https://www.youtube.com/watch?v=eR0sYLRx8Pk)

25 – LIGHTNING.

MORSE CODE

dit...dit...dit...dit	H
dit...dit	I
dar	T
dit...dit...dit	S

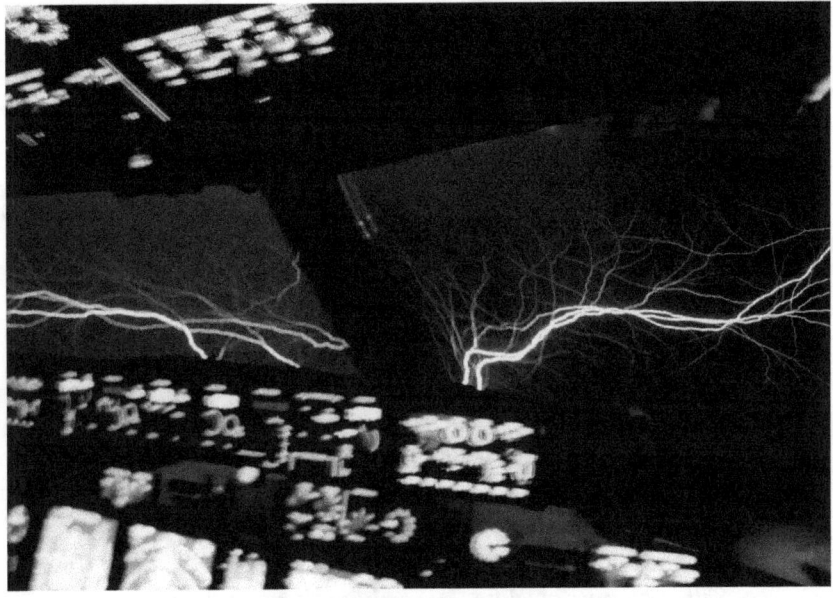

St. Elmo's Fire

St. Elmo's Fire videos
https://www.youtube.com/watch?v=B51GcGIqLlY
https://www.youtube.com/watch?v=P1luqXNqC1c

Lightning video
https://www.youtube.com/watch?v=m37z5R2rJ5E

Microburst videos (If you have a fear of flying don't watch!)
https://www.youtube.com/watch?v=HDfodeURad0
https://www.youtube.com/watch?v=xIHFP4oHvds

Self-explanatory. Note the earthing through the tyres.

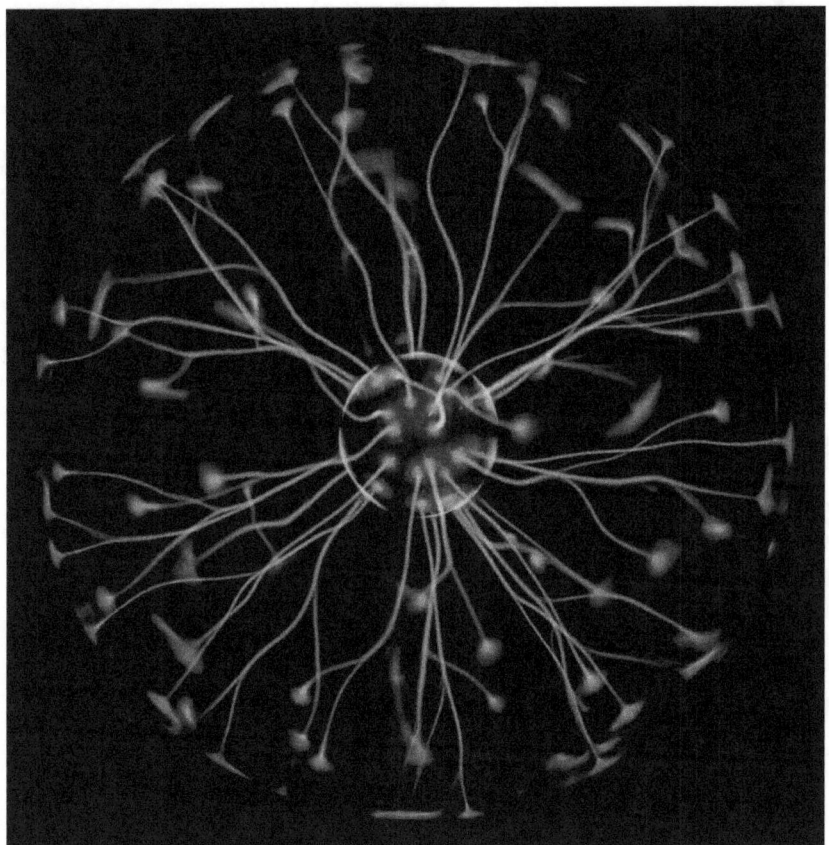

As for the undulating arms of electrical energy emanating from the nose of the 767 that sparkly night, check out a light ball like this above to get a little of what it looked like.

I've had one of these great toys for a long time; I probably bought it straight after my lightning experience as some weird subconscious effort to understand the universe I live in. Not really, it's just a fabulous moving light show.

26 – NOT ALL THE FUN WAS IN THE AIR.

*One way to operate an aircraft,
not the best Cockpit Resource Management.*

Videos of ground and water training. The first one has a flight attendant stripping her pantyhose off, presumably to prevent static on the slide. I refuse to comment further.

https://www.youtube.com/watch?v=fQoxIuio4Mc

This second one is actually shot inside the Qantas facility, just not with Qantas crew. If any Qantas crew were this reticent and slow, the firehose would have been used to blast a few into the pool. The music is great.

https://www.youtube.com/watch?v=NMDFOiLNUpk

Bill Austen

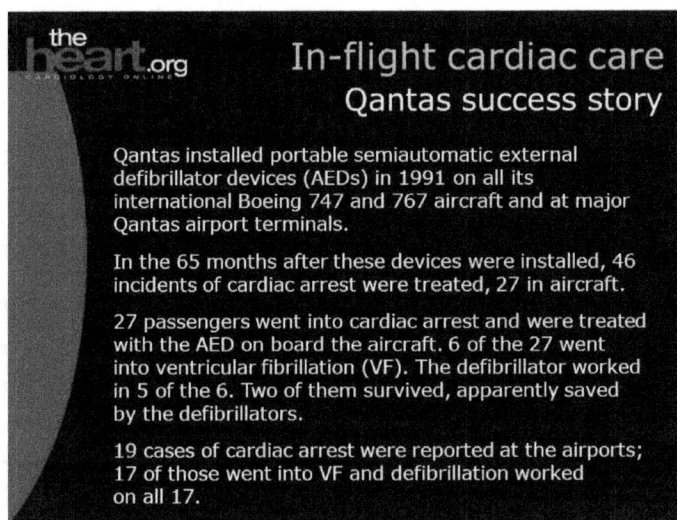

the heart.org

In-flight cardiac care
Qantas success story

Qantas installed portable semiautomatic external defibrillator devices (AEDs) in 1991 on all its international Boeing 747 and 767 aircraft and at major Qantas airport terminals.

In the 65 months after these devices were installed, 46 incidents of cardiac arrest were treated, 27 in aircraft.

27 passengers went into cardiac arrest and were treated with the AED on board the aircraft. 6 of the 27 went into ventricular fibrillation (VF). The defibrillator worked in 5 of the 6. Two of them survived, apparently saved by the defibrillators.

19 cases of cardiac arrest were reported at the airports; 17 of those went into VF and defibrillation worked on all 17.

Zappers!

Smoke!

When you get acrid smoke inside an aircraft, you can't stick you head out the window, so masks and goggles have to be used. When smoke does occur, like when a chiller fan short-circuits and catches fire, you better have practised donning the smoke protection beforehand; see photo of me and a S/O practising at 31,000 feet.

The electrical smoke incident between Brisbane and LAX was well prepared for. Familiarity with emergency equipment and knowledge of the electrical equipment and systems is a necessity. We were taught how to fight all sorts of fires and how to use the appropriate type of extinguisher – this was just a given. Your airline crews should all be well trained and tested in all these things. If you suspect they aren't, change your airline.

27 – FLYING SKILLS.

Best flying video ever filmed. I say this because shortly into the video the vision turns into what the pilot actually sees, namely the runway out in front and the minimum controls and instruments around him. Exactly what it feels like to the pilot.

https://youtu.be/VjS849ssgrw?t=634

Hot brakes "Old School Training" This video shows deflated tyres but the voiceover is great. Specially at the end where he realises that he has told people to not use the brakes and then tries to rectify that.

https://youtu.be/lFbQCZQqQ

28 – LONG-DISTANCE FLYING.

Website calculating great circle tracks. To do this from first principles with a slide rule is what we did. A simple calculation could take up to twenty minutes.

https://www.greatcirclemapper.net

A video of a big engine undergoing a catastrophic failure
https://youtu.be/9m7zRLJEIvw

A video of a Qantas 747-400 departing Sydney. I flew this aircraft a lot. This take-off is trouble free, as were the vast majority. The night departure from Buenos Aires was the one we pilots train for. Please note the noise the mike is picking up; explains why most pilots end up with significant hearing loss.
https://www.youtube.com/watch?v=2hbQH9J7LWE

29 – THE THREE-CARD TRICK.

Either this video is a trick or the card sharps do know what they're doing.

https://www.youtube.com/watch?v=LrQSTiCOOu0

30 – ANTARCTIC FLYOVERS.

Down over Antarctica, the clouds just parted for us.

An Alaskan glacier from the front seat of a light aircraft. The pilot didn't want his photo taken; I think a lot of characters on the run from something or someone end up in Alaska.

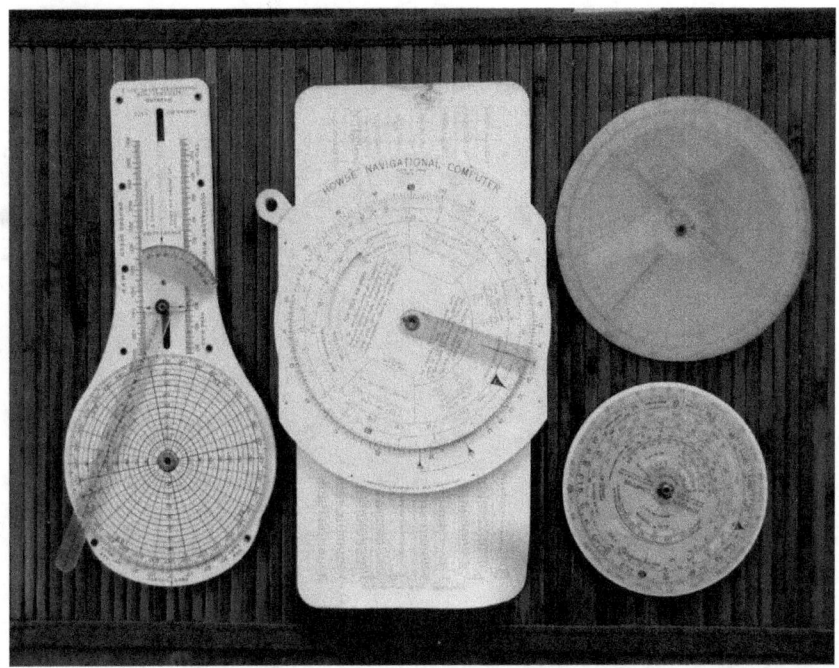

Pre-digital navigation computers – clever slide rules really. The one in the middle was designed by a Qantas pilot or navigator. This bloke knew his maths like Frank Brown did.

The bumpy bit you can see on the bottom right hand corner of the slide of that central computer is a result of an encounter with a light aircraft's fuel-driven heater. It meant I couldn't fully slide the insert in and out and, as a result, couldn't use it if the tailwind component got above a certain value. I spent the last few navigation check flights of the cadet course dreading any strong tail winds; the slide would only move so far.

31 - SAN FRANCISCO.

Parallel approach into San Francisco, 436 cubits apart. It looks way closer than that, doesn't it? Imagine what a Jumbo looks like at night on one of these approaches. Video of an approach to the same runways. https://www.youtube.com/watch?v=qfuwMBBfs0o

No fog, no clouds, no wind – no excuses.

Three pilots, late at night on the streets of San Fran and the new young one asks what's wrong with a particular bar and why don't they go in. The other two let him go in to check it out. He soon comes out and complains that they let him walk into the gayest bar he had ever seen. The older wiser blokes just point to the rainbow flag that all gay bars in San Fran proudly fly.

32 – TRAVELLING THE WORLD.

In the southern Philippines, there are lakes within islands. Google Earth it: Vulcan Point Island in Crater Lakes in Taal Volcano Island in Lawa Ng Taal in Luzon in the South China Sea. Zoom in and out on this Google Map (I note that after the eruption the map has already changed.)

https://www.google.com.au/maps/@14.0001336,121.0404788,10.73z

Taal volcano eruption from a Qantas flight deck a few days after it went up.

I mentioned an *inversion*. As you gain altitude the temperature usually goes down by 2 degrees Celsius per thousand feet. In an inversion the air temperature near the ground is colder than that above it until the inversion layer is reached. This usually happens on cold nights when the ground cools rapidly which, in turn, cools the lower air layers more than the higher layers. Smog gets trapped underneath the inversion level. In the good old days of coal-burning fires, places like Melbourne or London in the 60s would have a lovely layer of brown smog just sitting on all the people on a cold morning– ah, the good old days. A few thousand feet up the temperature gradient would become normal and a clearly defined surface of this smog could be seen like the surface of a sewage pond, above it the visibility was unlimited. In a light aircraft it was actually possible on a smooth day to feel a gentle bump in the control wheel when you went through the temperature change.

And you didn't believe me when I said the Japanese bombed mainland USA with balloons?

https://www.youtube.com/watch?v=0m9EqDlBBeg

Volcanoes smell – it's either H2S or SO2. H for Hydrogen, O for Oxygen and the S is for Smelly in both cases. Okay, the S may actually be Sulphur.

British Airways in a fight with an Indonesian Volcano, animation but fairly accurate.

https://www.youtube.com/watch?v=hFQjZoyYA8o

Circular rainbow with its double. Fantastic!

Circular rainbow videos. With glimpses of the elusive double rainbow.

https://www.youtube.com/watch?v=M-JSXKz6NSI
https://youtu.be/6GGzvikbJOA
This one is filmed from a drone.

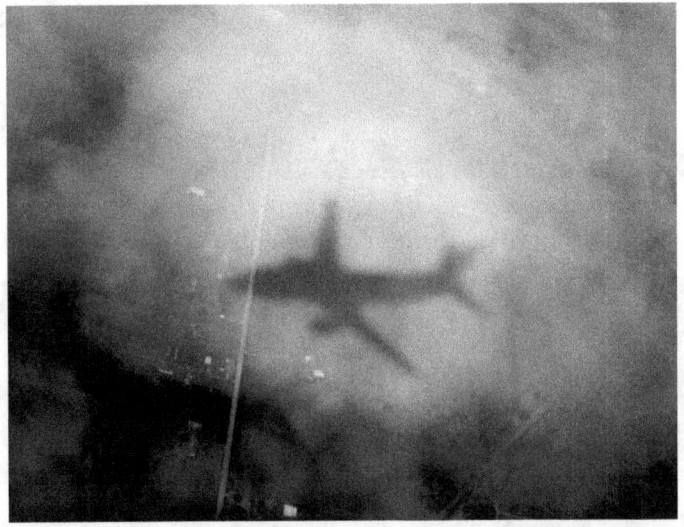

The Glory, with the sunlight turning the aircraft's shadow into a rainbow. Usually it's just a bright halo around the dark shadow. Great video of it.

https://www.youtube.com/watch?v=fDh7vHphmd4

Racetrack holding pattern video – and you thought it was simple. By the way, the Morse code soundtrack is all about the beacon the aircraft is holding over; the three-letter call sign is what the dits and dars are all about. Once identified the beacon's transmission would be silenced – pilots get annoyed like anybody else.

https://www.youtube.com/watch?v=sp4j-AYQZI4

My holding pattern was way better than this. It had the full moon right in the centre. This photographer had a camera though.

View out of a pilot's office window. This is at dawn. Imagine, after a couple more minutes of flying, the view would have changed into another equally magnificent vision. It was very easy to get all Tolkien about it. I wish I'd taken photos like JPC van Heijst; check out his website. https://jpcvanheijst.com/

Going into London it looked like this, except we were behind the aircraft and flew into the invisible swirls. It was turbulent enough to have to take over from the autopilot. Note the condensation forming on top of the wings and at the edge of the flaps. No fuel dumping or chemtrails, just water.

As I said it was easy to get all Tolkien about it all. I do miss the skies.

33 – EPILOUGE – HISTORICAL HILARITY.

My dad, late 90s (age that is) and still raring to go. He flew this aircraft through the desert in the 40s (decade that is.)

American veteran having a fly, this bloke passed away within a day of my father doing so. https://youtu.be/5thY5l4G2kg?t=247

Underfloor galley. You can see the one person lift with the two vertical windows that are there to stop you thinking you're in a coffin.

EXTRAS

Qantas 747-400 ferrying an engine.

Qantas was one of very few airlines that would do this. I had to carry an engine from Singapore to Sydney once; the aircraft flew like a *blevitt*. A *blevitt* is a 10-kilogram capacity bag filled with 20 kilograms of shit. This was just an old expression pilots used to describe less than ideal flying characteristics. Don't ask me why. The imagery is good though.

I flew this aircraft quite often. When you are on the flight deck you can't see the colour scheme. I wondered why on arrival into LAX people on the airport apron were staring, until I remembered which aircraft I was in.

Two older blokes trying to get into a Cessna (stop laughing.) My younger brother in the red shirt is a six-and-a-half-foot ex-pro-footballer. He does actually have a pilot's license and did manage to get in, eventually. You can see why pilots sometimes refer to some light aircraft as flying singlets. You don't get into them, you put them on.

One son learning to fly and falling in love with it all while over Sydney Harbour.

Why wouldn't he love flying? Look at the view from his new office.

Passing the baton on to the next generation on a 747-400 cruising over the Pacific.

On this trip, for the first time in my son's life, he had to do what I told him.

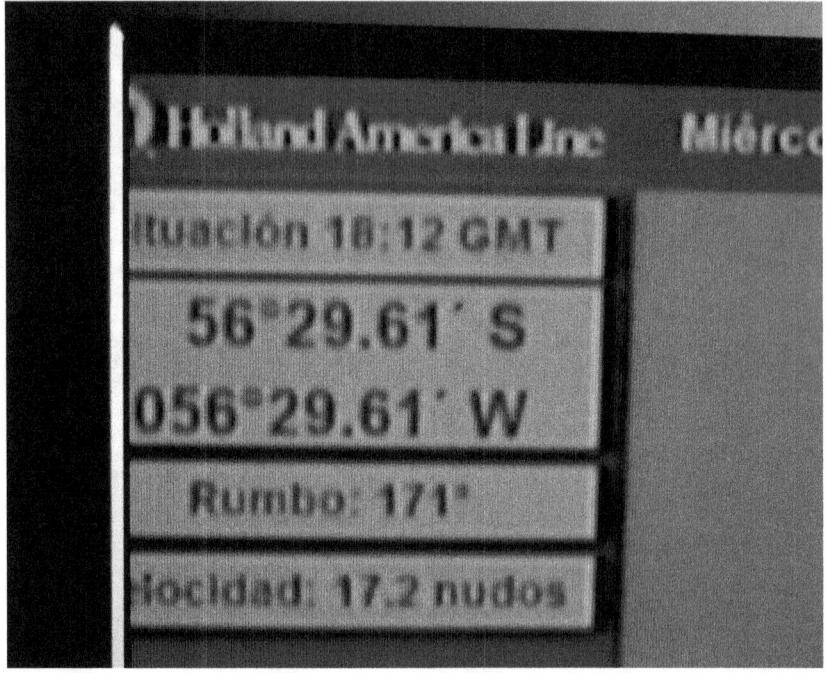

Snapshot of the navigation screen on a cruise to Antarctica. This is such a nerdy navigator thing to get into they have actually removed any references to it from the internet. Join the dots of all points of equal latitude and longitude and you get a figure 8 centred on the equator. Told you it was nerdy. (Nudos equals knots by the way. Rumbo means the 'course.' Indeed if you're not flying a great circle you actually fly a 'rumb line' on a map, a course of steady heading.)

Best website ever

At least for anybody interested in the planet he or she lives on it is. We have come a long way to get this worldwide information displayed and all you have to do is click your mouse a bit.

So, bring up the graphic Earth (I find that if you refresh the screen it comes up bigger) and move it around by the left click, hold and drag method. Zoom in and out with the little wheel. (iPads are different of course.) Right click on a point on the planet and you get the wind velocity (speed and direction) as well as the temperature for that position. It shows up on the left-hand side of the screen along with the Latitude and Longitude of the spot. You can change the units to suit yourself by clicking on the units; unfortunately, there is no 'cubit per egg timer' selection though.

By then right clicking on the word Earth on the left there you can bring up tables you can select from. I only play with the wind and temperature of the air but you can get info about the ocean currents as well.

From the Overlay line click on wind and temp to get the readout for the selected spot. Go onto the Height line and select 'sfc' for the surface wind and temp. The 250 hPa selection is close to where aircraft cruise. In checking it out as I write this guide, the jet streams are showing up as classically normal. It would take a balloon bomb less than two days to get from Northern Japan to Seattle. It's minus 56 degrees Celsius down in the middle of Antarctica by the way. Best website ever. Well, you can see why a pilot would think so anyway.

https://earth.nullschool.net/#current/wind/isobaric/250hPa/orthographic=-82.64,77.84,344/loc=74.668,-40.068

PILOT STORIES

I said in the book that all pilots have their stories. I loved hearing them while debriefing in the bar. Royal Air Force pilots' stories about flying through the rising columns of nuclear test bomb clouds through to wartime survival stories. One pilot was nicknamed 'Hotfoot Harry'. He'd been shot down three times after D Day and had made it back safely to allied lines three times on foot. He used to carry around the "missing in action" telegrams sent to his mother to prove his story.

The guys that had been in the forces had story after story. One F/O told me about the most embarrassing flight he had while in the Australian air force. He was the skipper of an anti-submarine patrol aircraft, a P3 Orion. He told me they found the Russian sub in the Indian ocean that they were looking for and just to confirm things they dropped a line of listening buoys near it. Sure enough number three buoy picked up a huge amount of noise. The sub was next to it. The only problem was the sub had surfaced right next to the top secret listening device and was indeed in the process of heaving it on board to take back to Russia. The F/O told me that as he flew really low and close to the sub the Russian sailor with the buoy in his arms put the sensitive microphone on the buoy up to his mouth and said in a heavy Russian accent to the low flying Aussie aircraft, "Fuck yoo Kangaroo!"

There was one pilot who was a fountain of information, you could ask him about any of the Goon Show scripts, he knew them off by heart. The episode where the Germans came over to the south of England to bomb the cardboard decoy tanks with cardboard bombs was his favourite. As far as I was concerned this bloke was radioactive and he had been since the nuclear test blasts in the Australian outback. Back then they had given him a shoebox of dust after one of the tests to take down to Adelaide for analysis. He had placed the box next to himself in the cramped cockpit and in his light summer flying shorts had carried out his task. He only grew concerned when standing outside of his aircraft with the shoebox in his hands he was approached by the scientists who were to do the analysis. He said the fact that they were in full silver hazmat suits with full facemasks and breathing tanks was bad enough but when they held out huge long tongs to take the box off him he really started to wonder.

The blokes who flew through the rising column of the mushroom cloud said they weren't too worried. They had special suits on and thought things should be fine. Two things changed their mind, they looked back after leaving the aircraft to see it being buried by a couple of bull dozers and the second disconcerting thing was all the skin sloughed off their hands the next day. Their gloves were a bit transparent to radiation it would seem. I thanked the bloke who told me this story and then asked if he minded if I moved away from him in the bar a bit.

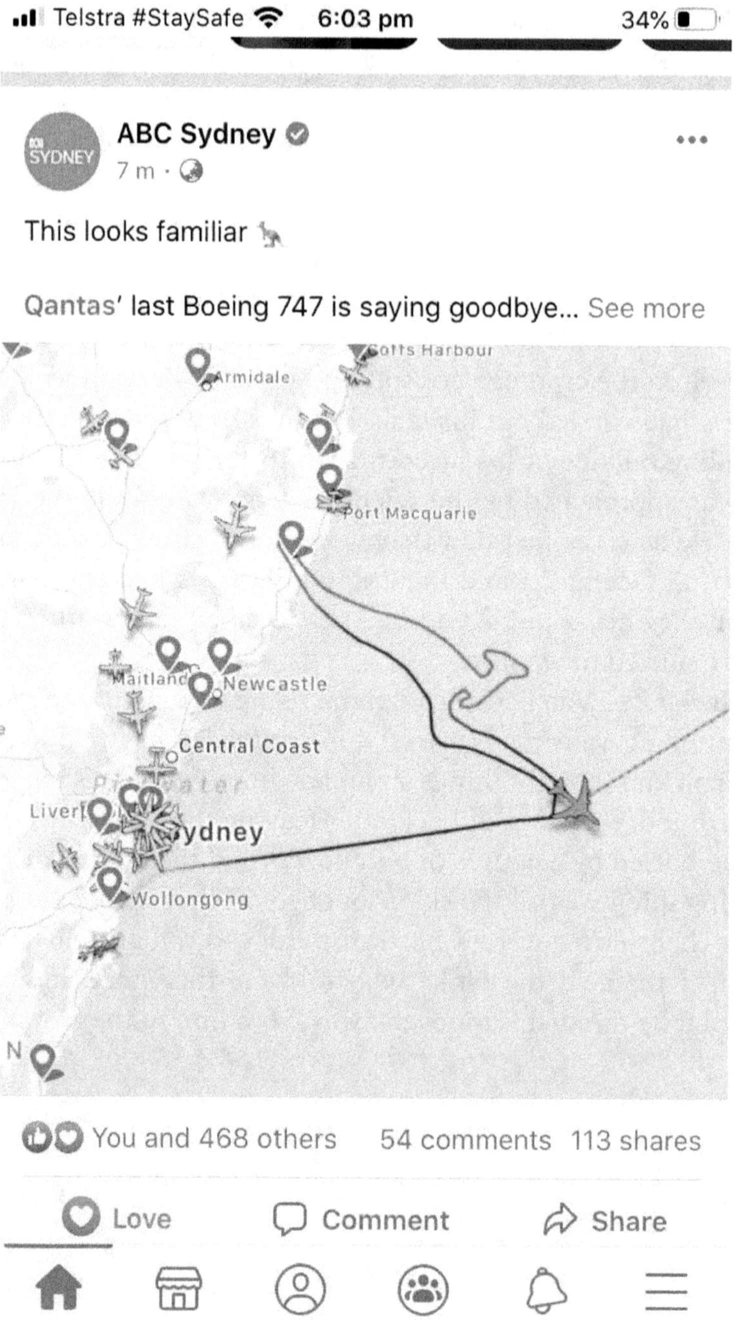

📶 Telstra #StaySafe 🛜 6:03 pm 34% 🔋

ABC Sydney ✓
7 m · 🌐

This looks familiar 🦘

Qantas' last Boeing 747 is saying goodbye... See more

👍❤️ You and 468 others   54 comments   113 shares

❤️ Love   💬 Comment   ↗ Share

I and a few hundred other ex-Qantas aircrew and engineers assembled in front of the Sydney Opera House to farewell the last 747 on its departure down Sydney Harbour.

After leaving the coast the aircraft followed a set of co-ordinates to complete the track shown above. The Qantas Flying Kangaroo.

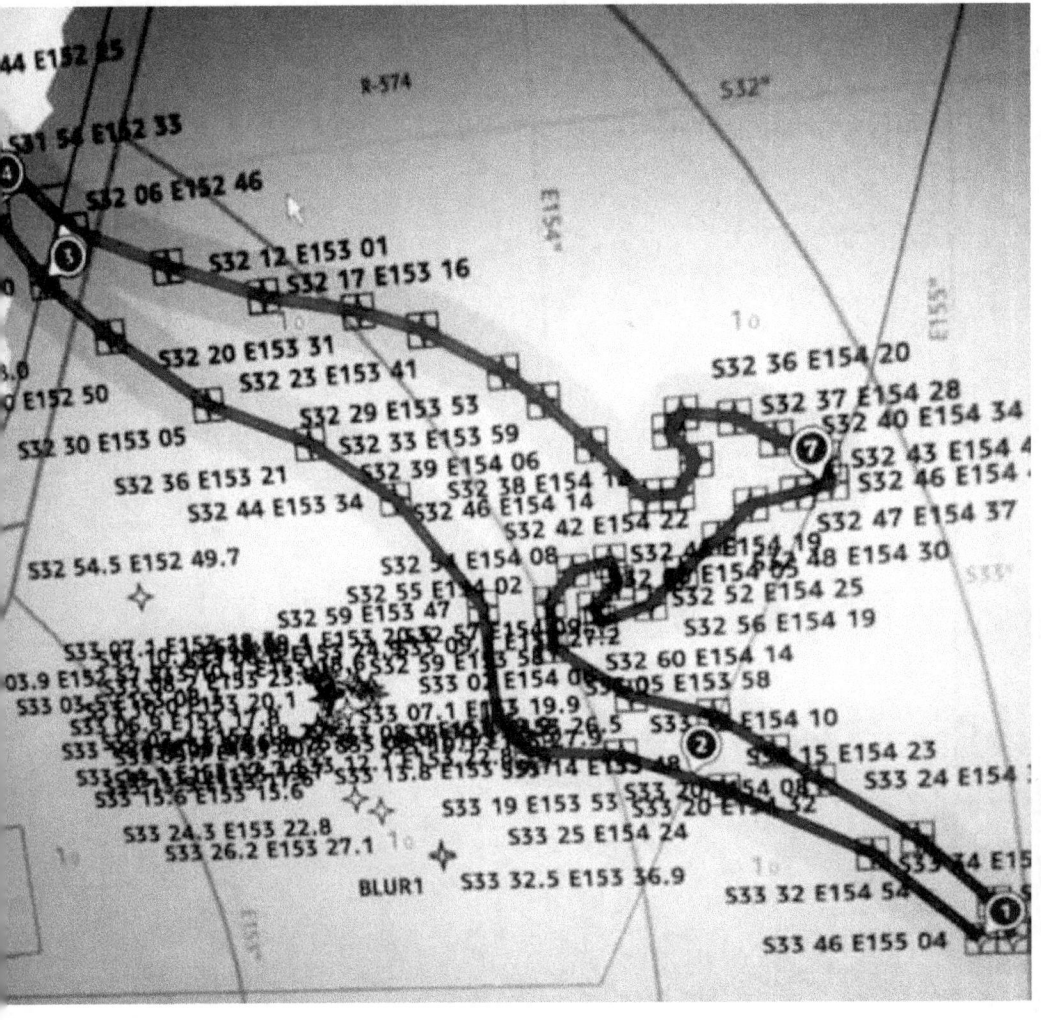

So the 'Kangaroo' was drawn on the radar screens when the aircraft followed a pre-calculated track fed into the navigation computer. Here are the Latitudes and Longitudes of the track. One of the pilots of that last flight told me they were spending a lot of time getting it right, this was weeks before the flight.

As an old pilot I was interested as to what altitude/speed/weight/flap setting and G-loading this was all done at. These are all important details.

https://youtu.be/tu-SUZJSk-8?t=398

Benediction for a Queen

*A*ircraft are just metal constructs, assembled on a factory floor But to the lucky few who fly you, you are always so much more When you joined us, newly gleaming, latest in a noble line.

Your majesty and grace impressed us, now had come your time to shine Quickly logging mileage, countless wishes granted on the way Thrilling, everyone who flew you. Hoping you would always stay Icecaps, oceans, deserts, forests. You have overflown them all.

Borne your subjects safely onwards, your reputation standing tall They were times some pilots cursed you, purge to say it, but it's true If you humbled them, the reason was because they disrespected you You have met our every challenge, explorer of the highest skies Surpassing all who came before you, unrivalled in your pilots' eyes Soon, your engines will fall silent, your time has come to finally rest

As you prepare to go and leave us, we say, thank you. You've been the best.

Qantas F/O Jeff Kale